Making IT Count

Making IT Count
Strategy, Delivery, Infrastructure

Leslie P. Willcocks
Peter Petherbridge
Nancy Olson

OXFORD   AMSTERDAM   BOSTON   LONDON   NEW YORK   PARIS
SAN DIEGO   SAN FRANCISCO   SINGAPORE   SYDNEY   TOKYO

Butterworth-Heinemann
An imprint of Elsevier Science
Linacre House, Jordan Hill, Oxford OX2 8DP
200 Wheeler Road, Burlington, MA 01803

First published 2002
Reprinted 2003

British Library Cataloguing in Publication Data
A catalogue record for this book is available from the British Library

ISBN   0 7506 4821 X

For information on all Butterworth-Heinemann publications
visit our website at www.bh.com

Composition by Genesis Typesetting, Rochester, Kent
Printed and bound in Great Britain by
Antony Rowe Ltd., Chippenham, Wiltshire

Contents

Contents

Contents

Leslie P. Wilcocks is Professor of Information Management and E-Business at Warwick University Business School. He has an international reputation for his work on evaluation, outsourcing, organizational and management issues in the IT field. He has co-authored 22 books and some 130 papers in *Harvard Business Review, Sloan Management Review* and academic journals. He is regularly retained as adviser by corporations and government agencies.

Peter Petherbridge has over 30 years of direct management experience. This has covered a diversity of roles in senior management and IT in large corporations and more recently in start-ups. Until 1993 Peter was General Manager of IT development for Mayer and Grace Bros. He has since consulted with organizations including Colonial, A.G.L., the RACV and the State Revenue Office of Victoria. He has held directorships in a number of eBusiness companies and is an Adjunct Professor at Swinburne University of Technology Centre for eBusiness and Communication.

Nancy Olson is a highly experienced management and IT practitioner who has worked on developing and delivering strategy for clients in a range of sectors including finance, energy, health and ebusiness. She is CEO of the consultancy Information Matters.

Computer Weekly Professional Series

There are few professions which require as much continuous updating as that of the IS executive. Not only does the hardware and software scene change relentlessly, but also ideas about the actual management of the IS function are being continuously modified, updated and changed. Thus keeping abreast of what is going on is really a major task.

The Butterworth-Heinemann – *Computer Weekly* Professional Series has been created to assist IS executives keep up to date with the management ideas and issues of which they need to be aware.

One of the key objectives of the series is to reduce the time it takes for leading edge management ideas to move from the academic and consulting environments into the hands of the IT practitioner. Thus this series employs appropriate technology to speed up the publishing process. Where appropriate some books are supported by CD-ROM or by additional information or templates located on the Web.

This series provides IT professionals with an opportunity to build up a bookcase of easily accessible, but detailed information on the important issues that they need to be aware of to successfully perform their jobs.

Aspiring or already established authors are invited to get in touch with me directly if they would like to be published in this series.

Dr Dan Remenyi
Series Editor
dan.remenyi@mcil.co.uk

Series Editor
Dan Remenyi, Visiting Professor, Trinity College Dublin

Advisory Board
Frank Bannister, Trinity College Dublin
Ross Bentley, Management Editor, *Computer Weekly*
Egon Berghout, Technical University of Delft, The Netherlands
Ann Brown, City University Business School, London
Roger Clark, The Australian National University
Reet Cronk, Harding University, Arkansas, USA
Arthur Money, Henley Management College, UK
Sue Nugus, MCIL, UK
Terry White, BentleyWest, Johannesburg

Other titles in the Series
IT investment – making a business case
The effective measurement and management of IT costs and benefits
Stop IT project failures through risk management
Understanding the Internet
Prince 2: a practical handbook
Considering computer contracting?
David Taylor's Inside Track
A hacker's guide to project management
Corporate politics for IT managers: how to get streetwise
Subnet design for efficient networks
Information warfare: corporate attack and defence in a digital world
Delivering IT and e-business value
Reinventing the IT department
The project manager's toolkit

1 Strategy, IT and the strange case of missing business value

'I worked under one CEO who only had two measures for IT: "Why am I getting all these complaints?" and "Why is it costing so much?"', CIO in a manufacturing conglomerate.

'Profit? Are you kidding? We're in Amazon.com mode', founder of Reel.com, a former video rental and sales site.

'I don't want to do much more user testing; it wastes valuable implementation time', project manager to a business CEO worried about the reliability and usability of the system being developed.

'Well, in truth we applied IT to a bureaucratic mess, and all we got was disaster faster', manager, commenting on a government social security system.

1.1 Introduction: positioning IT

What *is* the problem with IT? Why is IT so often regarded as a cash sink, a necessary evil, a black hole? From where do such sceptical views derive? Why do so many organizations continue not to get the business value they demand from their IT investments? Why, as we move to a so-called 'Real-Time' economy, can Information Technology actually seem to slow you down? In this chapter we deal with where the problems come from; what organizations look like when they are doing IT badly, in contrast to what they look like when doing IT well. Ensuing chapters then provide the roadmap for how IT strategy can be shaped and delivered. But first, we need to ring the alarm bells, to enable you to assess what you could be, but should not be, doing.

In 1998, ironically as what later became known as the 'Internet Bubble' gathered pace, one of the authors finally became convinced about the precise role of information and communications technologies (IT) in organizations. Being an academic he needed a lot of valid, empirical evidence, a study rigorously and objectively carried out, which compared like with like, which carried out sampling procedures and statistical analysis correctly, and which produced very strong pointers as to what was, and was not the case. As a matter of fact, it was something he already knew in his bones, and something that the other two authors had lived with for more years than they cared to remember in their consulting and managerial work.

That, *in itself*, IT has no intrinsic business value, other than what you can sell it for. That 'information' needs to be separated out from 'technology'. That data are records, that information is data with a purpose, a message, but if the purpose or message has no business value, then neither does the information. More recently the notion of knowledge has been introduced. And here you could say that information supports the development of knowledge in so far as information improves the model someone holds of how something in the world works. And that knowledge – that model of reality – has business value in so far as it is applied productively to business problems.

In an information and technology obsessed, indeed over-hyped, age, much comes from these seemingly simple observations that is counter to how IT is actually planned for, introduced and used – we hesitate to say leveraged – in our business organizations. One of the immediate observations is the dominant belief that, somehow, ever better technology will substitute for failures in developing and applying well information and knowledge to business issues. But let us widen the context further at this point. The particular study we referred to above, by Gus Van Nievelt and Leslie Willcocks, was called *Benchmarking Organizational and IT Performance*. Analysing database information on over 300 organizations, the study found empirically that IT as a coordinating, communicating and leveraging technology was capable of enhancing customer satisfaction, flattening organizational pyramids, supporting knowledge workers and improving productivity, Economic Value Added (EVA – a measure of profit) and Relative Customer Satisfaction (RCS – a measure of external competitiveness). At the same time, all too many organizations did not direct their IT expenditure into appropriate areas at the right time. Statistical analysis at the business unit level provided strong evidence for a significant, often positive, but multi-faceted IT effect on business performance. But timing and focus of IT investments emerged as all important. Moreover, IT is unable to add value itself, but does so only in interaction with other factors, for example organizational structure, competitive positioning, people skills (Nievelt and Willcocks, 1998).

In all too many cases the study found organizations adopting business re-engineering, total quality management, 'competitive edge' IT or 'best practices' benchmarking to achieve break-through improvements, despite scant evidence of their appropriateness and likely efficacy in specific circumstances. On IT, for example, the study found the optimum investment strategy following a complex path. When RCS is low, IT spending should be focused on improving operations, to bring the product and customer service to market acceptance. Only when RCS is average or better does it pay to invest in infrastructure. Moreover, investments in competitive edge IT are better timed when RCS is relatively high and basic IT infrastructure is in place.

This only hints at the richness of the straight and crooked thinking we have encountered on the subject of value for money from IT. Let us look in a lot more detail at eight major fallacies that all too often misinform how IT should be managed.

1.2 Fallacy one: ignoring the IT amplifier effect

Will investments in superior technology see you through to business leverage, especially if your competitors have not yet made those investments? Probably not. Much IT has been sold and bought on the premise that the more you spend on IT the more value you will get from it. It is difficult to find a single study that actually supports that correlation. A more perennial phenomenon, well documented by studies of the many waves of technology over the last 25 years, is what has been dubbed the 'amplifier effect' of IT. A good management is made much better by the application of IT, a bad management is made dramatically worse. This is hinted at in the study described above. Basically we find that it is management, both of the business and of IT, that makes the difference, not IT itself, however advanced that technology.

Consider an advertising agency that one of the authors once worked for. It commissioned us to spend some £200 000 on new accounting and market forecasting systems. Going back after these had been installed five months later, we found that the accounting system was not used. The head accountant rather liked the old system, and the effort of data conversion and staff retraining was too disruptive. The market forecasting system was used to impress the occasional client with its graphics showing 'maybes' and 'what ifs'. Neither investment addressed the essential problem, which was that the organization was losing customers in a recessionary climate. It emerged that a Board Director had commissioned the investment after seeing similar systems at a competitor. For him, the agency needed to demonstrate it was 'up-to-date', and had the right image. At the same time as implementing the IT, the agency was sacking 30 employees to reduce costs. Two years later the agency was taken over by a competitor. Here one can see the amplifier effect with a vengeance, with IT being applied in ways that have negative effects: disaster faster, in fact.

By contrast, Collins (2001) studied 11 great companies that consistently, and massively, outperformed their competitors over a decade or more. They were not concentrated in particular sectors, but what they shared were a set of six management practices. These are:

- a type of mature leadership he calls 'Level 5' leadership;
- a focus on 'who' before the 'what': people first, then what they can do;
- an ability to confront the brutal facts without losing faith in the end goal;
- a focus on one big idea, backed by a viable financial model, passion and ability to be world class in delivering the idea;
- a culture of discipline; and finally,
- seeing technology as an accelerator of business performance rather than a single cause of momentum and breakthrough.

In other words IT becomes valuable only in the context of the other five principles having been applied already. One executive from Nucor, the steel-maker, summed it up: '20 per cent of our success is the new technology we embrace ... [but] ... 80 per cent of our success is the culture of our company'.

Collins also looked at comparator companies in the same sectors as his great companies. He found R. J. Reynolds losing it position as the number one tobacco company in the world (against Philip

Morris), not because of its technology but because its management went into undisciplined diversification, and a later management buyout binge. A&P went from being the second largest company in the USA to irrelevance, not because it lagged behind Kroger in scanning technology but because it lacked the discipline to confront the brutal reality of the changing nature of grocery stores. Chrysler made superb use of advanced computer-aided design and other design technologies, but failed to link those to a consistent big idea, or what Collins calls the Hedgehog concept. Once again, the business and organizational context in which technology is applied explains success, not the technology characteristics themselves.

There is another dimension to the amplifier effect that is worth pointing out. IT is in fact a double-edged sword. Oversold invariably as breakthrough technology, what is less often pointed out are the possible consequences of moving IT into the core of business operations. Networks, high connectedness and speed have massive potential benefits, but what happens if the systems fail and the business is hugely over-dependent on their functioning? What are the downsides of the massive capability IT can already offer in the twenty-first century?

We already know some answers. For example, automated stock trading is known to have had an accelerator effect on the sell spree in stock markets during the 1987 global shares slump. In 2001 a simple misplacement of figures caused one broker to sell very low and lose £50 million in trading in the two minutes it took to discover the error and buy back the shares. On 13 April 1999 the Internet service provider AT&T had an outage of 2–6 hours that cost US$40 million in rebates. The cost of several viruses deliberately implanted into global networks during 2000–2002 ran into billions of dollars. The outlay on counter-vailing security measures is mounting every year. The moral of the story: IT needs to be managed as a two-edged, not a one-edged sword.

1.3 Fallacy two: riding to IT success by being first mover

In 1999, after concluding a presentation on strategic e-business to a water utilities company, one of the authors was thanked by the chief executive for one thing – *not* recommending that his company be the first big e-business mover in their industry. Yet the first mover rhetoric is persuasive. One of the constant themes during the Internet bubble years was summarized beautifully on the front cover of the widely read *Fortune* magazine of November 1998: 'Internet or Bust'. No mention there of the other possibility: Internet and bust. By 2002 it became more usual to talk of not being so much first mover as best mover.

To put some flesh around this concept of 'best mover', during 1999–2000 a study looked at 58 corporations moving to e-business (Willcocks and Plant, 2002). Almost all had first confronted the Internet with an attempt to seize a head start in their sector through technology leadership. But then what happened? Companies such as Lufthansa, Motorola, Citicorp, Royal Caribbean Cruises learned the technology in the context of marketing or customer service objectives, then moved on to profitable market share growth via e-business.

There were 18 such leaders in the study sample that migrated quickly out of the technology box. What distinguished them from the laggards and those who got stuck in the technology box were, firstly, their ability to listen to the technology and find out what it was telling them in terms of business application. Secondly, as in classic prime mover examples, such as the Sabre airline reservation system in the 1980s, it was the intelligent management of information that explained success. Thus Sabre used technology to improve the process for making reservations, tracking customer preferences, accurately pricing products and services, and responding to patterns of behaviour over time. By the end of the 1980s it was making more profit out of its information systems services than from flying people from A to B.

The leaders also:

- learned quickly and had the capacity to shift focus. They concentrated on building an integrated technology, marketing and information platform to enable this flexibility and reach;
- followed a business-focused, top-down approach to planning and an 'outside-in' customer- and competitor-focused route to business innovation through Web-based technologies (see also Chapter 2 and Earl's multiple methodology);
- based Internet strategy on established brands and business strengths;
- saw business-to-consumer (B2C) Internet use as part of a larger strategic investment in e-business, including intranet, extranet and supply chain applications.

Thus, yet again, prime mover success is not just about the technology. Being prime mover, and being over-reliant on the technology to see you through, is also a very risky proposition. Feeny (2001) points out three routes to sustainable competitive advantage through use of IT – generic lead time (being first and staying ahead) asymmetry of resources (for example, distinctive non-replicable information held on customers) and pre-emption barriers (for example, in one classic case Baxter Hospital Supplies locked in customers by putting computers on customers' desks for making and checking up on their Baxter orders – why would they want to switch suppliers and learn another system?). Of these three routes, Feeny concludes that generic lead time is the most risky and least sustainable.

Mike Vitale also pointed out as early as the 1980s the risks of information systems success (Vitale, 1986). His article points to examples where systems change the basis of competition to a company's disadvantage, lower entry barriers for other players, bring litigation or regulation, increase suppliers' or customers' power to the detriment of the innovator, turn out to be indefensible in competitive terms, are badly timed, transfer power and so are resisted strongly by other players, and may work in one market niche and not another. He could have added: systems that are a good idea but are implemented poorly or not at all. All this implies an over-reliance on technology, and an inadequate analysis of the competitive context to which it is applied. Such systems can become competitive burdens, that is sources of competitive disadvantage.

1.4 From dotty.com to dot.coma: the new rules fallacy

The 'Internet Bubble' was marked by extravagant advice and some correspondingly extravagant failures. Inherent in the whole affair was the notion that the Internet and Web-based technologies were so powerful and revolutionary that the old rules for running businesses, and applying technology, need no longer apply. The phrase 'e-business' means electronically enabled business, but too often the 'e' was interpreted to be *the* business. The result? Thousands of companies on the Web but, even by 2002, all too few profitable businesses. In many ways the 1997–2001 'dotty.com' years provided a master-class on how to get blinded by information-based technologies.

The new rules for this New Economy were the subject of many lists. A typical one appeared in *Business Week* on 22 March 1999:

- re-engineer the company;
- throw out the old business model;
- the buyer always wins;
- hold your customer's hand;
- go ahead, farm out those jobs (i.e., outsource);
- no Web site is an island;
- create an on-line sense of community;
- follow the money (see what investors are putting money into);
- a Web of nerds? Don't believe it;
- log on, Boss (only 25 per cent of CEOs were logging on according to a 1999 survey).

To these we could add many more that were circulating, but just three suffice to give the full flavour:

- brand doesn't matter (traditional brands can be easily challenged);
- content will be free (Internet-based businesses are that cheap to run);
- size doesn't matter (start-ups can take on anyone; the Internet gives global presence).

As the reader can see, typically the mood is upbeat, it's about innovation, and there is nothing to be seen about financial or business disciplines. What induced this fervour? In subsequent post-mortems, of which there have been many (where were these commentators when we needed them?) one commonly agreed factor was summarized by Michael Porter:

> *Companies that have employed Internet technology have been confused by distorted market signals, often of their own creation . . . Dotcoms multiplied for one major reason, they were able to raise capital without having to demonstrate viability.*

Or, as Warren Buffet put it more succinctly in March 2001: 'Nothing sedates rationality like large does of effortless money'. In his article Porter (2001) provides a sober and interesting analysis, showing how it should have been about competitive strategy and positioning, not the technology. A rebuff article appeared in *Strategy and Business* soon afterwards by Don Tapscott (2001), in which he says Porter really underrates the potential and implications of the Internet. Reading the two papers makes one think that Porter does not know much about the Internet and Tapscott is not an expert in competitive strategy and that the truth lies somewhere interesting between the two. They make a good pair of discussion papers to set a management team or an MBA class.

Unfortunately what the 'new rules' turned out to be were not that productive. One only slightly over-the-top version is supplied by Carton (2002). The annotations in brackets are ours:

- profitability can come later (most cases; e.g., Amazon makes first profit in the last quarter of 2001);
- we'll figure out who our customers are as we go (most cases);
- brand equals recognition (comes from large advertising campaigns, e.g., Click Mango);
- eyeballs equals customers (ignores the importance of the conversion into purchases rate);
- valuation equals permanent wealth (e.g., Webvan, Drug store.com, etc.);
- grow, grow, grow . . . (at any cost);
- inefficiency doesn't matter (most cases);
- extravagance is a right (see Boo.com and the three C's of Champagne, Caviar and Concorde – supposedly what some of the US$140 million was spent on in under two years);
- perks compensate for long hours and low pay (most start-ups);
- assume that stock options will make employees happy forever (Enron . . .).

From the heady dot.com years, if we paid attention, we learned some not-so-new rules for what is still in fact a not-so-new economy. For example, during Christmas 2001, in the developed economies only about 1 per cent of retail transactions went over the Internet – hardly yet a revolution. The not-so-new rules include financial disciplines, an issue hugely highlighted in late 2001 by the collapse of one of the New Economy figurehead companies, Enron. In this scenario IT investments need to be made in the context of business disciplines around such metrics as free cash flow, Economic Value Added (EVA), productivity of all assets used and Relative Customer Satisfaction – a competitive position measure.

Rangan and Adner (2002) usefully bring together what the fallacies and not-so-new rules might be. For them managers have had serious misconceptions about the power of Internet technologies. This has led managers to overestimate first mover advantage (see above); dilute fit with markets to take advantage of the reach capability of the Internet; unintentionally sacrifice focus in order to try to tap into ever larger customer bases; ignore Internet sector differences; rely on Internet partner leverage without examining the risks of going global prematurely (see below and Chapter 6); and treat technology as strategy (see above).

Many of the not-so-new rules have already been detailed above in these first few pages. It would seem obvious that there are limits on any organization's ability to outrun financial disciplines and to build market share at any cost, assuming an endless flow of relatively free cash. Good businesses, whether or not heavily IT-dependent, still need to provide outstanding service, have good staff relations, develop a brand customers trust, deliver their products/services at the right time to the right specification and use suppliers they can rely on. For IT management, we devote Chapter 2 to establishing the benchmarks for abiding management practices that make sense in the face of turbulent technology. But for now, let us look at one final way into understanding the not-so-new rules by considering what the successful Internet 'pure plays' did that was so different.

McKinsey and Co. (2000) reviewed over 250 Internet 'pure plays' from 1999 and found the profitable ones displaying seven attributes.

1 There was a genuine 'amplifier effect' with leaders achieving 12 per cent conversion rates (the average on the net has been around 2 per cent), 20 per cent churn rates (rate of loss of customers), and repeat purchases in 60 per cent of cases. These companies focused on well defined consumer segments and sustainable revenue models.
2 Typically they went for high gross margin (60 per cent plus) niches not needing large scale or unrealistic conversion rates. Such companies had an average revenue four times that of the whole sample.
3 They also developed the business by deepening and adding, that is, moving into complementary products/services aimed at the same customer segment. Conversion rates here tended to be double those of competitors.
4 They also avoided 'bleeding edge' technology. They ensured seamless operation of basic production presentation features, customer service tools and logistics. They practised disciplined outsourcing of IT. Their IT spend was 50–75 per cent less than the average for the whole sample.

5 They attracted customers by avoiding untargeted mass marketing. Instead they experimented and tirelessly tested the optimal marketing approach, went for affiliate deals in small customer segments and only paid partners for actual business results.

6 Leader 'pure plays' were very good at converting interest into transactions. They did this by having simple purchase processes; requesting limited details; offering real-time assistance; offering easy, safe, reliable payment methods; and following up abandoned shopping carts.

7 Finally, the leaders retained customers well. Practices included offering reliable basic operational execution including quick downloads; making exchanges/returns easy; responding to queries quickly, using customer profiles to drive promotions and personalization.

In all this, we once again see not-so-new rules being applied together with the deployment of powerful technologies that cannot be expected to do it all alone. These practices are not so different from those any self-respecting start-up or small business would employ. The truth was, people got blinded by the e- and could not see the word business anymore. It was like business would automatically be a result, would be a natural extension of the hyphen after 'e'. But getting suckered into the technology, and the new rules this seems to imply, has been a long and dishonourable tradition in the adoption and use of IT in our businesses and government agencies.

1.5 The 'all reading off the same hymn sheet' mistake: misalignment and performance inhibitors

Strategies and initiatives are wonderful things. Where do they all go to? Just looking at IT for the moment, studies in the mid-1990s found that often about half of what was in the original plan for IT never got implemented, and about the same percentage that actually got implemented was never in the original IT plan. Much gets lost, and found, it would seem, on the long road to implementation. This leads to our fourth fallacy: that we all understand the plan, that we all agree to it, and that the organization is structured and run in ways that ensure good communication of aims and relatively straightforward implementation of plans. In fact organizations are riven structurally by two major fissures. The one that has received most attention is the vertical functions most organizations are still divided into, for example human resources, purchasing, accounting, manufacturing, marketing. However, fissures also exist horizontally, however much organizations have attempted to reduce the layers in their pyramid structures. And these horizontal divides can be profoundly damaging in their displacement effects. As we shall see in Chapter 5, this is one reason why the balanced business scorecard has been brought to bear, in order to try to restore alignment.

Drawing on his wide experience, our colleague Robert White, director with Lucidus Management Technologies, sees the problem to be solved within an organization as the misalignment between the top of the organization, where business goals are set, and the bottom of the organization, which needs to do the work to meet and manage the goals. This sort of problem is endemic in organizations at a general level and, as the authors have seen many times, also exists between IT departments and business strategy. White explains:

> *The first thing that companies do is set a business goal . . . what it means, however they word it, is: 'shortest route to improve bottom line'. They then try to achieve that goal through normal operational activities and structures. The problem that they encounter as they push that down through the organization, is that the message actually gets blurred, which means that nothing happens. So in terms of achieving those goals, there are various degrees, but essentially they fail . . .*

White further describes the oft-chosen remedy to the failure to achieve such goals: a set of initiatives dictated, again, from the top of the organization. In theory, such initiatives could potentially solve misalignment problems: strategy is set at the executive level, sponsors are appointed to manage the initiatives, they in turn appoint project managers and set up projects, projects get their resources from the line, and the whole is aligned, and works – in theory.

In practice, such initiatives, be they within the IT department or any other part of the organization, rarely work effectively because of the same problems that cause the misalignment in the first place. The practice says something else. What really happens is that the strategy is usually poorly articulated and rarely communicated. So then some half-formed ideas aren't really communicated to anybody because if they're only half-formed, they're really hard to communicate anyway. Lack of accountability further complicates the issue: the sponsors fire off the initiatives then abdicate the responsibility by not getting involved in the detail.

Perhaps the key element in the problem is the failure to articulate the *value* of an initiative. Without an understanding of the value of an initiative, the line organization does not have the incentive to follow through with the 'initiative'. White likens these initiatives to 'smart weapons' (see also 'fire-and-forget' missiles below). The initiatives are not well thought-through, their value is not properly articulated and they are usually constrained by lack of resources. Thus initiatives are launched in the organization, but because strategy has not been formulated clearly, the 'smart weapons' have not been targeted very well: 'So it's a bit of handicap if you've a "smart" missile not to be clear about your target – you tend to wander about a bit'.

The ultimate result of such a situation is, initially, an organization out of alignment with its organizational goals, and secondly, ongoing misalignment because the initiatives launched to solve the initial problems still suffer from the same lack of unarticulated goals and strategies. The problems cascade through the organization. With initiatives running out of alignment, and probably out of control, typically there is little sense of the value coming from them. Often we see such value double-counted; we certainly see many occasions of double allocation of resources. Meanwhile project managers will focus on determinedly delivering their projects, which often means that the project and cross-project activity is poorly coordinated (see the Programme Office solution in Chapter 9). The line managers, who are the really important people in all of this, who are keeping the business going and generating the business as well, could be called the meat in the sandwich because now they have to give resources up to the project but of course, typically, do not have control over the project (see the Chapter 8 solution for this). So they give up resources and get on with what they perceive to be their 'proper job', namely keeping the business going. For White:

> *The real casualties in all this are likely to be the people that sit at the operational level who are the wealth-generating people . . . they have two jobs to do and two bosses. Because everything at the top was unconstrained by lack of resource or any kind of view of resources, they are now in an impossible position because they have too much to do and they have no real way of signalling back up the line that they are in distress.*

As we shall see, there are many ways of avoiding these all too typical sorts of misalignment – through establishing strategy in ways that set the conditions for success, through proper implementation processes, and by establishing navigation mechanisms throughout strategy shaping and delivery. In particular, in Chapter 5 we look at the balanced business scorecard and integrated performance measurement approaches that:

- provide a framework within which to develop the right management focus;
- provide a framework within which to develop the right measures regime;
- provide a framework for continuous improvement;
- create a common language across the organization;
- allow everyone to see how they contribute to corporate goals;
- promote a highly effective mechanism for interrogating and developing the measures.

1.6 Fallacy five: 'but we have strong planning processes'

When IT goes wrong, often the hunt for suspects traces back to sheer poor strategy and planning in the first place. As we shall see, one mistake is to conflate everything into something called an 'IT strategy' and then pass off responsibility for its development primarily to the IT function. Typically, such organizations will see business managers disengaged from IT management, an indifferent record on IT business value, and the IT director treated as a support, functional manager. Chapter 2 points out better strategy practice on this. Somewhat better organizations, such as the hi-tech company detailed in the case scenario below, tend to have a number of things going on, but are still self-confessedly rudimentary in their approach and are learning all the time.

Caselet example: hi-tech multinational

As at the late 1990s, the IT Department of the Test and Measurement Organization (TMO) within a hi-tech multinational had relatively rudimentary project assessment processes in place. According to one IT manager: 'I would characterize our assessment here as being pretty much on the front end of the learning curve. Most are not very sophisticated. The reason I say that is because on large investments, assessments tend to be more robust, and there's always a financial component. Increasingly, there is a business strategy, business impact component . . . and on the end of the spectrum, for smaller projects, there is often little return analysis in the traditional sense at all, because those projects may move very quickly, and there's not a lot of analytical framework around them. However, almost all projects go through a fairly disciplined project lifecycle process'. He does note that the decision process differs, depending on the part of the investment portfolio under consideration. For instance: 'At the highest level, overall infrastructure strategies are supported by the senior level executives in the business; the infrastructure investment is usually not based on a return to the business in the more traditional sense . . . There's a different set of investments that I would term project or solution based, and those decisions are usually based completely on business needs . . . Those are all business based, they are not based on an IT strategy by themselves, they are based on what we need to do in the business. In these cases, the IT investment levels are really part of the overall business programme. Those IT investments tend to be measured much more on a return basis'.

Strategic planning for IT continues to be an issue of significant concern to IT executives and CEOs alike. Planning should represent a combination of method (techniques, procedures employed, for example Application Portfolio or Critical Success Factors analysis), process (level of line management participation, user–IT relationships, degree to which general managers are engaged in IT) and implementation (do the strategies/plans get delivered?). As investments in information technologies have expanded massively, so a range of planning methodologies and techniques has been developed to guide and focus how and where the money is spent. Typically these approaches are intended to focus on:

1 aligning investment in IT with business goals;
2 exploiting IT for competitive advantage;
3 directing efficient and effective management of IT resources;
4 developing technology policies and architectures.

	Business-Led	Method-Driven	Administrative	Technological	Organizational
Influencer	IS Planner	Consultants	Committees	Method	Teams
Priorities	Board	Rational Analysis	Central Committee	Compromise	Emerge
IS Role	Driver	Initiator	Bureaucrat	Architect	Team Member
Metaphor	It's Common Sense	It's Good for You	Survival of the Fittest	We Nearly Aborted it	Partnership
Emphasis	The Business	Technique	Resources	Model	Learning
Basis	Business Support	Best Method	Procedures	Rigour	Process
Ends	Plan	Strategy	Portfolio	Architectures	Themes
Methods	Ours	Best	None	One Way	Any Way
Nature	Responsive	Top Down	Bottom Up	Blueprints	Interactive

Figure 1.1
Strategic information systems planning approaches (adapted from Earl, 1993)

Michael Earl's work on the strategic information systems (IS) planning (SISP) phenomenon is particularly useful for classifying practices, and suggesting their differing levels of effectiveness. He identifies five generic approaches: business-led, method-driven, administrative, technological and organizational (Earl, 1993)). Each approach includes a technique (method), a process, and a manner of implementation. More detailed characteristics of the five types of SISP are represented in Figure 1.1. While Earl's research indicates that the 'organizational' SISP approach is the most effective, it is useful, since we are also trying to identify ineffective practices in this chapter, to discuss briefly each approach.

Business-led: the basic assumption of this approach is that current business direction is the only basis for IT/IS plans. Consequently, business planning drives SISP. In other words, the business is leading IT and not the other way round. The upside of this approach is the recognition of IT as a strategic resource to the organization. The downside is the common finding that business plans are often not detailed enough to provide a basis for IT needs (see Figure 1.2).

Method-driven: adherents of this approach assume that planning is enhanced by a formal method or technique. IT managers influenced by this approach most probably believe that business management requires the profile and/or distinction of formal methodology or a consultant's blessing on the planning process. The benefits of this approach are dependent upon the organization, but may in fact raise the strategy profile and/or plug gaps in the strategy. On the other hand, the method may become more important than the results and implementation process. Unfortunately we have seen all too many organizations go down this route, with the plan rarely being implemented properly because organizational stakeholders fail to take ownership, especially where it has been consultant-driven (as opposed to consultant-facilitated).

Administrative: in this approach, the focus is on resource planning. It produces a one-year or multi-year development portfolio of approved projects; no project is undertaken unless resident on this resulting plan. While this approach encourages user input and generates system synergies as a result of the comprehensive portfolio view, administrative planning, unfortunately, can evidence a non-strategic direction and may result in a resource-constrained plan. This approach frequently results in user-led as opposed to business-led strategy and, in the terms we will use in Chapter 2, 'useful' rather than 'strategic' IT. The administrative process is often too 'bottom-up' and is easily politicized into those with most influence, persistence or persuasiveness getting the funds.

Technological: this approach requires analytical modelling methods to produce an information systems-oriented model (or models) of the business. It is a time- and resource-intensive approach, often engaging the use of CASE (computer aided software engineering) tools. The approach supports the development of a robust architecture based on rigorous analysis. It can, however, become too complex, losing management support and implementation support. It can also take too long and its results can often be out of phase with changing business requirements (see Figure 1.2). As we shall see in Chapter 9, increasingly infrastructure has to be developed through close liaison with business needs. This planning approach tends to be too inflexible for this to happen.

Organizational: this approach assumes that SISP is not a one-off, 'tidy' endeavour, but rather one that requires constant and ongoing integration between the IT function and the organization. Methods are employed but only on an as-needed basis. The emphasis is on the process of management understanding and

17

	Business-Led	Method-Driven	Administrative	Technological	Organizational
Strengths	Simple	Provides a methodology	System viability	Rigour	Become normal
	Business first	Plugs strategy gap	System synergies	Focus on infrastructure	Emphasis on implementation
	Raises IS status	Raises strategy profile	Encourages user input	Favours integrated tools	Promotes IS–user partnership
Weaknesses	*Ad hoc* method	Lack of user involvement	Non-strategic	Lacks management support	Generation of new themes
	Lacks management commitment	Too influenced by method	Bureaucratic	Only partial implementation	Soft methodology
	Depends on quality of business strategy	Implementation unlikely	Resource constrained	Complexity	Architecture becomes difficult

Figure 1.2
Strengths and weaknesses of SISP approaches (after Earl, 1993, 1996)

involvement. Its benefits include an emphasis on implementation and the promotion of IT–user partnership, while its risks include a 'soft', hard-to-quantify methodology and an increased difficulty in architecture development. While few organizations we have advised have had exclusively organizational approaches to planning, we have helped several to move in that direction. For example, in one country the Post Office IT Services group comprised a Business Systems Group (consultancy, systems strategy, technical direction, project management and implementation), a Group Centre (strategic framework for the whole organization) and an IT Services group (technical solutions, systems integration, infrastructure, enterprise service management). The planning process and ongoing review/ measurement process included sub-boards (effectively, cross-organization committees) with representatives from business and IT. Some of the weaknesses Earl uncovered with the organizational approach are shown in Figure 1.2.

In summary, we find organizations demonstrating varieties of planning practice, and all too many adopting less effective approaches. Earl's classification helps to diagnose why organizations might not be getting IT right at the front end, and what to do about this. Regardless of the approach, strategic systems planning, or some equivalent planning/prioritization process, should be the beginning of lifecycle evaluation. The research points to the 'method' and 'technological' approaches as ones to avoid: little is ever initiated in the method-driven approach, while the technological approach produces little in the way of business competitiveness. The 'administrative' approach is the most prevalent, and is more conducive to user commitment. Under the business-led approach undoubtedly some obviously necessary business applications get actioned. However, the 'organizational' approach is the most recommendable, with most of the 'themes' initiated producing competitive advantage. A latent problem here is making sure that delivering the IT for these business themes results in a consistent technology plat-form, rather than a 'spaghetti' one.

The organizational approach works through using such process arrangements as multidisciplinary teams, task forces, improve-ment groups and educational processes. Successful adherents tend to take an eclectic approach to use of techniques, rather than religiously sticking to *the* method. The organizational approach is correlated with dispersal of IT/IS attention throughout a relatively IT-literate organization. Implementation tends to be incremental, based on learning and evolutionary. This approach fits with a strong strand in the general strategic management literature that has moved way from competitive positioning analysis and rational planning. Thus Mintzberg (1990) is typical in arguing that strategy is more likely successful if it is strongly emergent and based on learning, and in fact a mixture of the formal and informal, the analytical and the emergent. Getting the balance right in applying the organizational approach, especially where large complex organizations inexorably move to bureau-cratizing most processes, always remains a challenge.

It is not enough to have strong planning processes; the question is – does the planning approach translate into effective use of IT? Manifestly, some approaches do not accomplish this well. However, such planning approaches are invariably deeply embedded in an organization's management processes, and our own experience suggests that SIS planning approaches need a lot of work and senior management attention to change.

1.7 Fallacy six: it's plug and play – IT as a 'fire-and-forget' missile

During 2002 we continued to read advertisements such as: 'Customer Relationship Management Globally in 90 days'.

Predictions of the soon-arriving 'real-time event-driven company' continued to be made. We noticed, and over the years sometimes advised on, government policy initiatives in areas such as health, crown prosecution, defence, local government, internal revenue service – all of them with massive IT implications for the delivery of the change and the new service. As one example, in December 2001 the UK government announced £85 million in new IT funding and set out a belated strategy to stress the importance of IT in plans to modernize the Health Service. In the face of over 1000 acute health trusts each with about 30 support teams, £85 million would seem to be too insubstantial to make much difference. It would seem that public–private partnerships with IT suppliers would be sought as a route to extra funding, but the record there has been mixed (see also Fallacy Seven below). But the plans for modernizing the NHS are still quite short on how any strategy actually gets funded so that it is implemented in ways that significantly improve management, and service to patients. As a general point, in no developed economy is this helped where politicians are in office long enough to begin initiatives, but often move on before those initiatives are scheduled to be implemented. Furthermore, few politicians have any interest in or understanding of the complexities and difficulties IT implementation represents to any organization.

In all this, we frequently find that IT is being thought of in terms of a 'quick technological fix'. The actual costs in terms of money, management time and effort, painful changes to the organization, people, processes and systems are, invariably, greatly underestimated. In many cases the result is that implementation itself is under-funded and becomes a self-fulfilling disappointment. In many other cases managers massively underestimate the difference between installing a new technology and getting it integrated into processes, ways of working, structures, and institutionalized into how goals are achieved on a daily basis at every level in the organization. This is why we devote Chapters 7 and 8 wholly to the issue of implementation. The case studies at the end of this chapter reinforce that IT can never be thought of as 'plug-and-play'.

Some sense of the difficulties can be realized by looking at the Internet arena, as organizations have attempted to evolve into e-businesses. We studied this ourselves, and the case history of Charles Schwab in Chapter 7 shows that evolving into an e-business is a very long haul indeed, involving a complex of factors and resources needing to be managed assiduously, in this case, over five years. In looking at just the issue of structure, we found organizations struggling to make decisions on whether to integrate or separate off their e-business initiatives (Willcocks and Plant, 2002). Famously, Tesco's e-retailing effort used existing retail outlets and stock. Barnes and Noble tried to compete against Amazon by setting up a 'pure play' largely divorced from the advantages of integrating with its parent firm; likewise Waterstones in the UK. Both subsequently changed their minds on the way forward. From our work we can suggest the occasions when it is better to integrate with the parent firm, namely when:

- the brand extends naturally into the Internet;
- current executives have the right skills and experience and the right people can be attracted and retained by the parent firm;
- executives are willing to judge and manage by different reward and performance criteria;
- the business, its distribution systems and IT platform translate easily into the Internet and play to its strengths;
- the integrated company continues to look attractive to potential alliance partners;
- cultures gel in a mutually supportive rather than a conflictual manner.

This could read partly as advice on how to respond and implement the challenges presented by any IT effort going to the heart of the enterprise. Likewise the findings of Kanter (2001). In looking at many hundreds of e-business change efforts Rosabeth Kanter came up with a 'How not to change' guide that has salutary messages for all attempting to implement IT, and which we summarize here.

1 Sprinkle Internet responsibilities throughout the company and let them all go forward as small and innocuous. Be sceptical if any seem to have potential and stress that the Internet is over-hyped.
2 Run Internet initiatives through a committee of people from unrelated areas, already overburdened in their primary jobs. Give its leadership to someone as a reward for loyal service rather than because s(he) knows anything about the Internet.
3 Go for the least demanding things you can do on the Web – a 'yawner app' rather than a 'killer app'.
4 Hand over the technical work to vendors who are most dismissive of your existing business but whose abilities you are least capable of assessing (see also INSUROR below).

5 Replicate on the Web what you do off-line. Duplicate your traditional business model and assumptions.

6 Make sure any Internet initiative meets every corporate standard; give it enough funding to keep it alive but not enough to risk it becoming an innovation (for an alternative, see Chapter 8).

7 Allow the organization to stay decentralized in its approach, and offer no extra incentives for cooperating in cyberspace. Stress the advantages of business unit autonomy and reward each unit for its own performance only.

8 Dismiss on-line competitors and keep comparing yourself with traditional competitors in the physical world.

9 Give people in the organization e-tools they are unable to use, requiring changes they will be confused about making. Do not allow on-the-job, or indeed much, training. Punish people for their 'resistance to change'.

10 Forget the customer. It is the company that is in control and the Internet provides a new opportunity for *us* to communicate with *them*.

In later chapters we spell out what needs to be done to move from such a recipe for disaster to institutionalizing deep change when it comes to IT, from moving to 'kill-the-app' to implementing 'killer apps'. As we shall see, to do so means going a long way from treating IT as a quick fix. It means considerable work in getting many resources to the right level and aligned, and it needs immense work on the softer side of the organization, requiring also great sensitivities over the political implications of IT-enabled business innovation.

1.8 Fallacy seven: outsourcery – become a virtual organization

Particularly prevalent from the early 1990s, and reinforced in the Internet years of 1998–2001, has been the notion of focusing on your own core competencies as an enterprise and outsourcing the rest to one or more 'world class' IT service suppliers. Outsourcing seems to provide a certain amount of magic in offering to take the IT pain away, reduce costs, improve service and allow management to devote themselves to strategic issues rather than be pulled away into IT operational firefighting. Prime effective users of the Internet such as Dell and Cisco are often cited as virtual organizations, or at least having high degrees of virtuality enabled by their external sourcing strategies. But as we shall see in Chapter 6, such companies in fact outsource very carefully indeed, and retain a lot of control internally.

In practice outsourcing runs many risks, as we document in Chapter 6, and needs to be very disciplined. For example, it is difficult to identify what any organization's core capabilities are, let alone what they need to be. All too often IT, for example, is dismissed as almost all 'non-core' and a prime outsourcing candidate. But we find in organization after organization that IT relates in complex ways to systems, processes, how work gets done, competitive advantage and whether any business initiatives will get delivered. There also seems to be an inordinate belief in the 'good offices' and capabilities of the IT services market. All too often we see the decision as not only that nearly all IT is 'non-core', but also that not much needs to be done in management terms to leverage supplier performance. Undue reliance frequently falls upon the contract for this. Chapter 8 provides an alternative view of the core IT capabilities needed to be retained in-house.

It is true to say that IT outsourcing has outlived the five-year period typical of a management fad. Global market revenues have grown from US$9 billion in 1990 to a projected US$150 billion-plus by 2004. The underlying compound annual growth rate has been 15–20 per cent in the 1992–2000 period, with the leading markets of USA and UK showing sometimes dramatic rises in a particular year when a number of mega-deals have been signed. Another leading market is Australia, which has shown rapid growth – AUS$2.2 billion in 1998, and an IDC estimated AUS$3.87 billion in 2002 with a 24 per cent annual growth rate from 1997 to 2002. Regionally, other predictions of annual growth for the 1997–2002 period are: Japan 6 per cent, Asia–Pacific 16 per cent, Latin America 20 per cent, Canada 14 per cent, Western Europe 9 per cent, USA 10 per cent and rest of the world 26 per cent. As we discuss in Chapter 6, this buoyancy is likely to be maintained by further developments in areas such as e-commerce, applications service provision, business process outsourcing, managed network services and supply chain management.

But is IT outsourcing *the* answer? IT Directors look to outsourcing for, for example, dramatic cost reductions, service improvements and/or an influx of hard-to-get-and-keep staff. Company Boards look to ditch their long-standing IT headache of perceived mediocre in-house performance and expensive headcount. They look to make their fixed costs variable, and pass on the costs of future IT investment to external suppliers. They also have seen outsourcing as an opportunity to restructure favourably the financial accounts. Happily, announcements of big IT outsourcing deals also tend to inflate the share price for a limited period as well. So, clearly, IT outsourcing can serve a range of purposes. However, we need to look a little more closely at the record.

One major source of evidence on IT outsourcing is provided by Lacity and Willcocks (2001). This establishes the outcomes from 116 IT sourcing case histories across the 1991–2000 period. The metrics used were: organizational objectives against results; cost reductions achieved against anticipated; and satisfaction levels established by the organization by, for example, user satisfaction questionnaires, level of disputes, invoking of penalty clauses. The results are shown in Figure 1.3.

Selective IT outsourcing emerges as the most effective practice, closely followed by the in-house route. We found successful selective outsourcers embracing several distinctive practices. They had more limited and realistic expectations, signed short (2–4 year) contracts for which the business and technical requirements remained relatively stable, kept in-house resource

DECISION	Success	Failure	Mixed	Unable To Determine/ Too Early To Tell	TOTAL
Total Outsourcing	11 (38%)	10 (35%)	8 (27%)	4	33
Total In-house Sourcing	13 (76%)	4 (24%)	0 (0%)	2	19
Selective Outsourcing	43 (77%)	11 (20%)	2 (3%)	8	64
TOTAL	67	25	10	14	116

Figure 1.3
IT sourcing decisions and outcomes – 1991–2000 (Lacity and Willcocks, 2001)

and knowledge to fall back on resulting in less power asymmetry developing in favour of the vendor and lower potential switching costs, often leveraged competition through using multiple suppliers, and found ways in the contract to give the supplier an incentive and to build in flexibility.

The track record of total in-house IT sourcing has improved from that before 1996. At that time, one-third were found to be unsuccessful because of an amalgam of in-house complacency, little sense of crisis, lack of external benchmarking and lack of threat from an external vendor outsourcing bid. The evidence suggests that in-house functions have been actively responding to marketplace developments in the last five years, and have been seeking to improve IT management, replicate vendor practices in-house, compete with potential vendor bids and benchmark performance against market developments.

Total outsourcing emerges as a distinctly high risk practice, a reason why, on our evidence, most organizations have not been going down that route. As Figure 1.3 shows, we have looked at outcomes from 29 of the 120-plus biggest IT outsourcing deals in the world, all of them involving outsourcing infrastructure, and they show a 35 per cent failure rate. It should be said that this is a significantly better result than we were getting from a number of early 1990s total outsourcing deals. Those unsuccessful deals shared certain characteristics. Virtually all sought primarily cost reduction. The organizations were in financial trouble, and saw total IT outsourcing as a financial package to improve their company's position, rather than as a way of leveraging IT for business value, and keeping control of their IT destiny. All were 10- to 12-year single-supplier deals, initiated by the company board with little IT management input.

The unsuccessful client organizations saw IT as an undifferentiated commodity, contracted incompletely and failed to keep enough requisite in-house management capability. They incurred significant hidden costs, degradation of service, power asymmetries developing in favour of vendors, and loss of control over their IT destiny. They did little to build and sustain client–vendor relationships, yet were reluctant to change vendor because of the high switching costs.

Most of the failing total outsourcing deals shown in Figure 1.3 were still following this pattern. The interesting group is that with 'mixed' results. Typically these are experiencing some success in one part of the deal, but little in other major parts. Thus one aerospace company signed a US$3 billion long-term contract, received a cash influx of US$300 million and transferred 1500 IT employees to the vendor. The infrastructure part of the contract was well managed, but some other sections had to be cancelled after the first year. Subsequently, the vendor was found to lack idiosyncratic business knowledge needed for designing and running engineering-based systems. Serious service and cost issues continued to plague parts of vendor performance.

Success in total IT outsourcing has taken a variety of routes. On the evidence:

- it requires a lot of management maturity and experience of IT outsourcing, as exemplified by BP Exploration in the early 1990s;
- it needs complete and creative contracting;
- a less long-term focus in the contracting arrangements, but a more long-term one in the relationship dimension; and
- very active and fully staffed post-contract management along the lines detailed in Chapter 8.

Among the successes shown in Figure 1.3, several were total outsourcing, long-term deals for IT infrastructure/mainframe operations. One involved a strategic alliance, where the company spun off its entire IT function in a shared risk reward and joint ownership joint venture with a software and services supplier. One involved a short-term contract to wind down a public-sector agency about to be privatized. Several went down the multiple-supplier 5- to 7-year contract route, while several were single-supplier deals that took on board the above prescriptions, had detailed contracts and were also high profile, with the vendors wary of adverse publicity in specific countries or markets. These issues will receive a lot more coverage in Chapter 6.

1.9 Fallacy eight: our distinctiveness makes comparisons irrelevant and learning unlikely

It continually surprises us in our work how internally focused organizations become, and how infrequently they seek external comparisons. Even more noticeable is the failure to compare across sites, business units or divisions within the same organization, let alone share practices and learning. This is especially true of how IT is planned for and delivered. In one multinational that had outsourced all its IT, ostensibly to develop a common technology platform, after five years we found seven different types of help-desk, a variety of software being used in different regions and a noticeable lack of interest in IT developments and management practices elsewhere in the organization. In fact the basic drive was to be different, not to converge. But can managers really seriously believe that there is nothing to learn from what succeeds and fails with IT elsewhere? The answer is, intellectually, probably not, but in their practices they frequently behave otherwise. Here then is a final test to bring the points of this introductory chapter together. Below we present three small case histories and their learning points. One is a failure, one is a success and the third compares a success and failure in a similar marketplace. Let us see what we can learn from these.

1.9.1 Case 1 – INSUROR, IT and business transformation

By the mid-1990s this insurance company was not reacting fast to the market, could not launch new products quickly, and could not build complex flexible products in a re-usable modular fashion. INSUROR (not the real name, changed by request) recognized that to be a major Life and Pension company, it needed to transform its administrative and operational way of working. It needed a new 'contract engine' for administering and developing existing and future insurance policy products, a 'client repository' data warehouse, improved speed and quality in customer service, a new call centre and improved communication channels. This amounted to what was acknowledged by senior managers as a business transformation agenda, in which IT was heavily implicated.

While the IT function had been streamlined and improved over several years, it was recognized that external IT-supplier help was needed. Of the two suppliers in the frame, SUPCO (name changed), a major multinational, was selected, essentially to transform the client administrative policy systems of the insurance company. An ambitious deadline of two years was agreed. The terms were tough on the supplier. SUPCO was given overall programme leadership, and had to deliver all components according to a strict schedule for a fixed price. The first deliverable – a statement of business requirements – was due within nine months. If it was not delivered, INSUROR reserved the right to invoke a termination clause, without penalties, before any payment. Any other late delivery was subject to liquidated damages. INSUROR retained rights in any requirements specifications developed. SUPCO signed because they believed that if they could deliver on this contract they could dominate the insurance market in terms of IT provision. They also believed they had developed a model (IM) of the insurance industry and the way it worked that could help to identify INSUROR's information requirements very quickly.

To get such a good deal INSUROR, in fact, through its contract negotiations, delayed the beginning of work for SUPCO, which ate into the supplier's already very tight time targets. SUPCO's CEO, who was the major champion of the deal, resigned in the first two months of the project, leaving what we will call the CAPS (client, administrative, policy system) project to be delivered by four different functions within SUPCO. The supplier found it difficult to commission its most senior project managers to work on CAPS, so the project managers appointed had little customer experience with such a large project. They quickly ran into difficulties, as it became obvious that SUPCO had greatly underestimated the size of the task, and the complexity of insurance products and administration. They also made little headway with using the IM to drive out detailed business requirements. Eventually they had to turn back to more traditional methods. While INSUROR supplied many staff to the project and appointed several managers to certain positions, these all tended to wait for orders and stand back and wait for SUPCO to make the moves.

A steering committee met frequently as an increasing number of problems arose. Six months in, SUPCO brought in a senior project manager to audit progress. He recommended de-scoping the project, changing the timescales, and moving many elements of the CAPS project to pilot mode. He was made project manager, but despite progress, SUPCO failed to meet the first deadline and, to INSUROR, looked like not going to get very far. The INSUROR CEO made the difficult decision to protect INSUROR's interest, pay no fees and terminate the contract.

Learning: what can we learn from this real-life case? We would suggest at least the following.

1 Don't sign 'Win–Lose' contracts with IT suppliers. INSUROR over-protected itself and drove far too hard a bargain with SUPCO, to the point that the contract was almost impossible to deliver. We have found that such contracts look like 'Win–Lose' to the client, but in three quarters of cases end up 'Lose–Lose', as in this case (Kern *et al.*, 2002). While SUPCO incurred

losses of many millions of pounds, INSUROR wasted one year and did not get its new administration engine.

2 A business transformation project is not a good one to hand over to an IT supplier to deliver. The supplier will be needed as a resource, but should be under internal management control. The business and IT function need to take much more primary roles in the delivery of such a project. At root, the problem was one of contracting. The deal was treated by INSUROR staff as an IT outsourcing arrangement when in fact it involved untested methodologies, a very high element of research and development, with the actual business requirements unspecified and probably changing over the two-year time period. Later we will suggest that a completely different way of delivering such projects is required (see Chapter 8). The low risk approach is to outsource tasks that you can write a detailed contract for, and that you understand and can measure. Otherwise the project needs internal sponsors, champions and business ownership.

3 The project needed much more pro-active participation and management by the client company INSUROR, especially given the complexity of insurance work and existing pro-cesses. It is difficult to drive out business requirements, for example, without not just tapping internal knowledge, but having knowledgeable people heavily involved in managing the projects, and committed to delivering the project benefits. Too much emphasis was given to standing back and letting SUPCO deliver on its contractual terms, while controlling their performance through relatively weak mechanisms such as the steering committee. Much better to pro-actively influence performance as it happens. The IT function could have been much more involved also, but was sidelined and reduced largely to auditing SUPCO performance.

4 Even 'world class' IT service suppliers need managing. In this case SUPCO was revealed as not a monolith but a group of disparate departments, none of which appeared to take ultimate responsibility for end performance. Provisioning the right IT staff is often difficult even for large suppliers such as this one. And sometimes tools and methodologies get over-sold, not just to clients, but even within the supplier itself, as was the case with the IM approach. This convinced the SUPCO negotiators that they could meet the aggressive deadlines they signed up to.

5 There were other projects being conducted more effectively at INSUROR at the same time as the CAPS project, some of them involving SUPCO. But the learning from those positive

experiences was not transferred into the CAPS project. IT-based projects are inherently risky, as Chapter 8 will make clear. Therefore create mechanisms for transferring learning on IT.

1.9.2 Case 2 – General Electric and its move to e-business

By mid-2001 this old economy winner was trading more through its private on-line marketplace – over US$20 billion in 2001 alone – than all the other business-to-business (B2B) marketplaces put together. In 1997 its GE Information Services (GEIS) had formed one of the biggest pre-Internet electronic buying networks. However, in GE's conservative culture it was difficult to win support for a new B2B business, not least because it involved cannibalizing the existing profitable GEIS business based on Electronic Data Interchange (EDI), rather than the Internet. By 1999, however, doubts set in about this focus, even though GEIS sticking with EDI meant that it met the CEO Jack Welch's criterion that all divisions must be number one or two in their markets.

Into 1999, the head of GEIS began agitating for a bigger role and a move away from the mainframe culture that dominated. In practice, e-business had already appeared in a few isolated spots, for example, GE Plastics had a Web site as early as 1994. By 1997 one of its divisions was allowing customers to make on-line orders. GEIS also operated a partly based Web service, which simplified and automated the bid and procurement process for other divisions, including GE Lighting. Progress was still slow. One could see why. For example, selling on-line would threaten to put the GE sales force out of business. Big Internet investments threatened the major measure by which all managers were assessed – the bottom line in each of their divisions. Moreover GEIS itself was wrapped up in dealing with Y2K (year 2000).

The big change occurred in 1999 when Jack Welch himself became sold on the importance of the Internet. By 2000 Welch had created 'destroyyourbusiness.com', which encouraged all divisions to reinvent themselves before somebody else did. In GEIS, the head decided in March 2000 to keep the existing operation as GE Systems services, an EDI provider, but split off a more entrepreneurial group – GE Global Exchange Services (GXS) as a software and e-marketplace builder. He chose to run GXS, which had fewer legacy obligations to hamper innovation.

A year later all GE's big divisions were running their own Web marketplaces for internal and external use. Three main initiatives were 'e-buy', 'e-sell' and 'e-make'. All three sought to extend the focus on quality inherent in GE's passion for six-sigma manufacturing and digitize to save money and reach customers faster.

Interestingly, the greatest hurdle was not technology, but culture (see also Chapter 7). Thus, fearing for their jobs, sales staff had to be offered bonuses to help customers use the Web sites to make orders. Employees were watched closely in case they used other routes – such as the telephone – to order supplies or make travel arrangements, for example. Some offices closed their mail rooms for all but one day a week to stop employees from using regular post, while others locked their printer rooms except for occasional carefully monitored days. Most of this started as about cost savings and quality. Subsequently the focus has moved also to new products, selling to new customers the old sales force did not reach, for example small businesses, and to expanding the supplier base by letting more firms bids on-line.

GXS still has some constraints on its ability to develop. It can invest in its own research and development, but during 2001 was not allowed to buy other firms with shares. Earnings-dilution acquisitions were still difficult for GE to accept. This meant that GXS could not profit much from the industry's consolidation, but must stick to organic growth and internal development. Clearly, developing an IT-based business from inside a large conglomerate is not easy.

Learning

1 Strategic IT initiatives need very senior management commitment and endorsement. They also need senior business line managers' commitment to deliver results. Nothing much happened at GE until Jack Welch bought into the Internet and the head of GEIS determined to head a new entrepreneurial venture. Earl and Feeny (2000) have produced a well reasoned piece on the importance of the top team in adopting a transformation agenda for IT, and describe well the characteristic behaviours of the CEO and top managers that make such initiatives successful.
2 The tasks of introducing and then institutionalizing IT-enabled change into a complex, conservative organizational culture are easily underestimated. Such change needs an

organizational and political, much more than a technological, focus – the subject of Chapter 7.

3 What has made the e-business initiatives successful in GE have been the strong business goals and imperatives established for applying the technology. This is endorsed strongly by our own findings in Willcocks and Plant (2002).

4 The issue of whether to integrate the e-business initiative, or set up a separate operation, comes through as a likely determinant of the levels of success achieved. At GE, semi-autonomy was selected and definitely produced results. However, it can be seen that even more autonomy might actually produce more success, but the risks and costs appeared unacceptable to the parent firm and its divisions. Trade-offs and politics are the ways of the big organization, in IT, as well as in many other areas.

1.9.3 Case 3 – drugstore.com versus Walgreens

Drugstore.com is one of the first on-line pharmacies. Walgreens is a much more traditional US-based drug store, that also saw itself as a convenience store. In July 1999 drugstore.com began selling its shares to the public. In August it had a market valuation of US$3.5 billion, despite having less than 500 employees, operating for less than nine months and planning to lose hundreds of millions of dollars before turning to profit some five years later.

This represented a real challenge to a traditional operator like Walgreens, at least in stock value terms. For example, Walgreens lost 40 per cent of its stock value in the lead up to drugstore.com going public; nearly US$15 billion in Walgreen's market value disappeared. But Walgreens did not react by jumping into Internet technologies feet first. One of his great companies, Collins (2001) tells the story of how Walgreens began experimenting with a Web site while engaging in intense dialogue about its implications within the context of its own strategic intent. Thus Walgreens had embarked on choosing physical retailing sites that gave customers maximum convenience in their neighbourhoods. How did the Internet fit with that? And how could these technologies be tied to Walgreen's major economic determinant of performance, namely cash flow per customer visit? How could the Internet enable Walgreens to do even better what they are best at and care most passionately about?

Gradually Walgreens began to find ways of bringing the Internet directly to bear on its home-grown inventory-and-distribution model, then its convenience concept. Thus the customer can fill in his/her prescription on-line, then drive to the local Walgreens drive-through wherever they happen to be, and pick up the items in question. The customer can also have it shipped to them if that is more convenient. By late 2000 Walgreens had launched a sophisticated Web site that was easy to use, backed by a highly reliable system of delivery. It announced a significant increase in job openings to support its sustained growth in business over the Internet. By then Walgreens' stock value had doubled within a year. Meanwhile drugstore.com continued to accumulate massive losses (US$124 million in the first year), and had to lay off many staff to conserve cash. By late 2000 drugstore.com had lost nearly all of its initial increase in stock value. As Collins puts it: 'Walgreens went from crawl to walk to run, drugstore.com went from run to walk to crawl'.

By 2001 Walgreens had pioneered the application of satellite communications and computer network technology, linked to its concept of convenient corner drugstores, tailored to the unique needs of specific demographics and locations. Its massive investment in a satellite system linked all stores together, forming in effect, a giant web of a single corner pharmacy. In this respect, as of 2002 Walgreens probably were leading its industry by at least 5–7 years.

Learning:

1 It is interesting to compare two companies ostensibly in the same industry over the same period of time, and their approaches to utilizing IT. Drugstore.com manifestly bought heavily into Fallacies One, Two and Three described above. In particular the New Rules orientation and the relatively easy capital available made drugstore.com believe it could trump traditional brands and lumbering large company competitors, because, moving first, the superior technology would see it through. Drugstore.com learned the hard way that the technology is *not* the business.

2 Walgreens demonstrates why it continued to outperform its rivals. It had a very robust business and financial model, a great business idea – what Collins calls its 'Hedgehog' concept – related to convenience, and used the Internet to accelerate its ability to deliver on the business and financial imperatives. Unlike in GE's case, for example, it is able to

innovate fast, provide large-scale IT investment and integrate the Internet applications into the heart of the enterprise.

3 Walgreens were not deflected by the hype surrounding the technology. Its real question was: 'how can this technology influence our strategic agenda?'. For drugstore.com, one is under the impression that the technology *is* the strategy, but until they work out how the technology can leverage a coherent business concept that has a differentiated customer service offering based on what customers really want, and a financial and operational model that can make profitable sales, little progress will be made.

1.10 Conclusion

The purpose of this first chapter was to make readers think about their own organizations, and whether they, too, are guilty of these fundamental fallacies. We need to make the point that these fallacies are not restricted to particular sectors, particular sizes or types of organization. Our practical experience supports what the research has long shown – that good IT management practice can be applied across the board. Accepting this, the first rule of thumb is to check out how IT is done in your organization against these eight fallacies. It is worth being brutal with the facts at this point. The second rule of thumb is to then measure your own practices against the seventeen benchmark good practices we describe in the next chapter. After that, the book dwells in detail on particular areas of practice. We show how to develop strategy, how to create navigation processes, how to source IT and how to deliver IT to the organization. Finally, we point also to the criticality of infrastructure in ensuring that strategy is not just shaped and detailed but delivered, but also how business requirements can be left more uncertain and open-ended than ever before.

References

Collins, J. (2001) *Good To Great*, New York: Random House.

Earl, M. (1993) Experiences in strategic information systems planning, *MIS Quarterly*, Vol. 17, 1.

Earl, M. (ed.) (1996) *Information Management: the organizational dimension*, Oxford: Oxford University Press.

Earl, M. and Feeny, D. (2000) How to be a CEO in an information age, *Sloan Management Review*, Winter, 11–23.

Feeny, D. (2001) E-opportunity: the strategic marketing perspective, in Willcocks, L. and Sauer, C (eds), *Moving To E-Business*, London: Random House, Chapter 3.

Kanter, R. (2001) *Evolve! Succeeeding in the Digital Culture of Tomorrow.* Boston: Harvard Business School Press.

Kern, T., Willcocks, L. and Van Heck, E. (2002) The winner's curse in IT outsourcing: avoiding relational trauma. *California Management Review*, Spring, 47–69.

Lacity, M. and Willcocks, L. (2001) *Global Information Technology Outsourcing: in search of business advantage.* Chichester: Wiley.

McKinsey and Co. (2000) Surviving in the aftermath of the B to C crash. *Business* 2.0, August 1st, 62–64.

Mintzberg, H. (1990) The design school: reconsidering the basic premises of strategic management. *Strategic Management Journal*, Vol. 11, 171–95.

Porter, M. (2001) Strategy And The Internet. *Harvard Business Review*, March, 63–78.

Rangan, S. and Adner, R. (2002) Profits and the Internet: seven misconceptions, in Brynjolfsson, E. and Urban, G. (eds), *Strategies For E-Business Success*. San Francisco: Jossey Bass.

Tapscott, D. (2001) Rethinking strategy in a networked world. *Strategy and Business*, **24**(3), 34–41.

Van Nievelt, G. and Willcocks, L. (1998) *Benchmarking Organizational and IT Performance*. Executive Research Briefing, Oxford: Templeton College.

Vitale, M. (1986) The growing risks of information systems success. *MIS Quarterly*, December, Vol. 10, 327–36.

Willcocks, L. and Plant, R. (2002) Pathways to e-business leadership: getting from bricks to clicks, in Brynjolfsson, E. and Urban, G. (eds), *Strategies For E-Business Success*. San Francisco: Jossey Bass.

2

Plotting the course:
where we need to be

'If you don't know where you are going, any road will do'.
Ancient Chinese Saying.

'The trigger point is articulation of a business issue or
opportunity which, if successfully addressed, would radically
advance the achievement of vision and strategy. If there is no new
idea associated with IT investment, then the most that can be
expected is that some existing business idea will operate a little
more efficiently as old technology (or IT provider) is replaced by
new'. David Feeny, Templeton, Oxford.

'We must stop thinking about IT from a cost point of view, and
start thinking about delivery and results. But this means the
business has to understand its own value propositions, and has to
be able to say to the supply side, this is what we want, and this
is how we measure it. A fundamental move is to separate the
information from the technology, and develop separate
achievement measures around each. Of course all this is
counter-cultural for a lot of organizations'. Robert White,
Lucidus.

2.1 Introduction

We are frequently asked, in our advisory and research work:
who is really good at leveraging IT for business value? How do
they do strategy? How do they deliver strategy? How and why
is IT managed so well? While we can point to specific
organizations, and indeed, throughout the book we provide

examples of these and their practices, the reality is that the benchmark of superb practice is rarely achieved in the vast majority of organizations we have researched and advised. Information technology management has shown slow improvement over the last decade but progress has been hamstrung by, in particular, rapid developments in technology, speed of change in business requirements, the sheer number of internal business change initiatives, IT labour shortages and developments in the IT services market not always matched by organizational ability to understand and harness those developments. But if IT management has an indifferent track record, the core of the problem has been a continuing, almost global, failure to address the central issue of managing information well.

The key to effective use of IT is to have a clear business strategy and business model, an information strategy that supports those, and use of technologies to make these business and information strategies efficient. Without the first two, all that IT can do is to make more efficient an inappropriate business strategy, an ineffective business model and organizational infrastructure, and mediocre use of information. In this chapter we set a benchmark of 18 practices that, together, enables an organization to gain demonstrable significant business value from its IT. We organize these practices into four headings that stretch across the lifecycle of any IT investment. These are: Direction; Organization, People and the IT Function; Development and Project Management; and Delivery of On-going Operations. In this chapter we provide an overview of what constitutes very good IT management, with the rest of the book providing much more detail and illustrations on specific practices.

2.2 The first benchmark: direction – strategy and the strategic use of IT

Practice 1 – there is a clear *business strategy* that has been agreed, understood and bought into by all key managers. The strategy is dynamic and flexible, may be expressed in terms of 'strategic intent', 'simple rules' or whatever, but essentially provides a clear set of business imperatives for action. The strategy is also based on a robust financial and business model. According to Jim Collins (2001), what distinguishes the great companies he studied is the eventual adoption of a 'Hedgehog Concept'. He found these companies had a deep understanding of three intersecting issues:

1 what the company could be best in the world at;
2 what drives its economic engine – what the key financial indicators are, and the vital business model;
3 what the company is deeply passionate about.

Great companies set their goals and strategies on these deep understandings, and did not move outside their 'Hedgehog Concepts', once formulated. Collins found no evidence that great companies spent more time on strategic planning than did comparison companies.

Practice 2 – strategy for IT is subdivided into Information Technology (IT) strategy (supply side, technology platform), Information Systems (IS) strategy (demand side, business applications, business information requirements), Information and Technology Governance (I&TG) strategy (information and communications technology leadership, how IT is managed, roles and responsibilities, how the IT function is structured), and IT Market Sourcing (ITMS) strategy. Appropriate managers are assigned to fulfil these tasks (see below).

Thus the IT function for the rapidly developing e-world has four major task areas.

1 The business task is concerned with the elicitation and delivery of business requirements. Traditionally the area of *Information Systems Strategy*, capabilities here are business-focused, demand-led and concerned with defining the systems to be provided, their relationship to business needs and, where relevant, the inter-relationships and inter-dependencies with other systems. A further focus here is on a strategy for delivery, together with actual implementation. The task here is accomplished primarily by business unit managers, with the IT staff providing secondary support on technical matters.
2 The technical task is concerned with ensuring that the business has access to the technical capability it needs – taking into account such issues as current price/performance, future directions and integration potential. This is the traditional domain of *Information Technology Strategy*, that is defining the blueprint or architecture of the technical platform that will be used over time to support the target systems. It presents the set of allowable options from which the technical implementation of each system must be selected. A further concern is to provide technical support for delivery of the IT strategy. IT strategy is the primary concern of the IT function and staff.

3 The 'governance' task is concerned with *Information and Technology Governance Strategy,* which defines the governance and coordination of the organization's information and technology activity. This strategy is reached through the IT Director and staff, in association with senior business executives.

4 The supply task encompasses understanding and use of the external IT services market. As such it is the domain of *IT Market Sourcing Strategy.* Particularly critical here are decisions on what to outsource and buy in and source in-house, on which external suppliers to use and how. A further concern is ensuring appropriate delivery of external services contracted for. There will be distinctive skills and capabilities in place to deliver on these requirements (see below and Chapter 8).

Practice 3 – business and IT management can navigate through the domains of IT hype (mostly created by media, suppliers and consultants), IT capability ('technical solutions in search of business problems'), 'useful' IT (endless uses and demands by users) and strategic IT (the business agenda – relatively few applications that underpin business strategy and create dis-proportionate advantage for the organization). This formulation is provided by Feeny (1997).

In more detail, David Feeny observes that ever since IT became important organizationally, he has found four perennial IT domains to exist in the face of turbulent technology. Reference to these domains enables executives to assess their organizational goals for IT.

1 *IT Hype* – this domain goes beyond the actuality toward a focus on potential capabilities and outcomes. The information highway, predicted to transform the existence of every individual, is a good example of where the IT rhetoric goes beyond what actually can be provided reliably. Many see much of the 1998–2001 Internet Bubble as fuelled precisely by this level of 'Internet or Bust' rhetoric about the power of Web-based technologies.

2 *IT Capability* – within IT Hype lies the ever-increasing domain of IT capability, comprising products and services actually available today for organizations to exploit. Within this domain, the counterpart to the information highway is the Internet: it does exist and is used by organizations. Clearly, other technology strands are more mature than the Internet; the sum total of this domain represents a vast toolkit of

technology. But what is this toolkit a solution to? What capability should you care about?

3 *'Useful' IT* – no organization uses everything available in the IT Capability toolkit; this domain consequently consists of all the investments that provide at least a minimum acceptable rate of return to the organization. However, the demand for 'useful' IT can be endless and 'useful' IT can be actually damaging in its ability to eat resources and distract attention and time from more strategic IT deployments.

4 *Strategic IT* – this domain comprises the subset of potential investments that can make a substantial rather than marginal contribution to organizational achievement.

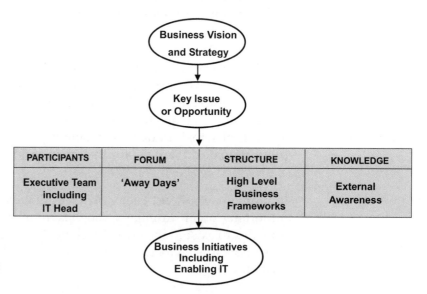

Figure 2.1
Business-led approach
(adapted from Feeny, in
Willcocks *et al.*, 1997)

Practice 4 – strategies detailed in the first two practices above are arrived at through a mutually informed process, are complementary and focused on agreed, common goals that relate to business value of IT. There are many ways this can be done. Feeny, for example, defines organizational exploitation of IT to be successful navigation through the domains, such that organizational resources become consistently focused on 'strategic IT' rather than merely on 'useful IT'. Contrast the following three approaches.

1 *IT-led* – in this navigation approach, senior management look to the IT function to professionally assess the domains and to propose an agenda for IT investment. Most organizations have operated in this manner at some point in the lifetime of

technology, and it may be accompanied by quite strong planning approaches (see Chapter 1, Fallacy Five). The difficulty with this approach lies in the inherent lack of application purpose for IT. In other words, technology's application is defined at the point of use, not at the point of manufacture. Consequently, the relevance of technology is a function of the user's imagination, not that of the product designer. The desire on behalf of the IT professionals to learn and understand new technology, and to attempt to apply it in a useful manner for the organization, results in 'IT Capability' or at best 'Useful IT' rather than 'Strategic IT'.

2 *User-led* – the natural response to the lack of application purpose is for the users to develop and argue the investment cases for technology usage. Unfortunately, this approach also commonly results in merely 'useful IT' for a number of reasons. First, only a number of users take up the challenge, and those that do tend to be IT enthusiasts (and so subject to the same issues as the IT professionals in making recommendations). Second, the users are operating within a bounded domain of responsibility. Consequently, their proposals may represent potential improvements to non-critical portions of the business.

3 *Business-led* – the business-led approach is represented by Figure 2.1. The business-led approach works on the assumption that anything is possible, envisions the ideal business initiative, then checks to see if the necessary IT is available. The second aspect of this business-led approach is that the IT investment evaluation flows naturally from the navigation process. Most organizations still operate investment appraisal processes that demand cost–benefit analyses of the proposed IT expenditure. The business-led approach assumes that, not the IT expenditure, but the adoption of new business ideas leads to business benefits, and consequently to 'Strategic IT'.

Feeny's approach provides a categorization of IT in the form of domains, a target domain for effective IT expenditure, and a navigational tool through the domains. The usefulness of the approach derives from its prescriptive direction.

Practice 5 – from these understandings managers can arrive at an IT strategic agenda, typically from:

(a) starting with business strategy and pinpointing IT needs;
(b) by also looking at the existing IT and establishing its technical quality and business value and making drop and improvement decisions; and

(c) by allowing innovation, which typically occurs close to the internal and external customer base at the margins or in the everyday operations of the business.

Indeed this is the basis of Earl's (1989) approach. Earl argues that a firm faces three issues when attempting to align and prioritize IT investments in the light of business strategy and opportunities. Let us consider these.

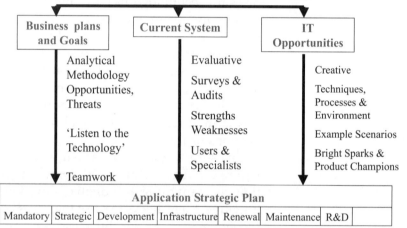

IT Strategy Formulation: A Multiple Methodology

Business plans and Goals	Current System	IT Opportunities
Analytical Methodology Opportunities, Threats	Evaluative Surveys & Audits	Creative Techniques, Processes & Environment
'Listen to the Technology'	Strengths Weaknesses	Example Scenarios
Teamwork	Users & Specialists	Bright Sparks & Product Champions

Application Strategic Plan							
Mandatory	Strategic	Development	Infrastructure	Renewal	Maintenance	R&D	

Figure 2.2
A multiple methodology (adapted from Earl, 1989)

The first issue is to *clarify* business needs and strategy in information systems terms. Earl's approach here is to use a top-down approach, shown as the first leg in Figure 2.2. Thus, a critical success factors (CSF) analysis might be used to establish key business objectives, decompose these into critical success factors, then establish the IS needs that will drive these CSFs.

The second issue is the *evaluation* of current information system provision and use (see insurance caselet example on p. 43). Senior managers need to understand the strengths and weaknesses of their current systems in order to facilitate drop or enhance decisions, and obtain an understanding as to where future investments in IT will be required. A bottom-up approach is needed here. This involves soliciting evidence from users and IT specialists on two major aspects: the technical quality of existing systems, i.e., their reliability, how easy they are to maintain and their cost-efficiency; and their business value in terms of impact on the business, ease and frequency of use. Such enquiries can reveal new insight and protect the organization from business exposures. For example, if an IT application has high impact but low technical quality it becomes immediately clear that investments need to be channelled into its maintenance, enhancement or replacement. Systems poor in both technical quality and business impact need to be divested. Our own experiences suggest that, even as at 2002, organizations are still very slow at making such 'drop' decisions. Notoriously, many systems can have high technical quality but are still not being properly exploited. This may be due to an initial failure to align the investment with strategic direction, or because the strategic thrust has changed over time. A new effort to realign the system is called for, or a divestment decision may be necessary. The bottom-up approach provides information and allows the opportunity for these type of decisions to be made.

Caselet example: operating division of a UK insurance company

A bottom-up evaluation of the existing systems portfolio for the Corporate Partnership division of this company was carried out. It revealed more clearly than before that most systems were of high business impact but of mediocre technical quality. These systems were between 10- and 14-years old and were taking 65 per cent of the IT budget in maintenance costs. Some replacement systems were being invested in, but it turned out that the size and spread of these new investments were too small. It also became clear that the replacement programme was on too long a time horizon and that the business was, in fact, seriously exposed to systems failures. It was resolved to outsource the running and maintenance of a high percentage of the legacy systems in order to refocus the internal development group on speedier development of new systems. Technical expertise would be bought in off the market to work on the development projects as needed.

The third issue is to ensure that other approaches do not drive out the *innovation* of new strategic opportunities offered by IT. In practice major innovative uses of IT for business advantage have rarely seemed to result from the application of formal planning approaches. Competitive edge systems frequently develop incrementally out of existing systems, from close contact and involvement between external customers and commercial managers. Once the idea is developed, it needs significant backing by those with resources and influence within the business. As a general rule, such applications have been pursued and developed outside formal IT administration procedures. An example of such development is shown in the Sterling Securities caselet.

Caselet example: Sterling Securities

In the mid-1990s this company provided security services to customers. It held about 5 per cent of the UK market and needed to grow market share. The security guarding industry had few entry barriers and had a reputation for poor quality and inconsistent service. Most companies had poor human resource systems leading to erratic, frequently inaccurate payment to security guards in their employment. This led to high labour turnover throughout the industry. Accepting customer perceptions of the service issues senior managers resolved to implement IS-based payroll, control and HR systems. These were developed with an independent software house. Once the systems were in, it became gradually clear that in dealing with an administrative problem, the company was also actually achieving differentiation in the marketplace. The systems were extended and included the ability of customers to use the facility for planning and control of the service. In time the software generated was marketed to other security companies as a standardized product without certain unique, differentiating features kept by the company. Two years into the development, Sterling appointed their first IT manager, and increased market growth was being achieved.

The multiple methodology provides three routes to achieving a strategic portfolio of IT applications. What is significant is that each route links IT investment to business needs. In fact there are three characteristics that makes an IT application plan such as that shown in Figure 2.2 strategic:

1 that the specific IT application has been successfully linked to business needs either through a bottom-up, top-down or inside-out analysis;

2 that the IT applications are suitably spread across the different types of application shown in Figure 2.2. The exact weighting will depend here on business strategy, the state of the IT inheritance and external events – for example changing competitor activity or customer requirements. However, there should be balance in the portfolio so that both existing and future business strategy are protected;

3 that the applications detailed in the strategic plan are fully committed to by those responsible for resourcing their implementation. This last requirement, in practice, is a very stringent criterion, and can provide some resolution to the problem all organizations experience – namely, too many ideas for IT applications, all with good business cases, but no real mechanisms, apart from political ones, for prioritizing investment in the face of resource and time shortages.

Practice 6 – measurement processes are in place that enable the organization to diagnose cost–benefit of potential IT investments and prioritize these investments to arrive at a risk-mitigated strategic applications portfolio. A set of measures are used to evaluate the technical, project delivery, financial, business process, user satisfaction and value, and learning payoffs from an IT investment across its lifetime. People are responsible for these metrics and driving benefits from the evaluation process. Results are tied to their performance appraisals and reward. These practices are discussed in detail in Chapter 5.

2.3 The second benchmark: organization, people and IT function

Practice 7 – the business and IT organizations, people and structures will have evolved through three phases, and will be mature enough in these areas to manage IT, including external IT service providers, maturely and strategically.

IT functions and the business typically evolve through three phases after a period of *ad hoc* proliferation of IT usage (see Figure 2.3):

1 *delivery* – how do we achieve IT service competence and deliver what the business wants?

2 *reorientation* – how do we get the business and IT people on a *strategic business* agenda for IT so that IT is managed as a strategic resource?

45

Growth Stages for the CIO, IT and the Business

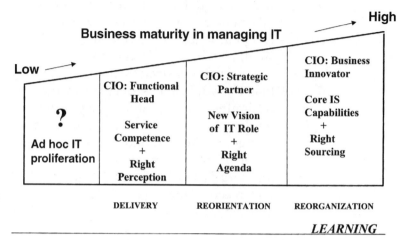

Figure 2.3
Evolution of the CIO, IT function and business (adapted from Feeny, in Willcocks and Sauer, 2001)

3 *reorganization* – how do we structure and decentralize now that the business and IT groups are sufficiently mature and what core IT capabilities do we need to retain in order to really leverage what the IT services market can provide for business advantage?

In the first phase, in seeking to control its use of IT, the IT function will focus on building its IT 'service to the business' delivery capability, probably bringing in external IT services to assist in this process on a selective basis. The IT Director typically will be very good at this process, and at managing technical people and the human resource policies that encourage staff retention, and very knowledgeable technically.

In the second phase the IT Director will be more concerned with liasing with senior managers as a peer, talking the language of business and showing how IT can create business value and change the way the business can operate. The credibility and reality of service delivery must be maintained. Business managers must evolve their ability and orientations to accept and deliver on their responsibilities and tasks in exploiting IT strategically.

In the third phase, where business units are sufficiently mature, typically IT responsibility is moved much more into those business units using a federal structure, with certain key restraining and enabling policies on IT retained at the centre. Our own work suggests that large-scale IT outsourcing only becomes effective when the organization has matured to this stage and it builds and retains nine in-house core IT capabilities (see below and Chapter 8).

In all this, it is key that the top business management team has evolved its capacity to manage IT strategically, from a business and IT perspective. This does not require technical knowledge. It does require a set of management practices, motivations and understandings that identify the business imperatives (e.g., cost reduction, better external customer service) and provide the business drive to achieve business value from IT.

Practice 8 – the structure of the IT function has been finalized and follows organizational structure. In large, complex organizations variants of the federal structure have been found to be the more effective. This is because a federal structure tends to minimize the disadvantages of becoming centralized, or decentralized, while capitalizing on the advantages of each.

Where federal structures are applied effectively the results gained are as shown in Figure 2.4. It can be seen that the role of the centre in such an organization structure is to provide both policing and enabling. Policing operates to prevent duplication of effort, reinventing of wheels, achievement of economies in purchasing, ensuring common standards and technologies. Enabling involves providing a critical mass of skills where required, funding, direction, links with corporate strategies and

The Federal IT Organization

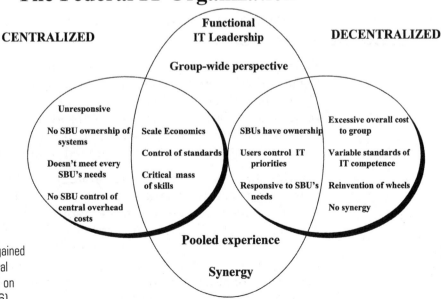

Figure 2.4
The advantages gained from the IT federal structure (based on Hodgkinson, 1996)

A Bank: Federal Arrangements

	Local	*Central*
Essential	•IS executive in Management Team •IS strategic planning •IS education of managers •Executive leadership for IT •Some IS development capability •Piloting new technologies •Relationship building •Service facilitation	•IT vendor, acquisition monitoring and •development - Policy and Management •Architectural & technical standards •Technical & quality assurance •Delineation of local responsibilities •IS human resource development •Chargeout & control policies •IT leadership, business systems thinking
Possible	•Some IT operations capability •Some business systems thinking •Contract monitoring (local needs)	•IS development consultancy •IT operations capability (pooled skills •Common systems development •Co-ordinating IS development • throughout the function •Co-ordinating IS across divisions and • business units •Relationship building (pooled) •Service facilitation (pooled)

Figure 2.5
How federal arrangements can be distributed (illustration only, adapted from Willcocks *et al.*, 1997)

sharing of knowledge. These are only examples. In all this, what is fundamental is that the centre and the business units have agreed on the distribution of tasks and personnel. A not untypical distribution of rights and responsibilities is shown in Figure 2.5.

2.4 The third benchmark: development and project management

Practice 9 – project management should be an in-house organizational, core capability, not restricted to IT projects or the IT function. Modern organizations need to be much more project-based, but their capacity to absorb change and deliver initiatives will be severely hampered if their project management capability is restricted to a limited number of functions.

Practice 10 – a risk-mitigating strategy is applied, of only outsourcing mature IT tasks that are well understood, and for which detailed contracts can be written and that can be monitored in detail. The same applies in the sort of tasks that can be left to any IT supplier, including the internal IT function. Development is a risky area, especially where it is a new, unstable technology or a radically new application of an existing technology/software, where the business does not know quite what it wants from the technology nor what the technology can do, and/or where there is lack of relevant IT expertise in-house, and amongst external IT service providers. We call these situations of *low technology maturity*.

Practice 11 – where technology maturity is low, projects should be seen as business projects, and delivered by credible, experienced project managers with a track record of delivering this size and type of project. A project needs a senior executive as a project sponsor who initiates the project, establishes its business imperative, provides its key resources (including managers) and protects the project. There is also a need for a project champion who communicates the vision, motivates direction, deals with political issues – s/he is typically a senior executive who has a lot of credibility and who will reap the business benefits from the project. The project team will be a multifunctional team with requisite full-time IT specialists, full-time good users, bought-in external IT people as needed, and business managers seconded as required.

Practice 12 – such projects are delivered quickly using a 'time-box philosophy'. Typically all projects have to be:

- delivered within a 90–120 day deadline (best practice organizations regularly drive these time limits down even further);
- are not started if this is not likely to be achieved;
- composed of a multifunctional team;
- are consistent in what will be developed and delivered, with overall IT strategy and the technology platform blueprint for the future;
- use a prototyping approach with regular IT developer–business user contact;
- with business executives making key decisions, and responsible for deriving business value from what is delivered.

This subject is so important, we devote Chapter 8 to spelling out the critical dimensions of making the approach work. In Chapter 7 we also describe the importance of taking a whole-organization approach to delivering large-scale change.

2.5 The fourth benchmark: delivery of on-going operations and infrastructure

Practice 13 – the IT function retains nine core IT capabilities that deliver on the four essential tasks described in Practice 2 above.

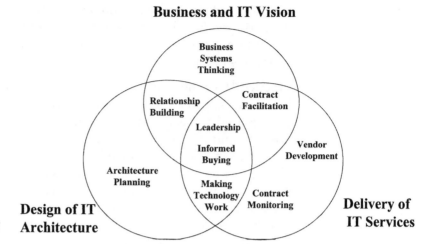

Business and IT Vision

Figure 2.6
Core IT capabilities
framework (from Feeny
& Willcocks, 1998)

The nine capabilities populate seven spaces in Figure 2.6. These spaces are not accidentally arrived at. Three are essentially business, technology or service facing. One is a lynchpin governance position covered by two capabilities (see Figure 2.6 – Leadership and Informed Buying). Finally, there are three spaces that represent various interfaces between the three faces. The capabilities that populate these spaces are crucial for facilitating the integration of effort across the 'faces'. We now move to detailing each of the nine capabilities.

- *Capability 1 – IS/IT Governance.* IT leadership is required to 'integrate IT effort with business purpose and activity'. The central task is to devise organizational arrangements – structures, processes and staffing – to successfully manage the interdependencies, and ensure that the IT function delivers value for money. Provision of IS/IT governance capability is the traditional role of the IT Manager or Director, the Chief Information Officer or 'CIO' of the local business.
- *Capability 2 – Business Systems Thinking.* This capability is about 'ensuring that IT/e-business technologies capabilities are envisioned in every business process'. In best practice organizations, business systems thinkers from the IT function are important contributors to teams charged with business problem solving, process re-engineering, strategic development and delivering e-business. The information systems/e-business strategy emerges from these teams' recommendations, which have already identified the technology components of solutions to business issues.

- *Capability 3 – Relationship Building*. The need for relationship building is symbolized by the overlap between business and technical faces in Figure 2.6. While the business systems thinker is the individual embodiment of integrated business/IS/IT thinking, the relationship builder facilitates the wider dialogue, establishing understanding, trust and cooperation amongst business users and IT specialists. The task here is *'getting the business constructively engaged in IT issues'*.

- *Capability 4 – Designing Technical Architecture*. This is about 'creating the coherent blueprint for a technical platform that responds to present and future business needs'. The principal challenge to the architect is to anticipate technology trends so that the organization is consistently able to operate from an effective and efficient platform – without major investment in energy-sapping migration efforts.

- *Capability 5 – Making Technology Work*. Operating the overlap between the technical and supply faces of Figure 2.6 is the technical fixer. The fixer requires much of the insight found in the technical architect role, allied to a pragmatic nature and short-term orientation. In today's environment of high complex/networked/multi-supplier systems, the technical fixer makes two critical contributions: to rapidly troubleshoot problems that are being disowned by others across the technical supply chain; and to identify how to address business needs that cannot be properly satisfied by standard technical approaches. The need to retain technical 'doing' capability is recognized even amongst organizations that have 'total' outsourced IT.

- *Capability 6 – Informed Buying*. This involves analysis of the external market for IT/e-business services; selection of a sourcing strategy to meet business needs and technology issues; leadership of the tendering, contracting and service management processes. In an organization that has decided to outsource most IT service, the informed buyer is the most prominent role behind that of the CIO. One respondent described their role in this way:

  If you are a senior manager in the company and you want something done, you come to me and I will . . . go outside, select the vendor and draw up the contract with the outsourcer, and if anything goes wrong it's my butt that gets kicked by you.

- *Capability 7– Contract Facilitation*. *'Ensuring the success of existing contracts for IT services.'* The contract facilitator tries to ensure that problems and conflicts are seen to be resolved fairly within what are usually long-term relationships. The role arises for a variety of reasons:

- to provide one stop shopping for the business user;
- the vendor or user demands it;
- multiple vendors need coordinating;
- enables easier monitoring of usage and service;
- users may demand too much and incur excessive charges.

One contract facilitator noted:

> *They (users) have been bitten a few times when they have dealt directly with suppliers, and it's a service we can provide, so now we do.*

- *Capability 8 – Contract Monitoring.* Another consequence of IT/e-business outsourcing complexity is the need for contract monitoring. While the contract facilitator is working to 'make things happen' on a day-to-day basis, the contract monitor is ensuring that the business position is at all times protected. Located in the exclusive space of the supply face, the role involves holding suppliers to account against both existing service contracts and the developing performance standards of the services market.
- *Capability 9 – Vendor Development.* 'Identifying the potential added value of IT/e-business service suppliers.' The single most threatening aspect of IT outsourcing is the presence of substantial switching costs. To outsource successfully in the first place requires considerable organizational effort over an extended period of time. To subsequently change suppliers may well require an equivalent effort. Hence it is in the business interest to maximize the contribution of existing suppliers – the role of vendor development. Anchored in the supply face of our model, the vendor developer is concerned with the long-term potential for suppliers to add value, creating the 'win–win' situations in which the supplier increases its revenues by providing services that increase business benefits.

Practice 14 – the in-house group should consist of high performing individuals who operate as a team, who are relatively few in number, with distinctive capabilities, orientations and motivations. Appropriate human resource policies, including reward systems will be in place to attract, retain and have a succession plan in place. High performers require challenge and specific attention to their career planning needs.

These nine core IT capabilities can be evolved gradually as the organization itself evolves through Delivery, Reorientation and Reorganization phases. Note that the IT director role and capabilities also change over this evolution. The type of IT Director needed for Delivery will not be the same for each of the other phases.

The model presents a number of serious human resource challenges. It requires high performers in each role. Furthermore, in contrast to the more traditional skills found in IT functions there needs to be a much greater emphasis on business skills and orientation in all but the two very technical roles. There is a significantly increased requirement for 'soft' interpersonal skills across all roles, all roles demand high performers, and each role requires a specific set of people behaviours, characteristics and skills. In the research, we regularly found that where a particular capability was missing or under-staffed, then problems arose. A typical issue was to conflate several of the capabilities and appoint one person to fulfil them. For example, at one large bank we found a 'contract manager' responsible in practice for contract facilitation, contract monitoring and IT governance. Not surprisingly, he underperformed in all these tasks.

Practice 15 – there have been put in place, before outsourcing, the following capabilities to manage any large-scale IT outsourcing arrangements proposed:

- ability to arrive at an IT sourcing strategy (see above);
- ability to diagnose the IT services market, understand individual IT service provider capabilities, limitations and strategies;
- ability to arrive at a contract and measurement systems that ensure that the organization gets from its outsourcing what it required and expected;
- ability to post-contract manage all IT service providers engaged so that their services are leveraged for business value.

Practice 16 – the core IT capabilities model expresses the minimum required in-house to leverage IT for business purposes. It may well be that there are also advantages for keeping non-core capability also in-house. Good practice organizations do this when it is cheaper to do so, and/or when they cannot find an IT service provider capable of accomplishing non-core activities to the required standard.

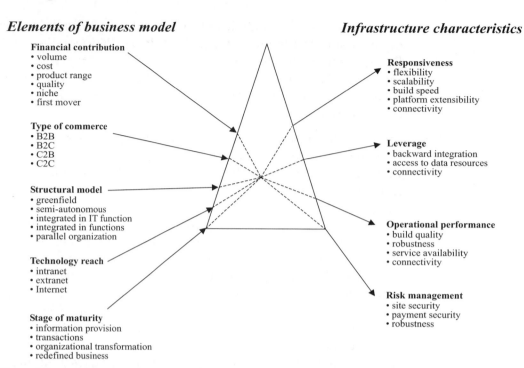

Elements of business model

Financial contribution
• volume
• cost
• product range
• quality
• niche
• first mover

Type of commerce
• B2B
• B2C
• C2B
• C2C

Structural model
• greenfield
• semi-autonomous
• integrated in IT function
• integrated in functions
• parallel organization

Technology reach
• intranet
• extranet
• Internet

Stage of maturity
• information provision
• transactions
• organizational transformation
• redefined business

Infrastructure characteristics

Responsiveness
• flexibility
• scalability
• build speed
• platform extensibility
• connectivity

Leverage
• backward integration
• access to data resources
• connectivity

Operational performance
• build quality
• robustness
• service availability
• connectivity

Risk management
• site security
• payment security
• robustness

Figure 2.7
Relating the business
model to infrastructure
(based on Sauer and
Willcocks, 2001)

Practice 17 – in good practice organizations business managers are operating on leveraging IT for business value on a daily basis and have incorporated their responsibilities and task into their daily work. The IT function is also identified and operates as integral to the way business is done. Business managers will be setting business direction and leading business initiatives that have integral IT components. They send out positive signals about the potential value of IT and how they seek to harness that value. They will have elements of IT decentralized to them, for example involvement in projects, monitoring IT payoff, some local IT knowledge, will work on boards and committees overseeing and monitoring IT direction and effectiveness in close liaison with IT people, including IT service providers.

Practice 18 – infrastructure is regarded as more than a technology platform and architecture. It is seen as the complex of technology, skills, processes and suppliers. It is also treated as a part of overall organizational design, and the foundation of strategic flexibility. Infrastructure investment and design receive constant senior business management attention. Investments are made to retain robustness, strategic and customer reach, process and management enablement, support for individuals and merger/acquisition capacity in the face of changing business requirements.

In well managed organizations IT infrastructure is seen as an integral part of the business, such that senior managers, including the CIO, regularly participate in translating their specific business needs and designs across into the implications for IT infrastructure – as shown in Figure 2.7. This translation process provides a detailed understanding of the types and size of investment needed for IT infrastructure.

In recent research into e-business infrastructure we found the most effective users of infrastructure saw infrastructure funding and design as a boardroom issue. They also employed in-house technology architects and technical fixers to work in this area. They behaved in ways that, in a business heavily dependent on IT, made sure that infrastructure provided a critical enabling platform for the delivery of business and for future reach and range, and strategic directions possible. Typically such organizations went through a planning process something like that illustrated in Figure 2.8.

A further common characteristic of these organizations was that they were moving to one single infrastructure. Companies such as Oracle, and the ones we describe such as Dell (Chapter 6), and Citipower and Macquarie Bank (Chapter 9) had, or were in the process of, ridding themselves of the disparate legacy, ERP and e-business inheritance, and building an integrated technology platform that was consistent with business processes, organizational design and able to deliver on business imperatives.

Finally, all these organizations were also flexing and developing their infrastructures on a regular basis by working much closer

What is Required for E-Business?

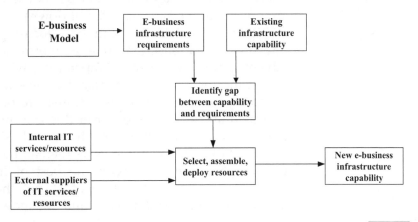

Figure 2.8
The process of arriving at a single e-business infrastructure (adapted from Sauer and Willcocks, 2001)

to the business units and their dynamic needs than ever before. The age of the IT infrastructure Five Year Plan, for them had come and gone, and was replaced by two year plans with constant adjustments and developments along the way. Again, this subject is so important that we give it sustained treatment in Chapter 9.

2.6 Conclusions

Frequently we have found organizations taking IT very seriously indeed, and resolving to undertake a range of initiatives to 'sort out IT once and for all'. Less productively, often much of the effort and resolve is located as the responsibility of the IT department. Since 2000 we have even seen several global e-business initiatives located as primarily the responsibility of the IT function, or of an IT services supplier. Our finding is that where business managers are disengaged, where IT initiatives are under-funded and under-resourced, where the CIO is not part of the top management team but is regarded, and behaves, as a functional manager, and where all this is justified on the basis of the indifferent past track-record of IT – in these circumstances the organization will always be a laggard when it comes to managing IT strategically for business value.

However, there are also risks in taking IT very seriously. The biggest risk, here, that we regularly encounter, is the under-estimation and underprovision of the time and resources required to deliver on what is in fact, very often, a set of very ambitious plans and targets. All too frequently the resources and the time are not forthcoming, and the need for process, organizational and behavioural change are misunderstood. Too many organizations do not realize the need to evolve into an effective, strategic user of IT, nor do they know how to do this. We give them the starting point of downscaling their effort and ambition and much more limitedly focusing on the relatively few business applications that will provide disproportionate advantage in how business imperatives will be achieved. This buys time for evolving an organization's and business units' capability for managing IT as a strategic resource along the lines indicated above. In the long run this is a much more strategic issue, and will result in much more business value being delivered over the next five years than all the IT initiatives and projects that might be, with the best of intentions, coming through. It is the *management* of IT not the technology that delivers pay-off. And it is sound business and information strategy that provide the primary direction, for which, important as they are, IT outsourcing, IT strategy, technical innovations, technology infrastructure and 'world class' IT service providers cannot provide substitutes.

References

Collins, J. (2001) *Good To Great*. New York: Random House.

Earl, M. (1989) *Management Strategies For IT*. London: Prentice Hall.

Feeny, D. (1997) Introduction, in Willcocks, L., Feeny, D. and Willcocks, L. (eds), *Managing IT As A Strategic Resource*. Maidenhead: McGraw Hill.

Feeny, D. (2001) The CEO and CIO in an information age, in Willcocks, L. and Sauer, C. (eds), *Moving To E-Business*. London: Random House.

Feeny, D. and Willcocks, L. (1998) Core IS capabilities for exploiting IT, *Sloan Management Review*, **39**(3), 9–21.

Hodgkinson, S. (1996) The role of the corporate IT function in the federal IT organization, in Earl, M. (ed.), *Information Management: The Organizational Dimension*. Oxford: Oxford University Press.

Sauer, C. and Willcocks, L. (2001) *Building The E-Business Infrastructure*. London: Business Intelligence.

Willcocks, L. and Sauer, C. (eds) (2001) *Moving To E-Business*. London: Random House.

Willcocks, L., Feeny, D. and Willcocks, L. (eds) (1997) *Managing IT As A Strategic Resource*. Maidenhead: McGraw Hill.

<table>
<tr><td>**3**</td><td></td></tr>
</table>

Baselining the enterprise

'The shift to Web services architecture for corporate computing is not only a matter of adopting new technology. It will require broad organizational and managerial changes as well as the development of new kinds of capabilities. A particularly big impact will be felt in the corporate IT department. CIOs will face new challenges and assume new roles'. John Hagel and John Seely Brown (Harvard Business Review, September 2001)

'I just like to know . . . so that I can say to myself: "I've got fourteen pots of honey left". Or fifteen, as the case may be. It's sort of comforting'. Pooh Bear

3.1 Introduction

Within industry and business today, strategic IT development now involves far more than finessing the existing investment in technology. Experience within the contemporary business scene suggests that for most enterprises the task is one of organizational transformation as they grapple with the challenges of moving to e-business. Change of this magnitude will impact every aspect of the organization. In particular it will require of its enabling technology an agility and a readiness to adapt at what is being called 'Internet Speed'. Developing a coherent business strategy, therefore, is not least about preparing the organization for life in the fast lane of technology. Within this context, developing a strategy for IT is about (a) identifying the relatively few applications that give disproportionate business payoff (covered in the first two chapters) and (b) ensuring IT readiness by planning and putting in place the necessary people, alliances and infrastructure, that is, creating the IT conditions for business success. Given the way IT penetrates so many business processes, it is fairly obvious that this cannot be done without taking in the broader organizational, and indeed external context, and this is the approach we take here.

Strategic positioning and preparation, however, must be done without impacting the continuity and the profitability of the ongoing business. It is therefore essential for strategists to understand what exists within their own organization, what must be preserved, and what needs to be changed. Such an exercise will also identify the potential problems that lie ahead. This exercise of risk analysis is a vital part of the planning process as, once a risk is identified, contingency plans put in place to both minimize the chance of failure and to limit the impact on the programme if such risk events occur.

Within existing organizations it is likely that there will already be a considerable investment in technology and information systems. These may range from legacy systems of considerable age to the latest hardware and software platforms. There may be an underlying systems and data architecture that has been planned and followed with care or, as is more likely, an accumulation of disparate platforms and applications cobbled together over the years, utilizing a variety of communications protocols. Data may be duplicated, replicated or possibly the outputs from one application re-keyed into another. We saw all these possibilities alive and well – in some cases not so well at all – during 2002.

Before beginning any significant undertaking it is necessary to have a realistic assessment of the resources and infrastructure that are available and our capability to effectively deploy them. Whenever we set out to achieve goals, or to plan to move in a given direction, or to create a 'strategic plan' we embark on a programme of change. A programme that presumably will move us forward from where we are to where we want to be. It is therefore a useful exercise to spend some time at the commencement of the endeavour to understand clearly the point of departure. The distance between the rhetoric and the reality of IT in organizations again never ceases to surprise. Which is why the baselining exercise to establish where an organization really sits, is a fundamental exercise.

Such an exercise encompasses a range of subjects. This chapter will explore several areas that need to be understood if a true baseline is to be obtained. A useful framework for targeting the areas that need to be understood before embarking on a process for change is set out below. We will revisit this framework in Chapter 7 when we look at the process of managing change. For the moment, however, we are concerned with baselining where the enterprise is. Throughout, it is useful to bear in mind our basic assumption that e-business was, and is, not a fad, but actually a long-term change in the way enterprises will be doing business. In this regard, what we are seeing, albeit slowly, because technologies change quickly but their absorption into organizational ways of working happen at a different speed, is discernible moves towards utilizing Web-based technologies, and rolling these into a single technology infrastructure, embracing all other related technologies. For examples of this see Chapter 9.

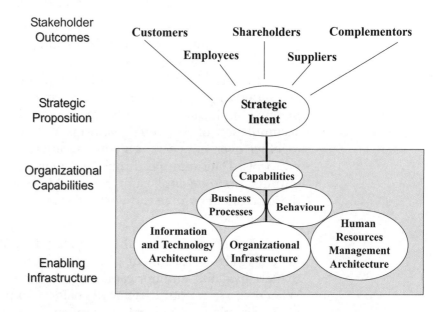

Figure 3.1
A framework for targeting change (based on Keith Ruddle's work in Willcocks and Sauer, 2001)

The baseline commences with a realistic appraisal of the organization and resource capabilities, together with other stakeholders. Experience has shown that a strategic transformation challenges traditional organizational structures and demands new skill sets and behaviours that may not be present in the existing enterprise.

As we indicated in Chapter 1 (see Fallacy Seven) the world of e-business has also created new challenges and opportunities for *alliances and partnering agreements*. These may be with vendors and suppliers or may involve completely new relationships as the organization explores new ways of aggregating and engaging with its customers. It is necessary to understand what strengths or weaknesses exist within the organization if it is to fully participate in new partnering arrangements, an issue we also deal with in more detail in Chapter 6.

E-business is underpinned by the investment an organization makes in the *IT infrastructure and functional architecture*, and, because a seamless transition to any new replacement platforms is necessary for business continuity, it must be understood in detail (see also Chapter 9). Whilst this may sound like a motherhood statement, in the experience of the authors, many organizations that have undertaken such a review have been surprised by how little they did in fact know about what they had, and what it really cost. One insurance company in 2001 outsourced most of its IT and made an estimate of its IT base and costs and, subsequently, in due diligence with the supplier, discovered that its actual costs were 50 per cent higher.

It is also recommended that two further areas are fully reviewed and their strengths and weaknesses frankly assessed. The first of these is the *readiness for the introduction of new technology*. In Chapter 2 we introduced Feeny's notion of the four domains as organizations move from 'IT Hype' to 'Strategic IT'. Significantly the second of the domains, called by Feeny, 'Capability' is characterized by technical solutions searching for business problems. Many of these solutions are the products of sustained vendor marketing. In our experience, this often leads to the organization being driven by its technology investments before other conditions of readiness have been met. This can be seen, for example, in the cases of INSUROR and drugstore.com in Chapter 1. In Figure 3.1, the importance of aligning technology investments with human resources, behaviour, organizational infrastructure and processes can be readily appreciated.

The other area to be considered is the capability of the organization to ensure *proper governance and management of projects and resources*. Strategic transformation will frequently involve the management of multiple concurrent projects and managing the competition for scarce resources. Such skills are often not available within the organization nor are the necessary processes often implemented. A realistic appraisal of this area of organizational competence will lessen the risk of costly mistakes down the line. This links with further exposure we give to this theme in Chapters 8 and 9.

3.2 An appraisal of the organization and resource capability

People are at the heart of strategic transformation. In *People in E-Business: New Challenges, New Solutions*, Wright and Dyer (2000) introduce a new paradigm for 'agile' organizations. They identify the characteristics of organizations likely to survive in the turbulent environments of e-business as those of Initiation, Adaptation and Delivery, at Internet speed. These characteristics are not usually those of traditional organizations. And even those sceptical of the need for 'Internet speed' will readily admit that technologies and markets seem to be more uncertain and volatile than they ever were, with competition not easy to predict, nor the right initiatives and responses.

Without appropriate skills and competencies there can be no initiation, adaptation or delivery. An essential part of the planning process is a detailed analysis of the current capability of the available resources. An assessment of the skills and competencies necessary to deliver and implement in a world where change is continuous and where the contribution of the IT department is measured as much by its intellectual capital as by the reliability of its systems.

Organizations arise out of the need to get things done. They are human institutions that have no real meaning apart from their efficacy in achieving the goals of the people who form them. The word, organization, comes from the Greek word *organon*, which means a tool or an instrument. Organizations can take many forms and will usually reflect the social and cultural norms of the society in which they are set. As with other human institutions however, organizations develop certain characteristics of their own, and once established create their own form of inertia and resistance to change. You only have to refer back to General Electric (Chapter 1) to appreciate the levels of conservatism an organization can exhibit – and GE is number one or two in most of its markets. As new challenges arise we need to adapt the tools we use to meet them and our organizations need to adapt and change as well. Commercial organizations still reflect many traditional patterns that have been evident for generations. New modes of doing business are creating new challenges to these traditional structures.

E-business itself demands differing technical skills than are usually present in traditional IT departments. Some people can adapt, can learn new skills and rise to new challenges. Some will have difficulty with change. Some skills will be better sought from alliances and from partners. Some may be outsourced. The role of consultants and contractors will be an important consideration when planning the capability and skill base of the organization. The increasing complexity of technology platforms as businesses move from legacy environments will mean that few organizations will have the resources to ensure complete self-reliance. Not only new skills but new forms of employment contract; a fresh approach to remuneration and new working arrangements will be needed to support the truly agile organization.

The era of 'new economy' businesses at least gave a new lease of life to innovation, and the importance of some fundamental 'sea changes' in the nature of work and organizational culture. By 2000, Willcocks and Plant (2002) were finding organizations, by no means all of them dot.com start-ups, that were adopting new cultures with the following characteristics:

- operating at net speed;
- executing dynamic strategy;
- reaching globally and virtually;
- engaging in internal collaboration;
- integrating with partners.

The failure of many dot.coms should not hide the fact that there have also been a number of organizations across sectors that finally got the message about speed, change and culture, and that have analysed carefully where information-based technologies fit in. The challenge that more traditional organizations face is to manage their own organizational transformation in the light of changing competition and employee expectations. E-business will come to change the way in which an enterprise relates to both its suppliers and its customers. It has already begun to remove many of the existing barriers to new entrants, and reduced geographic borders and time zones. Potentially e-businesses can operate with dispersed teams and with virtual organizations. It demands new sets of skills and competencies and, to be successful, makes incredible demands on management. E-business can transform entire industries as well as individual enterprises. Because it is such a new phenomenon its course is unpredictable and, of course, the 2000–2002 experience would suggest that it was all a bit of a bubble anyway. But we argue that when you see organizations quietly going about building their e-businesses – the Walgreens, the General Electrics, the Dells, the Macquarie banks – you will realize that we are just beginning to experience the nature of the challenge (see also the Brown Brothers caselet below). The response must of necessity be uncertain, flexible and subject to rapid adaptation as circumstances change. Chaos theory is alive and well in this environment. Those organizations lulled into a false sense of security by the dot.bomb phenomenon may well have their senior management facing salutary questions by 2004 such as: 'What did we achieve in the recession to build our ability to compete in the upswing? And why is our IT so unprepared for meeting our new business needs?'.

Caselet example: Victorian Winery

Brown Brothers is a significant name in the Australian Wine Industry. Situated in the northeast of Victoria the family business has developed a reputation for quality wine and for the number of 'varietals' that they produce. With an expanding market and strong forecasts for growth the business has begun to venture down the road to e-business.

Significantly, their first step was to implement an ERP platform to provide a sound base for integrating their systems and business processes and to replace a legacy of old systems. This task was a very big one for the business and made large demands upon those responsible for the implementation. The business, however, was anxious to make the next step.

Conscious of their inexperience with the Internet and with on-line business, Brown Brothers decided to take a relatively small step first so that they could gain experience with this new channel of communications and begin to tailor their infrastructure. Because the IT department was fully engaged with bedding down the ERP platform, the job of getting their first on-line initiative up was given to staff from Marketing.

Brown Brothers's reputation for good food and wine had led it to establish an 'Epicurean Club', with members scattered throughout Australia and some overseas. This group was chosen for the first on-line development and, using a software partner, an interactive and functionally rich site was built for the members. Many of the staff members were involved in this project, helping to design the site, determine the functions and the content it would provide.

> Vignerons and winemakers, chefs and marketing repre-
> sentatives all participated in this project and all had the
> opportunity to learn not only the demands such a develop-
> ment makes on an organization, but the ongoing responsi-
> bilities for maintaining its freshness and currency.

Our experiences with companies suggest that roles and jobs
that people in e-business undertake are dynamic. In several
organizations few employees had a job description that
remained constant long enough for the ink to dry! They
frequently took on a number of roles and worked within
multiple teams within their organization. Often they had more
than one person to whom they reported. Project type work and
activities used to be distinguished from routine work because of
its unique characteristics. In modern enterprises moving to
e-businesses, this distinction breaks down as the many activities
exhibit project characteristics and the emphasis on outcomes is
more marked than in traditional brick and mortar businesses
(see also Chapter 2).

In these businesses, where human capital and intellectual
contribution is measured and rewarded, new skills, behaviours
and competencies are demanded of those engaged in the
enterprise. Management of these people introduces its own
challenges, particularly in organizations that may have a mix of
traditional business and e-business enterprises (see GE in
Chapter 1, for an example). The task of managing such a
workforce itself demands consideration. How adequate is
existing management to the new task? A detailed analysis of the
strengths and weaknesses of the management team will reveal
the gaps that need to be filled by new talent or by a development
programme.

3.3 A review of alliances and partnering agreements

The demands of developing e-business environments and the
challenge of maintaining freshness of content and the reliability of service is such that few organizations can be fully self-
sufficient. More and more tasks are shared with key alliance
organizations or outsourced to reliable partners. Indeed the
downturns experienced across the developed economies during 2001–2002 saw relatively more attention being given to

external sourcing as the rate of growth of expenditure for other IT needs slowed (see Chapter 6 for further information on this topic).

A good relationship with all such partners and vendors is an important ingredient of success for IT managers, but one that is not easy to achieve. Key suppliers can provide valuable input to the strategic planning process. They can assist with the education of the organization as it prepares for change and the implementation of new technology. They can add value in many ways, but we have plenty of evidence, personal and academic (see Kern and Willcocks, 2001), that the relationship must be managed carefully. Suppliers and vendors do have their own agendas. They may be driven by sales quotas, but most also understand the need for the development of long-term relationships with their clients. Most will recognize that their own success depends on their client's success and will work to help them achieve it.

There are some guidelines that can assist in the development of sound vendor relationships.

- *Cultivate a dual supplier policy.* It is wise to remember the old adage 'Don't put all your eggs in one basket'. Over-dependence on a single supplier can put your business at risk if that supplier either goes out of business or has a major change to their product range. Wherever possible it is to your advantage to have access to more than one supplier for each of the core services or products that you require. It can be wasteful of your time and resources to endeavour to cultivate too many suppliers. That will be a drain on your resources. A balance is essential and a dual supplier policy can provide that balance.
- *Develop and maintain clear rules for communication.* The interface between your organization and the supplier must be clearly identified. One person from your organization should act as the gatekeeper, control the access by the supplier to your information and your people and manage the relationship. The supplier will normally themselves nominate an account manager or representative to manage the relationship from their side.
- *Build a level of trust* that enables the sharing of information. Within the rules of confidentiality you can establish your reliability as can your supplier. Where this exists there can be a degree of openness and frank exchange of information that can assist in framing policy and in avoiding costly mistakes.

- *Maintain a professional relationship.* The point of supplier relationships is to derive the optimum results for your organization. Your personal relationships with supplier representatives must be governed by that objective. It is for this reason that many organizations have rules that govern the degree to which their employees can enjoy hospitality or receive gifts from suppliers.
- *Ensure rules of confidentiality* that are understood and followed by all parties. If you are to derive real benefit from your key suppliers they will certainly gain access from time to time to confidential information about your business. Equally your people may gain information about their products or plans that are not yet in the public domain. All parties need to understand the rules that will govern confidentiality. Some organizations will require the other party to sign a confidentiality agreement to guard themselves against disclosure.
- *Ensure that your business procurement policy is understood* and followed in all business dealings. All dealings should be honest and open to scrutiny. Most organizations will have established rules that govern procurement. These may involve a process of tender. Where this is a requirement for established vendors then the rules must be followed scrupulously to ensure fairness and equal opportunity.

Caselet example: Colonial Ltd

Colonial, a major Australian all finance company merged in 2000/2001 with the Commonwealth Bank. In the mid-1990s, Colonial had embarked on a programme of growth that was so successful that it ultimately made it attractive as a merger target. When the growth programme was commenced, a new CIO was appointed to transform an inappropriate system base and IT organization with an infrastructure that would take the organization forward.

Right at the start of this process, he called in his major vendors and consultant suppliers and set about creating a significant alliance. His first task he perceived to be to fix the baseline. Because his own resources were stretched in keeping the current infrastructure going, he sought assistance from these alliance partners. They all were anxious to gain business from the re-development programme, so they could well play a part in the detailed analysis of the current platforms.

He further asked their cooperation in forming mixed teams and this was readily agreed. Several teams were quickly put together with resources drawn from multiple sources. Many of these were self-managed teams, relying on the professionalism of the members to ensure timely and accurate results. The programme worked, and worked so well that several of the suppliers involved continued to jointly bid for work where they believed that their combined skills were appropriate.

3.4 An assessment of the current IT infrastructure and architectures

This is likely to be one of the hardest of the 'Baseline' assessments. If it is to be done well it requires a degree of objectivity that may prove difficult to obtain. It may, in fact, be an area of analysis that can most benefit from the use of an external consulting resource or third party to achieve that necessary detachment and objectivity. Alternatively, it might be workshopped within the organization, making use of the skills and experience of as wide a group as possible and, preferably, facilitated by someone from outside the organization.

The aim is to produce a realistic assessment of the various strengths and weaknesses of the IT organization and its infrastructure. This review should extend to include an assessment of the identifiable opportunities and threats recognized by the participants. It must be conducted in such a way that those participating will feel entirely free to express their views frankly and openly. As in a 'brainstorming' exercise, it is better to get it all down for subsequent culling and rework than to stifle the flow of ideas and the frank exchange of views. Properly conducted, the group itself should have the capability to sift and weigh the contributions, and come to a consensus. In a large organization this exercise may have to be conducted across a number of sub-groups in order to really dig into some of the specialist areas and provide the widest opportunity for participation.

The review should not allow itself to get bogged down in fruitless discussions about the relative merits of a particular technology or methodology. This is a frequent weakness of such exercises and one of the reasons for using experienced facilitation. It should, in fact, concentrate on the processes that are in place, or the lack of them, together with the way in which the resources of the organization are structured and utilized. Some of the key areas for review will include the following.

- *Customer Relationships and Satisfaction*. There are few, but fortunately some, IT organizations that have developed a sound reputation with their customers for delivering quality IT solutions, on time and within budget. There are even fewer that have the same reputation for providing responsive, friendly, timely and understandable support to their customers. The reasons for this state of affairs are complex, but customer relationships can be turned around.
- *Education, and Learning With Customers*. Part of the answer lies in the role that IT departments should play in providing education to their clients and customers. Part also lies in IT giving up some of its pretence to a sort of alchemy that allows only initiates into the secret world of technical competence. IT managers now need to recognize that many of their customers are joining the workforce with excellent degrees and sound understanding of the role technology can play in business. An understanding that may well be better grounded than that of some IT professionals. One of the essential tasks of establishing a Baseline is to review the status of the customer/client relationship and to develop strategies to strengthen the positive aspects and to turn around the negative ones. The CitiPower caselet below points out how an IT director took responsibility for educating business users and managers on the IT role in the organization.
- *Charging Systems*. One key area that should be reviewed is any causes for dissatisfaction with the performance of IT within the organization. In our experience, dissatisfaction often relates to how the costs of IT are apportioned within the organization. Are they 'off-charged' to business units or does IT have its own budget from which business group priorities have to be met? We have seen several major IT outsourcing deals sunk because of the arbitrary charging systems they imposed or inherited, and resulting user revolts (see also Chapter 6).
- *IT Literacy*. Another critical area for review is the degree to which the role of IT and technology are generally understood within the organization? How much effort has been put into educating the organization on technology and the processes associated with its delivery? On this point, review the relevance of business maturity on IT, as discussed in Chapter 2.

Caselet example: CitiPower – educating the business on a new e-business infrastructure

As in many other countries, in Australia the utilities marketplace has been progressively opened up to competition. From January 2001 the industry faced full retail contestability, and unprecedented levels of uncertainty. What implications does this have for building e-business infrastructure that gives significant advantage? Is such advantage even possible, or is the race merely to keep up with the existing and unforeseen competition?

From its headquarters in Melbourne, CitiPower provides electricity and other energy-related products and services to over a quarter of a million business, residential and industrial customers in the city's business district and suburbs. It is also licensed to sell gas in New South Wales and its home state of Victoria, and has offices in Sydney, Brisbane and Adelaide. CitiPower thus runs an energy distribution, but also an energy retailing set of businesses. CitiPower resulted from the break-up and privatization of the State Electricity Commission of Victoria in 1994. Subsequently it has faced some daunting challenges. There have been rapid changes in ownership, increasingly fierce competition and constantly changing political climates and regulatory regimes in the different states in which it operates. There is a constant need for product innovation. At the same time CitiPower has been learning how to operate in a commercial environment, and trying to understand its markets – all of which implies on-going cultural change for its long-term staff.

The challenges are summarized by the newly appointed CIO in January 1999: 'As an organization we have to become incredibly flexible, at the same time as getting a new identity and culture, and supporting that with tools and capability'. The solution, starting from March 1999, has been to build a technical and process capability that enables e-business, even before many of the applications are known:

'Everything we do, every dollar we spend in applications development or purchase, on technology spend, is cognisant of the fact that we will move progressively to e-business.'

At the same time, in order to educate senior business management, occasionally the CIO has not wrapped pure technology projects, for example the middleware and the Aus$5.5 million server/database projects, into the various business cases for building business applications. Why is this education necessary? Because, for the CIO, executives have to know intimately about IT, its contribution and the components that make it up:

> 'IT is not a single specialization, it is multi-disciplined. I had to find a way, and continue to find ways, of exposing things like architecture to the Board and into the Executive management team, as part of the on-going education.'

At the same time there are a number of people throughout the organization who come up with opportunities in the IT and e-business areas, and these opportunities get widely exposed, including at senior executive meetings, but the opportunities are always judged against a business case. But the CIO, with a somewhat more back-door approach, was also able to argue successfully for the adoption of an Intranet. The existing Intranet had been poor, and the CIO pointed out that if you can't do IT or e-business internally, and cannot set up all the processes, ownership and disciplines necessary, then you are not going to do it externally, for example with customer-facing systems or B2B operations. Over time the Intranet has become more entrenched and used, whilst it also forms an integral part of the infrastructure being developed. This case is continued in Chapter 9, which focuses on Infrastructure issues.

3.4.1 Standards and quality

Most IT organizations aim to build a reputation of excellence. That their standards of delivery are not only timely and within budget, but that the delivered product works as it was expected to work. That all deliverables conform to recognized standards of quality. Only a few of these organizations in our experience have put in place the procedures and metrics to inform themselves of how well these standards are met.

A commitment to quality and to its continuous improvement must be supported by all within the organization, particularly its management, if it is to succeed. Without management commitment the programme will die of inertia. We have seen organizations that do take quality seriously and exhibit the characteristics of a learning organization. Not only are they concerned to systematically test and review their deliverables, to provide feedback and to correct defects, they are also committed to a thorough review of the processes and to the involvement of all stakeholders in suggesting improvement. They also measure their improvement and give recognition where it is merited.

There is a plethora of well-defined and documented industry standards that are meant to guarantee that IT deliverables work as they should and that data is both reliable and recoverable. There is a fundamental requirement that all the deliverables should be fit for the purpose for which they have been designed. Standards need to be in place to ensure that they are fit, but also that the standards are affordable. The concept of affordable quality is important. Quality costs, both if quality controls are not applied at all but also if they are so overdone that unnecessary time and money are wasted once an acceptable level of quality has been attained and acceptable levels of risk achieved.

Begin by examining how quality standards are defined within the organization and if all staff are aware of the standards and how they should be used. In particular it is important to review what procedures are in place for quality reviews and if staff have been trained in how to conduct them. If quality metrics are taken how can they be improved or better utilized for continuous improvement?

3.4.2 Software testing procedures

The testing procedures used in the development of new software should be reviewed. Most of these testing regimes and standards have grown out of the hard-won experience of the era of 'software engineering'. It is often now apparent that these same standards have not always been maintained in the development of software that is designed for the Internet. More attention is often given to the graphic design than to the fundamentals of performance. Are test plans currently prepared for each module and each component of the architecture or infrastructure to test for conformity with established standards and against the agreed requirements?

3.4.3 Useability testing

The development of e-business initiatives has renewed the focus on acceptance and useability testing as a user-directed activity that tests the delivered product or system against the agreed requirements and quality attributes. Useability testing of the user interface is particularly important as a means of ensuring 'ease of use'. Techniques for useability testing include the use of laboratory situations where a user is required to complete a series of tasks whilst viewed by those responsible for development. It is one thing to design a system according to technical standards, it may be another for the user to navigate their way through a variety of prompts and screens to perform their routine tasks. Useability laboratories can give a sobering experience.

3.4.4 Integrated systems testing

This follows a process or transaction from beginning to end to ensure the integrity of the total process and the validity of the data across all systems. During an extensive change programme where the components and systems are implemented in stages integrated systems testing should be carried out each time the environment changes. This in itself can be a complex and sometimes costly exercise. Its value to the organization is the guarantee that no change to the environment will put the business at risk as rigorous testing ensures the integrity of the overall process.

Three other areas relating to IT performance need to be included in fixing the organization's baseline.

1 *Change Management Procedures.* The first of these is the ability to manage change within production environments in a professional manner that does not impact service and preserves the integrity of data. This is another discipline that has been well understood in traditional 'mainframe' environments, but has had less emphasis in development associated with on-line environments. It is important to review the appropriateness of the standards and to upgrade them where necessary.
2 *Disaster Recovery.* Are there well-understood procedures to safeguard the data assets of the organization and to recover both the environment and service delivery in the event of calamity? This involves more than disciplines for back-up and off-site storage of data. It also involves the identification of

key human resources for the recovery process and the preparation of detailed plans that indicate the order in which recovery should be done with agreed priorities. It is too late to argue about these things when disaster happens!

3 *Prioritization of Change Requests.* The third of these areas has to do with how change requests for enhancement or maintenance of existing systems are prioritized and managed within the organization. It is worthwhile investigating the percentage of total IT resources that are actually committed to maintenance tasks. In our experience with some organizations this can run as high as 75 per cent. Where such a high proportion of an organization's resources are committed to propping up the existing infrastructure the capacity to release resources for new development is severely impacted.

3.4.5 System and data architecture

This of course should be well documented, as it is in every well-run organization! The problem is that, in our experience, such awareness is most often not the case. Hopefully, the detailed Y2K reviews brought about by fears of transition to the new millennium did bring much of the documentation up to date. But then that was two years ago! There can be no clear baseline without some stakes in the ground, and very sound knowledge of the existing systems and data that are supporting the organization. Start by undertaking an audit of the existing systems and develop a system profile for each one. The following information on each system will complete the profile.

1 *Identify each system or application.* This may sound simple enough but it may prove more complicated. Sometimes information systems have a formal and a common name, often an acronym and sometimes may be referred to by different names in different parts of the organization. It is best to have this sorted out at the start than to find it out well down the planning process. The documentation should include 'Version and Release numbers' if they are used and any information about current development, which may include outstanding enhancement or maintenance requests. It is also necessary to be clear about system ownership. Identify the person or persons whose approval is necessary for changes to be made to each application, system or their associated business rules and data. In large organizations

complex systems may impact many different functions and ownership may not be clear. Any such ambiguities or lack of clarity will complicate plans for future development or replacement of these systems and should be resolved early in the planning process.

2 *Describe the system.* Explain its origins and purpose, what it does and why it exists. Who uses the application and where does it fit in the overall architecture. In a large organization this may prove more difficult than it sounds. People are often inventive in the way in which they source and use data to support existing or new business functions. Often the users of a system will extend well beyond those for whom it was originally designed to include new users who have found uses for the information or processes it provides. These new uses for the system may now require preservation or replacement when planning for change. This description should include its key features to provide detailed information about the way that the system is used. It will include details of how the system is administered, the number of users, peak transaction periods, and rules for security and recovery. If it involves an on-line component there will be details relating to content management, inbound and outbound e-mail, and moderation of discussion boards and commercial transactions.

3 *Identify all system interfaces.* Identify any other systems that interact with the system you are describing. This will include any system that provides or receives data and those that provide or receive transactions. In fact all inputs and outputs need to be identified, both electronic and manual. This information should include all information about the volume, frequency and business rules that govern such interfaces. This information is critical for any systems that may have to interconnect with the systems of your suppliers, customers or other alliance partners.

4 *Where is the data?* It is essential that all data stores be clearly identified, together with the means of storage, size and all information relating to back-up and recovery. It is appropriate at this time to consider the nature of data within the organization and the way in which it meets the information needs of the enterprise. Its accuracy should also be questioned. As businesses begin to exploit the opportunities for more customized service offered by the Internet and investment in Customer Relationship Management (CRM) systems it becomes essential to have clean data. Data 'cleaning' becomes an essential task.

3.4.6 Data privacy

The question of privacy is now an important one in many societies. This includes consumer access to the information that corporations and other organizations may hold about them, together with their right to request that data not be passed to a third party without their permission. Any review of current status should examine the ability of the organization to respond to any legislative requirements for privacy. These would normally include the requirement for any customer to be fully informed of any personal data that the organization may hold about them. Customers normally must be able to ask for incorrect information to be corrected. While these requirements may sound simple, for large corporations where data are held in many places the compliance tasks can be enormous. Desktop applications should not be neglected in this exercise. They often provide 'critical' information but are not always covered by the enterprise requirements for back-up and recovery and may well escape the attention of the IT department.

3.4.7 Documentation

This task of discovering and documenting the applications that support an organization can be time consuming. Its difficulty should not be underestimated, particularly in large organizations where information technology has evolved over a long period of time. It will require considerable detective work in many cases and much of the information will need to be checked for accuracy before it can be relied upon.

The task will be complicated where organizations have allowed the development of 'desktop' applications by individual users to support their own business functions. The proliferation of such applications will complicate the task of baselining the organization's information infrastructure, but they cannot be overlooked. They often will be providing necessary functionality that is missing from the core systems or they may be providing data in a more timely fashion.

The risk with such desktop applications is the opportunity they provide for the duplication of data and for the application of different business rules. Can it be assumed, for example, that if customer records are duplicated, all customer data relating to name, address, billing data, etc. will be the same in all such applications? Will all such applications utilize standard business formula for calculation of such things as gross margin, stock turn, volume discounts or any other calculation? In other words, if we take data from two desktop applications, will we be comparing apples with apples? The problems are magnified where the outputs of one such application are printed and then re-keyed into another because there is no appropriate interface.

Caselet example: data in an energy company

In preparation for the year 2000, this large energy distributor and retailer undertook a detailed review of its entire system base, partly to ensure readiness for the new millennium and partly in preparation for migration to a new ERP platform. Several surprises were uncovered.

They found that data on customers was held in some 27 separate locations. Some of this was replication because of governance issues that required distribution and retail to be at arm's length. Much, however, existed in desktop systems built, for example, by energy traders, who had developed their own techniques and tools and, consequently, databases! Attempts to analyse this data were frustrated by the use of different business names for customers, different addresses and different means of calculation of fundamental business metrics.

They also found that some systems continued in production, without anybody using them, because either they performed an integral step in processing or their interfaces formed a necessary part of the architecture. One system that was still running because of its interfaces to other systems (systems that would fall apart if the interfaces were turned off) had in fact acquired new users as its outputs had been adapted to new purposes. It was discovered that the functionality it now provided had become necessary and would need to be provided by the new platform.

Such discoveries were not uncommon in the run up to the year 2000. That is now history. But be warned. Several years of subsequent diligent desktop use has undoubtedly continued the proliferation of data.

Experience has taught us that diagrams best describe the data and application architectures wherever possible. There are well-established standards for functional, data and system diagrams. It is wise to follow these standards, as they are widely understood. They are also useful tools for explaining to non-technical audiences the complexity of the infrastructure. One CEO of our acquaintance was so taken by the high-level data model of his organization that he had it framed and hung in his office. No one had the heart to tell him it was already out of date by the time it was hung.

3.5 Readiness for the introduction of new technology

There is an old adage that says, 'if it isn't broken, don't fix it'. Whilst this may be underpinned by considerable common sense, in IT terms it may lead to dependence on outdated technology to the detriment of the organization. There are three chief reasons for investment in new technology. They are to increase productivity, to reduce costs and to gain competitive advantage. New technology alone, however, will not produce any of those three outcomes. Indeed, as we pointed out in Chapter 1, with IT capability there is also enormous potential for harm. Not only is new technology expensive, its impact on the organization can be great. Like a large meal, the digestive process can take a while and upset the normal functions. The introduction of new technology therefore always involves risk. The risk needs to be assessed and appropriate contingency measures put in place whenever such an implementation is planned.

Increases in productivity are usually defined in terms of our ability to do things faster or more easily, which is often the same thing. There are also opportunities for an organization to increase its ability to be productive though increased integration of systems, better utilization of data or the use of more automated tools for development, testing and maintenance of the organization's IT.

The opportunities that now exist for e-business create increasing pressure on organizations to introduce the necessary infrastructure. This may come from a need to participate in industry portals, to communicate better with suppliers, customers and employees, or simply to respond to competitive pressure to provide facilities for electronic commerce. There are also perceived, often big opportunities to reduce the cost of the infrastructure. This may involve changes to licensing arrangements for software or the use of tools that are either easier to use or tools for which the necessary skills and competencies are in greater supply. Many older technologies not only become increasingly difficult to maintain, they also are subject to a diminishing supply of skilled people who become hard to find and expensive to retain.

The merits and demerits, the risks and constraints of the current technology base need to be clearly understood. There is no value in migrating to new technology for its own sake. You also need to check whether the real problem is not the existing technology, but the failure to exploit its potential. For example, what are desktops used for in your organization? And what could they be used for? On average, we reckon only between 10 and 30 per cent of existing IT potential is utilized in most organizations we advise and research. Vendors will work hard to espouse the value to your organization of the latest release or new product. As with any other significant expenditure such claims need to be tested, confirmation sought and values weighed. When a decision is made to invest in new technology it should be for cogent and well founded reasons based on a detailed financial and impact analysis.

It is not simply matters of cost and technical integration that should be considered when contemplating new technology. There may be a requirement for new skills and competencies. The organization's willingness to change core practices also should be considered. There is often an 'inertia' within organizations that, without intervention, will always return to known ways and procedures. Huge investments in ERP type systems have often failed to produce the business benefits forecast because of this inertia, as the caselet example of a manufacturing company, below, indicates (see also Chapter 8). Old applications, systems and business methods find extraordinary ways of preserving themselves and running in parallel with the new technology for extended periods.

Caselet example: manufacturing company

In this large organization a new ERP system was introduced at great cost and with significant impact on the workforce. Senior managers discovered, however, a year after implementation, that the predicted benefits were not being obtained, many users were openly critical of the cumbersome nature of the new platform and that several legacy systems were still running in parallel with the new.

External consultants were called in to review the situation. Among the key findings they reported was one that showed the organization's directors still insisted in seeing a particular report in a form they were accustomed to. That particular report could only be provided by a legacy system. The result was that the system was kept in production and data re-keyed into it from output from the new system every month to produce the one report.

When the cost of continuing with this report format was brought to their attention the directors were very quick to accept change. What is interesting is that the culture within the organization was one such that senior staff felt unable to challenge the directors' request for reports from the legacy systems.

Many of the other problems could be traced back to an almost total absence of any change programme to ready the organization for the change, or to involve the users in process re-design.

Organizational readiness is even more critical when considering substantial investment in new technology to support e-business opportunities. The integration of e-business into the overall operations of a business involves far more than the integration of the technical platforms. It can have a large impact on business processes and change the way that the business interacts with suppliers, customers or staff. Traditional business organization will guarantee that many business roles and functions are impacted by changes to any business process. When we begin to talk about the changes inherent in areas such as 'Supply Chain Management' or 'Customer Relationship Management' (CRM) the impacts become quite wide and general.

A significant problem has recently emerged in relation to the implementation of CRM. It goes to the heart of many issues that have impacted successful e-business initiatives. The question is one of ownership. In particular, the relationship of Marketing and IT departments in decisions about CRM investment is often unresolved. It is apparent to the authors that such decisions, and indeed all decisions about the move to e-business, must be endorsed at the highest levels within an organization. For this reason the organization as a whole needs to sign on to technical change with both public and active commitment to the goals of the strategy. There needs to be a preparedness to adopt the new technology and to adapt the way business is done to incorporate its benefits into each functional area.

3.6 Governance issues for the management of projects and resource utilization

As part of the benchmarking exercise it is worthwhile assessing the capacity of the organization, and particularly its IT departments, to deliver quality outcomes and to do it consistently within budget and on schedule. The delivery of a strategic programme makes use of large resources and places stress on the organization, as well as risk, if things do not go as planned. Some of the key areas to be explored include a review of how effective the organization is in delivering projects on time and on budget with both a satisfied client and a satisfied team. Are there processes in place to properly initiate projects with clearly agreed objectives and a standards governance process? That is, a process that will ensure proper project planning, monitoring and control.

If not in place, appropriate processes should be developed to ensure that sign-off takes place at regular project milestones and that the project 'owners' are identified and included in the governance procedures. This can help to resolve potential disputes about ownership down the track. Similarly there should be an established process for Change Control, whereby requests for change to any requirement or the scope of any project can be documented and reviewed for impact on cost and time schedules. The caselet example below provides some insight into the sort of unexpected issues that can arise, requiring good governance procedures to be in place. Chapter 9 also shows the usefulness of a Programme Office approach (see the CitiPower case, above).

Caselet example: software development company

This relatively small organization, with a staff of less than 20, has a reputation for developing good quality software to support e-business initiatives. In particular, complex interactive Web sites have been developed for a number of service organizations with significant membership providing a range of services as well as e-commerce facilities. Most of the work undertaken for these clients is performed on the basis of a fixed price contract.

Difficulties arose in protecting the gross margin on these jobs because of the enthusiasm of the staff to provide the best quality product. Management found it hard enough to manage the range of changes to specification requested by the client, as is always the case. What proved more difficult was to manage staff members who conceived more and more ways to add value to the end product or whose desire for technical perfection frequently caused re-work and damaged productivity.

Whilst the clients were delighted with the results and eagerly recommended the software company to others, its financial results did not meet management expectations and put the business at risk. A total review of governance procedures was necessary as well as the re-education of the staff to ensure a professional approach to the development process and a recognition of what was 'affordable' quality.

3.7 Conclusion

The task of establishing the Baseline can be time consuming and difficult. Its pay-off comes in organizational readiness to move forward. The completion of the task should help the organization define its strengths and weaknesses. It will enable the identification of opportunities to move forward and the charting of potential risks to success.

If carried out with the involvement of team members the review will enable their input both in the identification process and the creative planning to exploit the recognized strengths and overcome perceived weaknesses. This buy-in by team members is perhaps the most valuable aspect of the exercise, particularly for their ongoing involvement in risk minimization.

It can also enable the entire organization to have a realistic appraisal of the size of the task before it. As with many other aspects of life the migration to e-business does not take place on a level playing field. All organizations carry some form of weight in their saddlebags. These 'handicaps', when recognized, can be compensated for or overcome. Unrecognized, they create major problems and make the task of organizational transformation much more difficult than it already is. The Baseline forms a solid basis for developing the plan to move forward, which is the focus of the next chapter.

References

Hagel, J. and Brown, J. (2001) *Your next IT strategy, Harvard Business Review*, October, 105–113.

Kern, T. and Willcocks, L. (2001) *The Relationship Advantage: information technologies, sourcing and management*. Oxford: Oxford University Press.

Willcocks, L. and Plant, R. (2002) Pathways to e-business leadership: getting from bricks to clicks, in Brynjolfsson, E. and Urban, G. (eds), *Strategies For E-business Success*. San Francisco: Jossey Bass.

Willcocks, L. and Sauer, C. (eds) (2001) *Moving to E-business*. London: Random House.

Wright, Patrick M. and Dyer, Lee (2000) *People in E-Business: new challenges, new solutions*. Cornell University Center for Advanced Human Resource Studies, Working Paper 00–11. New York: Cornell University.

4

Putting the pieces together: getting IT from A to B

'In this world, where rapid change and transformation are becoming the norm, organizations face new challenges. In addition to planning and executing tasks in an efficient rational way, they face the challenge of constant learning, and, perhaps even more important, of learning to learn'. Gareth Morgan (Images of Organization).

'What we call results are beginnings'. Waldo Emerson.

4.1 Introduction

In Chapter 2 we saw how, from a variety of considerations, we need to arrive at an IT strategic agenda. Starting with a business strategy to pinpoint IT needs, by looking at the existing IT infrastructure and organization to establish its capabilities, and by encouraging innovation. When these tasks have been completed a fundamental task remains, the matter of delivery. Here we focus on what Chapter 2 refers to as IT strategy. The authors, in the capacity of IT executive or consultant, have often been at this point of the strategic process. In some ways it is like beginning a race. The goal is more or less clear, and the weight we are carrying is understood. There is an eagerness to begin. This chapter is about 'getting on with it' and about 'delivery focused management'.

The goal of those responsible for IT within an organization can usually be defined as: 'the delivery of affordable innovative IT solutions continuously aligned with business needs together with the processes to respond to changes in business priorities'. The development of IT strategy is to put in place the processes, people, alliances and infrastructure to achieve this goal.

Having undertaken the task of understanding the current status of all factors that are relevant to the achievement of the goals, and fixed the 'Baseline', the next step is to resolve the steps to be taken, the tactics to be employed to achieve these goals. This provides the 'flight plan' for getting from A to B, from today into the future. It will need to be documented in a variety of forms suitable for differing audiences, costed and agreed.

It will be more than a simple list of functional requirements, enhancements or replacements for existing or new applications. The plan must cover each of the areas of strategic significance that will establish the conditions necessary for successful achievement of the overall plan. These areas will include the following:

- A *delivery plan* is required that details the order in which the various components of the overall strategic agenda will be delivered. This is a must, to ensure sound planning for implementation and change, as well as ensuring the ongoing integrity of the business. It will detail what has to happen in each area of the organization. It will also safeguard the ongoing delivery of information systems, ensuring continued viability of the organization and its data as new components of Technology Architecture are introduced and as new connections are made and old interfaces switched off.
- A *resource plan* to ensure that the right people are available at the right time and to optimize the use of scarce and valued resources. Labour is likely to be one of the greatest costs, typically at least 35–40 per cent and, in our experience, one of the resources most often wasted by poor planning.
- A *communications and education plan* that will address two issues. The first is to manage the expectations of all stakeholders. The second is to assist in the overall management of change so that the organization and its people are progressively readied for change. What Kurt Lewin (1951) described as 'unfreezing' the organization ahead of the desired change (see also Chapter 7 for more detail on this).

Other matters to be covered include the matter of *risk mitigation*, and the question of *business process re-engineering*. There are also some more mundane matters that must be attended to at the beginning. This chapter will begin with them, as, in our experience, getting them right is essential to the success of the programme.

4.2 Rules of engagement

Because the intent is one of delivery, before beginning the task it is wise to have some fundamental issues decided and agreed by all those involved. Whilst some of these sound deceptively simple, experience has taught us that often people do have differing expectations. It is better to ensure that all expectations are in line at the outset, rather than discover at a late stage in the programme that significant differences remain. The following key issues should be resolved, agreed and documented.

First of all, we need to be clear about the scope of the work to be done and the deliverables required. These need to be clearly understood and agreed by all involved. It is not sufficient to rely on an assumption that all parties understand what is to happen. Much of IT still remains somewhat of a mystery to many in business. Their expectations about the complexity of the task and the order in which work will be undertaken may be at odds with the plans. As with most complex projects, time spent at the start to ensure understanding is time well spent.

It is also important to know what resources will be made available to assist with the task. Whilst the resources within the IT domain may be identified and their time scheduled, there will be demands made upon the time and commitment of a great number of people within the organization. This needs to be made clear at the start and plans made for their availability, backfilling if necessary with other resources. In our experience the amount of time and input required by business representatives in definition, review and testing of deliverables often comes as a nasty surprise and one which can impede progress and even bring the programme to a halt.

It is also useful right at the start to have agreement about the form in which plans, progress reports and documents will be constructed, and the procedures for review and sign off at key milestones. Who will be responsible for these regular points of approval will be important as deadlines crowd one another, and dependencies begin to pile up. Wherever possible, make approval a progressive exercise. It is pointless delivering to a busy person a large document for review at short notice if delays in approval will hold up progress.

At the same time the detail of financial monitoring and reporting of the programme must also be understood and processes put in place to ensure compliance. Exactly what authorities do individuals have for approval of expenditure and how are these to be exercised? What must be reported, how and when? It is particularly important that estimates of forward capital expenditure are clearly flagged, so that provision for payment can be made. In our experience, accountants as a general rule disapprove of surprises relating to large sums of money suddenly falling due without prior notice.

It is also important to establish any standards or guidelines within the organization that must be followed. Whilst it is always possible to find and blow the dust off a set of standards for IT in an organization, it is another thing to determine if they are in fact being followed. As organizations move toward e-business, they discover a whole new range of standards associated with new products as well as operations in the new domain. The demands of an 'interconnected' world, particularly in business-to-business transactions often require attention to standards for the interconnection. In late 2001 there were some 2233 e-marketplaces globally, and plugging in suppliers and customers was proving a significant barrier (Laseter *et al.*, 2001). The increasing demands of new partnerships and alliances also raise issues of compliance and performance that can challenge traditional approaches to standards.

If these questions can be clarified at the start of the process, then the opportunities for the project going off the rails can be significantly reduced. The strategist will often find that there is a significant job to be done in educating the organization about what is possible and in helping its decision makers deal with the issues of technology. This can be a time consuming task, but a necessary one. In practice it is often skimped, and this can lead to immediate problems being handled at the expense of generating bigger ones down the line. There is little point in documenting plans that are not understood or are impossible to achieve. An education programme is an essential part of the strategic planning process.

We have also made it a practice right at the start to establish guidelines for all documentation associated with the strategic project. These guidelines cover matters such as font size and document identification with version and release rules so that all can be sure at any time just which is the latest version of a document. Guidelines for document storage, use of directories, restrictions on access and other matters associated with management of the documentation need to be addressed. For standard documents it may be advisable to establish templates so that a common look and feel is provided. The programme will not benefit from allowing options in the way status is reported. Particularly financial status!

Lastly, the matter of accommodation and facilities such as phones, computers, work rooms, white boards, coffee and all the other little things that will enable the efficient achievement of the programme's objectives, should be considered. All this done, we can begin. None of this is glamorous; all of it makes delivery more probable.

4.3 The delivery plan

The demands for IT support can originate in a variety of ways. Not all will be relevant in every situation, but the following should be considered. Once there is a clear understanding of the new applications or functional changes that are needed, the next step is to establish the precedence of work, the order in which they will be delivered. This task is not a simple one. Often there will be vigorous, if not cogent, argument about the priorities to be assigned to each piece of work. At its simplest, then, clearly the work that delivers the greatest benefit to the business and that is the easiest to deliver should have the highest priority.

Alas, it is not always that simple! There are many other factors to be taken into consideration. Sometimes the need for legislative or regulatory compliance will force a priority. It may be that there are technical reasons that require a sequence of implementation steps giving priority to infrastructure systems lower in perceived business benefit. There may be sound reasons relating to implementation and the ease of use that dictate the sequence of delivery. As Chapter 8 makes clear, there are also inherently political issues related to change that need addressing right from the strategy formation stage. Several other issues need to be considered.

Firstly, it is important to determine if there are any legislative or regulatory requirements that are mandatory for the organization that will be addressed with the strategic plan. These may be a prime motive for change if the current technology or functionality cannot meet the new requirement. They are also likely to have firm dates for compliance and must be given priority in the delivery plan.

Will the organization develop new products or services that cannot be supported with the existing technology? There may be competitive or other timing pressures that need to be met. Often such programmes will include many areas, of which IT may be only one. The overall business strategy should highlight these business drivers, which need to be reflected in the IT strategic agenda.

What timing issues are associated with core components of the infrastructure or the systems development? There may be delivery constraints or issues associated with precedence in installing new hardware or software. There will always be competition for scarce trained resources both internal and external, from the key vendors, for example. With regard to suppliers, one IT Director in charge of a major outsourcing deal told us that he saw himself in competition against all the supplier's clients, on a daily basis, for the supplier's best people. All potential timing issues need to be considered in developing the delivery plan.

Will there be demands for any on-line technology or change to the infrastructure to support e-business? This may include new ways of doing business with customers, suppliers, employees or any other group of stakeholders. There may be timing issues associated with implementation by these key stakeholders that will impact your own delivery plan. If so, they must be considered and given the appropriate priority.

Once these things have been considered, the task of determining priority can proceed. It is a key responsibility to determine the sequence of steps necessary to deliver the strategic outcome, and to be able to present sound arguments to support that sequence. Within the constraints dictated by the considerations outlined above, the programme of delivery that is determined should facilitate early wins wherever possible to sustain commitment. This is a tactic that minimizes the risk inherent in massive implementations and projects that, having very long lead times, are likely to encounter massive changes in requirements before delivery. It is better to deliver in incremental chunks that offer real benefit to the business and minimize the risk of failing to deliver anything. We return to this theme in Chapter 8, but see also Figure 4.1. Such a programme of incremental delivery will provide flexibility and agility for a future with uncertain outcomes. It also provides options for superior management of risk and return than a single big bet, and allows for Web and technology mandated partnerships supporting rapid and unpredictable change.

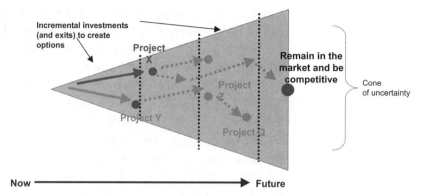

Figure 4.1
Incremental delivery

It is our experience that the plan should also minimize the amount of re-work or interim solutions. It is not always possible to be fully free of interim steps. Particularly if the plan is as advised for progressive delivery. Because of the complex interfaces to be found in many system architectures (and not always old ones) it may be necessary to provide for interim feeds of data to or from systems as their interfacing systems are sequentially replaced. There is clearly a tension here between the need to provide valued functionality and the need to sustain business processes with interim solutions that will have to be replaced with more permanent solutions. Such interim steps also complicate the overall task of implementation, adding to cost and potentially confusing the users. The delivery plan must consider where such interim steps are required, and do all that is possible to minimize their necessity.

The delivery plan should also aim to ease the impact of implementation on the organization. Change needs to be both planned and managed. It is too important to be left until the last minute, and needs to be conducted as any other project. In preparing a Delivery Plan, the ability of people to absorb change must be considered. Wherever practical, the implementation should be incremental, with each stage of implementation building on the last, and arranged in a sequence that facilitates ease of learning and optimizes the technical implementation.

The programme must be affordable and meet the budget requirements of the organization. Certainly it is not the hardware and software costs alone that have to be accounted for. There is the very significant cost of labour, of training and education. Not only the IT resources need to be included. We regularly find, in fact, that the non-IT resources cost anything between two and four times those of technology such as hardware, software, cabling. These are regularly underestimated at the strategy-making stage. Any programme of technical change has great impact on the business and its staff. The time needed for people to state requirements, to participate in workshops, meetings, reviews and presentations as well as contribute to design and testing can be very great. This feeds into extra costs. We estimate that more than 60 per cent of all costs associated with new IT projects is in the implementation stage.

The delivery plan must deliver real outcomes in terms of business benefit. It is important that these benefits are clearly identified right up front at the commencement of the programme. It is even more significant if the anticipated benefits can be tied into real budgets to ensure that they materialize, and that there are people who will be accountable for them (see also Chapter 5). These are the people who in the organization will accept the responsibility for reaping these benefits, and driving the associated changes in process or procedures through the organization. Too often in programmes that involve comprehensive change, or those where no clear accountability for achieving the benefits is assigned, they fail to materialize or are unrecognized because of poor measurement techniques. We deal with corrective processes for this in Chapter 5.

An aim should always be to reduce the risk of outage through technical change or corruption of the business core data assets. It must be expected that change will always impact the existing technical environment and the greater the change, the greater the impact and the risk to daily operations. The delivery plan must, therefore, anticipate that things might go wrong, and at each point of change provide contingency plans. These plans must facilitate checks to ensure the same values for data passed prior to, and after, the change, as well as detailed plans for roll-back and recovery in the event of unexpected results.

4.4 Planning and prioritization

The world of contemporary IT is one where the agreed programme will be subject to change as new challenges and business opportunities emerge. All too many organizations never build this contingency into the way they do strategy. This is because maintaining a healthy balance in strategy making between control, rigour and flexibility is something of an art form, or craft, dependent on experience. The natural tendency is to err on the side of control, but much of it is really, as Mintzberg (1993) suggests, about crafting strategy.

The process for prioritization of work must be a rigorous one, where these competing initiatives can be evaluated and placed within the programme in accordance with their priority. This process, which is well established in many organizations, is usually known as gating and relates to the 'gatekeeper' functions that control the initiation and resourcing of business-justified projects. They establish a framework that will ensure that once recognized, potential projects are initiated and conducted in a professional manner so that:

- each potential project is assessed in relation to its place in the strategic plan together with other current and proposed projects;
- appropriate resources are deployed to complete a project in a timely manner;
- projects are aligned with the organization's objectives.

Central to these procedures is a framework that ensures, for each project, several key roles and responsibilities. Whilst different businesses have used various titles for these roles we have usually recommended the following. An *advocate* or *sponsor*, namely the head of a Business Unit who will argue strongly for that initiatives share of the scarce resources and who will be its champion within the organization. Secondly a *results manager*, nominated by the Advocate who will accept responsibility on behalf of the Business Unit for the delivery of the project and its benefits. It can be useful if any benefits detailed in the business case are also written into the key performance indicators of the results manager who can then be held accountable for their achievement. These are the minimum necessary, and in Chapter 8 we locate such roles into a larger scheme for managing projects.

The 'gating process' normally allows for five 'gates'. Gate One – *Concept* – takes the newly conceived initiative and broadly documents it so that a decision can be made as to its future and to seek approval within the Business Unit to devote the necessary time to progress the concept through the next stages of approval.

The second gate is *Feasibility*. This step takes the initial project concept, explores its feasibility and, in conjunction with the Project Office (see Chapter 9), develops the documentation required for the project to be registered and allowed to move forward. During this step the project Advocate and Results Manager will be nominated, the project objectives are detailed and, at a high level, the project costs, benefits and capital requirements estimated. Resource requirements, particularly the Project Leader, can be forecast and an impact analysis is undertaken.

The third gate is *Prioritization*. Any initiative can only proceed when approval is given and resources formally committed. Rarely these days do IT initiatives fall within the province of a single business unit, and prioritization therefore must be carried out with a view to the organization as a whole. If this procedure is circumvented then resources can be committed to initiatives dictated by 'he who shouts loudest' or who has the budget to get an initiative up – a potential weakness in the Administrative approach described in Chapter 1. For a real life example of this in action see the caselet example of the finance company below.

Caselet example: a finance company

This was a traditional business where its Information Services were built upon an architecture of ageing systems, some of which were aligned with powerful business units. The IT staffing had over the years been organized in support teams associated with these complex systems. Built over several years, the systems had been constantly enhanced and their interfaces multiplied. Documentation had not been kept up to date and the teams of experienced staff supporting each of these systems had over time developed strong links to their business unit colleagues.

All requests both for maintenance and for functional development came to the teams directly from the business unit who exerted some proprietary ownership over them. They prioritized their own work with the business unit, and frequently had sufficient backlogs of work to keep them going for months. There were no staff available to the business for other work and any initiatives that sought to use some of the resources allocated to these business unit systems were strongly resisted.

Where the business as a whole takes seriously the task of deciding what work will gain priority, then it will consider a range of issues in deciding priority. Some of these – issues of compliance, technical precedence, business necessity and customer retention – should always take precedence. Other factors, however, need to be considered. Firstly, is there a strong fit with

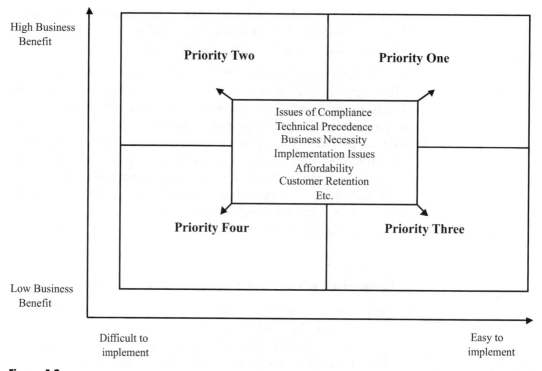

High Business
Benefit

Priority Two

Priority One

Issues of Compliance
Technical Precedence
Business Necessity
Implementation Issues
Affordability
Customer Retention
Etc.

Priority Four

Priority Three

Low Business
Benefit

Difficult to
implement

Easy to
implement

Figure 4.2
Priority matrix

the strategic business drivers and the availability of funds and resources? Is there dependence on, or interfaces to, other projects? Will there be benefit to the business through coordination of implementation plans, and are there appropriate technology resources?

Our experience has taught us, however, that when all of these things have been taken into consideration there is still another important question. How can we get quick wins to give business benefit and sustain business enthusiasm? Figure 4.2 indicates a matrix that is useful to evaluate such initiatives. Those that will get the highest priority are those high in business benefits and also easiest to implement. Other considerations may force initiatives. Keep in mind that it is also possible in some cases to 'unbundle' initiatives and deliver some functionality ahead of the remainder, and in that way gain real business benefit.

The fourth gate is *Planning and justification*. This step covers the scope of the initiative together with detailed plans for approval and, if required by the Investment Guidelines, a Business Case. The initiative will only proceed beyond this step when the appropriate approvers have signed off these deliverables (see Chapters 1, 2 and 5 for suitable planning and prioritization methods).

The fifth gate is *Final approval*. Once approval is given to proceed, the Project Office take over the governance of the initiative that may then proceed in accordance with its Terms of Reference and Plan. A revisiting of the gating procedure would only be required if there was:

- substantial change to the project scope;
- evidence that the project costs and benefits will vary from those submitted in the Business Case;
- a substantial change in the risks associated with the project; or
- the project will substantially exceed its schedules.

Figure 4.3 below provides a typical approval table.

PROJECT ACTIVITIES	Project Leader	Advocate Sponsor	Project Steering Committee	Business Owner	Project Office	Related Project Managers	Regulatory Officer	General Manager IT	General Manager HR	Chief Financial Officer	User Representatives
Project Concept		R		P	R						
Terms of Reference	P		S*	R	R	R	C	C	C		A
Requirements Definition	P		S	R	R						A
Business Case	P	R	S*		R				R	A	A
Graphic Design	P			S							R
Design & Specifications	P				S	R			R		R
Test Plans	P				S				R		
Acceptance Test	A			S	R	R					P
Useability Testing	A			S	R						P
Implementation Plans	P		S	R	R	R	C	R	R		A
Final Review	A		S*	S	P						R

Figure 4.3 Example of an approval table; sign-off and approval chart (S, sign off; C, consult; R, review; A, assist; P, perform. In the case of strategic projects, the steering committee will sign off Terms of Reference, Business Case, Final Review)

4.5 The resource plan

Having the right people available at the right time is both the secret for successful delivery and also one of the most difficult things to achieve. There will always be competition for scarce resources within the programme itself, let alone for other organizational priorities. Planning for the resource requirements of the programme will be an important component of the total plan. This is not a task to be done in isolation. A better result will be produced if as many informed team members as possible can be involved. Vendors and other alliance partners can also assist with this part of the planning. Their experience with similar programmes can be of great help. It is particularly important to identify the range of skills and competencies that will be needed at different times within the programme, and for how long they will be required.

Two important questions have to be answered in relation to the resources. Where will they come from, and how will they be managed? Obtaining the right answers to these questions is vital to the delivery of the strategy. If the resource plan falls down there will be an immediate and possibly catastrophic impact on budgets and schedules for the programme.

The Baselining exercise undertaken in Chapter 3 should have provided a detailed assessment of the human resources available within the organization. That baseline, when compared with the requirements of the programme, will almost certainly prove inadequate. This will almost certainly be the case where significant e-business initiatives are concerned, as few organizations can afford to retain in-house the mix of specialist skills that are required for such a development.

There are several sources for the human resources that will be required. Some of the key ones are covered below. As with investing, however, it is important not to put all your eggs in one basket (see also Chapter 6 on sourcing issues). Do not rely on one source alone to obtain the resources that are required. Make the best use of the variety of sources to obtain the best mix of human talent for the funds that are available. Look to the following.

- *Recruitment* is always an option. It means that the organization can directly employ key skills. It also usually implies permanent employment that can become a problem once the programme has been delivered and the need for the resources disappears. Permanent recruitment should therefore be used with care. It is best used for leadership roles or for key skills for which there will be an ongoing requirement within the organization.

- *Assignment* of resources from elsewhere in the organization can prove a valuable source of people with real knowledge of the business. Though perhaps lacking in technical skills, their knowledge of how the business operates, who are the decision-makers and how to manage communications can significantly contribute to the success of the programme. The downside is the need to supplement their skills in technical areas and to provide them with the education and supervision to ensure their effectiveness. If this is planned, and the people selected early enough, they can quickly pull their weight.

- *Training and education* is a means of developing skills within the organization. It also provides significant motivation for existing employees who see themselves as valued and who may have other skills critical to the enterprise. It is also a risk, for often training in skills that are in short supply will furnish the staff member with an updated résumé and a new sense of their market worth. A worth that if not recognized within the organization may well be recognized by a competitor.

- *Vendors* can be a valuable source of critical skills, particularly where the successful delivery is important for the vendor's on-going sales and marketing programme. With new technology, vendors are keen for the implementation to succeed and will often urge key resources upon the purchasing organization. These resources may sometimes be sourced locally or may be drawn from the vendor's wider network. Such resources can contribute much, but they also have the potential to cause problems within the programme. It is important that it is the organization not the vendor that has the final say on whether individual resources have both the technical and human skills to become a contributing member of the team. Identification of the right people, and agreement on their rates and availability, should be included in the contract negotiation for the vendor's product and should be as enforceable as any other component of the contract.

- *Consultants* and contractors can be used to provide specialist skills or to supply additional resources in peak periods. While they can be expensive, they do provide a degree of flexibility in the resource plan. They need to be selected with three principal criteria in mind: first of these is that they should contribute specialist skills that are not otherwise available within the organization or they simply provide short-term support for peak workloads. The second principle is that wherever possible, especially if they have specialist skills, they should be willing and able to add value to the team by transferring skills to other team members. And thirdly they need to have the people and communication skills that will enable them to become valued members of the team.

When appointing contractors or consultants, it is important to meet and interview the people offered prior to contracting their services. The contracts need to be specific in terms of the nominated resources, the period of contract, rates and rules for termination or renewal. It is increasingly important that the rules relating to confidentiality and intellectual property also be spelled out and the scope of work to be undertaken clearly specified.

4.6 Managing the team

There was a time when we would differentiate 'Project Management' from other forms of management by certain of its characteristics. These normally included its time, budget and deliverable constraints as well as its use of teams that were formed specifically for the task. Increasingly these are the characteristics of everyday business whether in the 'new economy', in the 'not-so-new' economy, but particularly in e-business. People in e-business developments will often fill multiple roles. We have seen them become members of multiple teams and work on several tasks concurrently. For some of us who have been a while in the IT industry this may be a well-remembered scenario. It was ever thus, we might say. Even allowing that this may have been partly true, the change these days is the pace at which things happen.

With a clear focus on outcomes, the delivery of a strategic programme is a significant exercise in complex management, and it is easy to lose sight of the people. Concern for the team and their well-being is essential for the maintenance of good morale and, as a consequence, high levels of productivity. In programmes of this sort, team members will often work extended hours for long periods, and will be under considerable pressure. The roles can be stressful as they will work with unfamiliar people, be up against tight time schedules, and frequently meet with unexpected technical and, importantly, human problems.

There are a number of simple things that can be done. First among these is ensuring that those responsible for leading and directing the teams are experienced managers of people and that they have sound interpersonal skills. Other basic rules of the road include:

- ensure that each team member has a job description and a clear understanding of the programme's objectives and the importance of their own role in achieving success;
- clearly identify the quality standards and the work practices that are to be followed and the methodology to be used;
- define the reporting relationships and where the individual is placed in the overall team. What will be the rules for escalating problems and for reporting progress? If there are rules for time recording, communication or any other procedural matters they need to be documented and explained;
- give them a 'home'. The delivery of strategic programmes often means both a rapid increase in numbers of people to be accommodated, and a degree of itinerancy in work practice. Everyone needs a place to hang their hat and the tools to do their job. If team members are widely distributed or working in cramped conditions, sharing desks, PCs or other tools the productivity and the morale will suffer;
- build team identity. If the team members are committed to the task and their success as a team they will develop a supportive environment that will contribute to the quality and the success of the programme. Provide the team with the opportunity and the logistical support to foster its group identity and to strengthen team spirit. Allow the team to contribute to the planning of its tasks, to reviewing its work and to contributing to the overall assessment of progress. By their taking on a sense of ownership of the results, their commitment and motivation will be positive.

4.7 Communications plan

Whether planned or not, the process of change begins right at the start of the strategic delivery process. It begins with the expectations of individuals as they begin to comprehend what is involved and they begin to anticipate its impact on their jobs and the organization as a whole. It is for this reason that planning for the management of change must become an integral component of the whole programme (see also Chapter 7 where we deal with this issue in much more detail). A well defined communications strategy is an essential component of any programme for the delivery of IT strategy. We have learned over several such programmes that the following ten rules for sound communication work.

4.7.1 Rule one. Identify the audience

With IT, it is certainly not the case of one size fits all. What might be appropriate for an audience of technical staff who may have carriage of the operational systems will fall on deaf ears if directed at a group of end-users. There may be multiple audiences, each with their own expectations and degree of IT literacy. It is important to identify them and to tailor communications to their needs. Yes, it is time consuming! Yes, it adds to the workload! The pay-off is in informed and supportive people who understand the programme, and their part in it. They will not fear surprises and they will be better prepared to take on board the organizational transformation. To make this point, we provide a caselet example of actual practice at an automobile club. One can see that Phase 2 of reorientation (see Chapter 2) is being entered into with the Directors here.

Caselet example: automobile club

Following a decision to develop an on-line presence this automobile club was faced with the need to educate its Board of Directors, who, as a body, had little experience with the Internet. The directors themselves, while appreciating the need to provide such a service for their members, were conscious of their own lack of knowledge and their responsibilities as decision makers.

With the assistance of an alliance partner, an information programme was organized for each of the directors. One-on-one appointments were made with an experienced professional who developed a series of guided tours focused on areas of interest for each director. As they became more familiar with the basics of the Internet, question and answer sessions were facilitated to develop a greater understanding of the technology and the opportunities it might afford their business. Following this simple beginning, the Club embarked on a series of e-business initiatives. As these have developed, so has the capacity of the directors to engage with the new technology.

4.7.2 Rule two. Communicate often

This is not a once-only matter. For communication to work, it must be regular and sustained. Far better to provide a small amount of information frequently than one or two major presentations. You can use the information flow to provide frequent updates, and address those frequently asked questions that, if not addressed, can build a climate of apprehension. Here again, there is a need to recognize the differing audiences and their need for particular information.

4.7.3 Rule three. Make use of your vendors

They can provide enormous assistance. Not only do they have access to a wide body of knowledge that is pertinent to your programme, they also have resources that can be made available to you to help communicate. It is also a way to build the partnership, and to link your various alliance partners in the programme. They have almost certainly been down the road before you and their experience, together with their probable marketing expertise, can be a source of material that otherwise would be difficult to assemble.

4.7.4 Rule four. Manage expectations

The communications programme is probably one of the best means for confirming the agenda and preventing people from forming unrealistic expectations. At the commencement of major projects it has been our own habit to assemble the key stakeholders and get them to write down what they perceive to be the objectives of the project. Each person is then invited to stand and read what he or she has written. It can be an illuminating experience. Usually there are as many different objectives as there are people. Organizations can ill afford to have such confusion. Use the communication channels to ensure that there is a common understanding and that any misconceptions are quickly put to rest.

4.7.5 Rule five. Build anticipation

As there is bound to be significant training and education, developing a readiness to learn can be a great advantage. Regular communication can build up the level of excitement and using the model of Kurt Lewin (see Chapter 7), help to 'unfreeze' the organization and ready it for change. It will encourage and build change agents and, properly managed, help to break down any apprehension that exists within the organization. Don't overdo it, though. It can be counter-productive to build up false expectations and ultimately destroy any value the communication programme may have.

4.7.6 Rule six. Put someone in charge

A communication programme demands coordination and cannot be run by a committee. In a large programme it can be a full-time job for someone, and one that will pay for itself if it is done well. Use the best person for the job, not the best available person. There is a difference! With the right person in charge the programme can be a dynamic force for change within the organization, and can greatly simplify that whole change programme.

4.7.7 Rule seven. Use the technology

It can be a great learning tool. In fact there is a wide range of tools and techniques that can be used for good communication. It is not sufficient to simply rely on one mode of communication. The use of multimedia, presentations, newsletters, e-mail and Web sites can all contribute to the spread of information. Choose the mode that is most appropriate to the subject matter and the audience.

Caselet example: a winery

A major wine maker, having implemented its ERP platform, was preparing to initiate its e-business activity. They had chosen to move forward using incremental steps and had selected their 'Epicurean Club' as the first step. Providing an on-line environment for club members would enable the organization to gain experience in managing the environment and in the back office procedures necessary to support it.

Throughout the development programme, in conjunction with their consulting partners, a Web site was established to provide regular updates on progress and first-hand glimpses of the site as it developed. The input and feedback that was generated made this a valuable tool in the development process and contributed to the ultimate ease of implementation.

4.7.8 Rule eight. Involve the users

Information technology has, hopefully, moved out from behind the curtain and no longer can pretend to alchemy. We cannot pretend to have all the answers. The involvement of those who will use the delivered technology is vital to its success. The development methodologies that we now use demand the joint involvement of developers and users to achieve quality outcomes. These same users can be the best advocates for change and can communicate with their colleagues with greater credibility than others can.

4.7.9 Rule nine. Timing is important

As with most aspects of education, efforts at teaching are largely wasted if they do not come at the 'teachable moment' when conditions and motivation are right for the individual to succeed at learning (Havighurst, 1953). We do waste a lot of time and effort in trying to teach people before they are ready. In the task of communication, therefore, it is important to be clear about the objectives of each step in the communication process. Over the years we have learnt to differentiate between providing information of interest and trying to do the job of training. They are different. One can assist the other, but they should not be confused.

4.7.10 Rule ten. Stay agile

We are convinced that one thing is certain. The more detailed the plan, the more likely it is that there will be change! As organizations enter the dynamic world of e-business, it is difficult to forecast more than six months with certainty. This needs to be taken into consideration in the communication programme. Do not lock-in expectations. Keep the communication flow open, and be honest about the possibilities of change. This is a game that needs to be played on the front-foot.

4.8 Risk management plan

Risk is a necessary component of all serious endeavours. Certainly it is a familiar companion in all IT projects, as we shall see in later chapters. The delivery of IT strategy that involves significant change has implications for time and cost as well as quality. Sound risk management involves the strategies by which risks are identified and contingency plans put in place to either prevent their occurrence or to minimize their impact if they eventuate. There are several areas of significant concern for any delivery plan. We have found that some of the most common are those that follow.

- *The introduction of new technology* – particularly where this is leading edge and there is little industry experience to use as guidance is always risky. It is not just the reliability of the new technology that is at risk, but all the factors associated with its integration into existing environments. New technology also brings an associated skills vacuum. Periods where trained and experienced resources are in short supply and high demand. Can you guarantee that there will be the skills available to solve complex technical problems as they arise, and arise they will (Murphy's Law), often at the most inconvenient time.
- *The calibre and experience of the key resources* available for the programme is critical. If the organization and those respons-ible to deliver have had significant exposure to similar programmes then the risk is reduced. Where these levels of experience diminish, then the levels of risk rise dramatically. It is as important for the organization as a whole to have the experience of large IT implementations as it is for the technical resources. On this issue, revisit the INSUROR caselet in Chapter 1. Such programmes place considerable stress upon an organization and its people. Business has to go on, but there are also a range of ownership tasks associated with the delivery of strategic IT projects that impact everyone to a much higher degree than is usually expected.
- *The association of multiple vendors* – where they are involved in the delivery of the strategy, either as suppliers of components, as integrators, or project managers – this increases the risk. Particular problems may arise where there are technical problems, and cooperative endeavour to fix them proves difficult because of tribal boundaries and turf protection strategies that each vendor puts in place. The rules for problem solving and cooperation need to be agreed and documented right at the start of the delivery programme and escalation procedures put in place to resolve such potential conflicts.
- *Dependence on third parties* – where delivery of components of the overall solution is not under the direct control of the programme managers can always be guaranteed to increase tension. When schedules are tight, and completion depends on the delivery of such a component, the level of risk rises dramatically. In this case, also, detailed contractual agreements need to be in place early, contracts that are enforceable and that

provide for penalties for late delivery or for failure to meet the defined requirements and standards for quality. But beware of writing 'lose–lose' contracts, as in the INSUROR case.

- *Lack of an identified 'Owner'*. Where business processes, data and applications can be linked to well-defined owners who have the authority to approve change, the task of delivery has considerable advantage. Then the agreement of requirements and approval at agreed milestones should flow smoothly. Where this is not the case, then the delivery can be delayed by endless debate and resolved only by compromise, or by the balance of power within the organization. In more traditional business areas, such as finance or purchasing, these lines of authority have been well recognized. It is particularly in the new areas of e-business that boundaries are unclear. When we introduce technologies for Customer Relationship Management (CRM) who owns the customer? When we introduce an on-line presence, which department is the owner? Some organizations will say that it is IT. Others will choose Marketing. If these issues are sorted out up front then delay will be less frequent.

- *The overall impact of change on the organization* can sometimes cause indigestion. Both the volume and the duration of change should be considered. In e-business, change is almost constant and, with strong management focus on outcomes, there is often little time to think about the impact on the staff of the organization. However, the delivery of strategic IT solutions involves major business transformation and it is wise to ensure that the process of change is planned and that its impact on members of staff is optimized. There should be, for example, an overall plan for the retraining of staff that considers all the changes, rather than a plan for each one that may lead to confusion and duplicated effort (see also Chapter 7).

4.9 Business process re-engineering

It is not really possible to talk about the delivery of strategic IT without talking about business process re-engineering (BPR). They go together like a horse and carriage! While it is not the purpose of this book to treat this subject in detail, there are a number of points that must be made. When we discuss organizational transformation we are talking about people and the way they work, about Information Systems (IS) and, only to a lesser degree, about Information Technology (IT), which is the enabler (see also Chapter 2).

There has been a great debate over the past few years about the value of ERP systems. Much of the debate has arisen because of the pain many organizations have endured with their implementation. Much of this pain has been self-inflicted through poor planning and lack of attention to process re-engineering, as revealed in the case of the energy company described in the caselet example below.

Caselet example: energy company

This company implemented an ERP platform in 1999, partly to meet the challenge of the millennium, and partly to replace an aging and disparate suit of systems. Strategically, the new systems would provide a base for both supply and sales chain management that the legacy systems could not do. The business case was predicated on significant savings from the efficiencies the new systems would bring, and the information that would be more readily available.

One year after the implementation of the ERP platform the benefits had not been obtained, and many of the legacy systems were still in production. The senior management team of the organization were less than impressed and a major review was commissioned to see what had gone wrong. The review revealed a familiar story.

Whilst the strategic direction that underpinned the implementation of the ERP platform was well articulated in the business case and understood by the senior managers, little attempt had been made to spread that vision down the line. The teams that worked on the project, drawn in the main from outside the organization, had limited access to those with this vision. They worked almost solely with the users of the legacy systems who were the ones who specified the requirements for the new.

The consequence was an ERP implementation tailored as nearly as possible to replicate the legacy systems. No attempt had been made to re-engineer any business processes. The new ERP platform was force fitted into a configuration that caused problems both for its users and for the operation of the system. For the users, performing the familiar business processes with their new tools was

---

time consuming, cumbersome and difficult. It was a bit like switching from a five-speed Hilux truck to a Mack truck with 27 gears, just to do the shopping.

The great opportunity to review the businesses processes and tailor them as well as the new platform was lost. Going back to attempt this after the implementation would nearly double the already expensive exercise. The legacy systems, by the way, had to be maintained in the main to produce reports in a familiar format for senior management that the ERP platform could not produce.

We are aware of many similar cases! (See Chapter 8.)

Business process re-engineering is a complex task and one that requires a high degree of competency in those who undertake it. Without this focus on the way organizational processes work, and the jobs of the people who use them, there will be little in the way of benefit to be gained from large expenditures on new technology. New platforms alone cannot optimize the supply chain, though they can provide the means of doing so.

This is particularly true for e-business initiatives where the expenditure on the Web site can be wasted if not backed up with sound business procedures. Even something as simple as handling of inbound and outbound e-mail from a company site needs appropriate business rules and procedures in support. Truly here the devil is in the detail. Too often the handling of such mail is delegated to perhaps the marketing manager's personal assistant, who may or may not get round to it depending on other priorities.

Our traditional processes and work practices are invariably not sufficiently flexible to deal with the demands of e-business. They require as much attention, if not more, to their re-engineering as is given to the development of the technology. Those who face the challenge of delivering IT strategy in these times really must give process re-engineering the attention it deserves.

4.10 Conclusion

Whilst the essential problems of delivering an IT strategic programme remain as complex as they ever were, the challenges that accompany any migration to e-business have made the task even more difficult. The speed at which the opportunities occur, the drive to achieve 'first mover' advantage, the 'hype' of the industry and the more subtle pressure from vendors can often create circumstances in which IT must respond or be seen as an impediment to organizational progress.

It is in these circumstances that some of the lessons that IT has learned the hard way over its short history can assist. In the main these come down to people. People who can demonstrate both a structured approach to problem solving together with the flexibility to adapt their processes to meet the new challenges, will be needed. These same people will need to work well in multiple teams and to perform a variety of roles. They will be people who are good communicators and who not only want to grow, but who will also encourage the development of their colleagues.

They are not the typical IT professional of the past, of brick and mortar organizations, though some of these may have made the transition. They will have inherited the lessons of the 'glass-house' and the 'not-so-new' rules but have the capability to re-interpret them. Above all, they will have the enthusiasm and the intellectual capacity to focus on the business and its imperatives first, and then on technology as a tool to help achieve them.

References

Havighurst, R. (1953) Human Development and Education. London: Longmans Green and Co.

Laseter, T., Long, B. and Capers, C. (2001) B2B benchmark: the state of electronic exchanges. *Strategy and Business*, Vol. 25, 36–42.

Lewin, K. (1951) *Field Theory in Social Science*. New York: Harper Rowe.

Mintzberg, H. (1993) *The Rise and Fall of Strategic Planning*. London: Prentice Hall.

Morgan, G. (1996) *Images of Organization*. Thousand Oaks: Sage Publications.

5

Dealing with the IT strategy navigation challenge

'Industrial-age control ratios persist as a way of thinking about IT costs ... [but] the effects of computers are systemic'. Paul Strassmann, 1997.

'Business does not stay static and neither does technology ... so if you are going to use technology to change the way people do business, then you need some kind of model to give you flexibility to match dynamic business problems, with dynamic technology solutions'. California Franchise Tax Board Project Manager.

'It's like gaining another day every week'. Manager at Frito-Lay (snack foods) after the implementation of a new decision support system.

'Outsourcing [IT] imposed on us evaluation disciplines in the business, not just in IT, that we should have had before; but now seeing all that money going out of the door, we really had to do it'. Manager, major utilities company.

5.1 Introduction

To keep strategy flexible but focused is a real navigation challenge. But strategy itself is nothing if it is not implemented. This raises further difficulties. How do we keep the strategy on course to ensure actual delivery? In practice our research has consistently shown that all too few organizations manage this well. In particular few operate evaluation and management practice, in an integrated manner across the IT systems investment lifecycle. The result is regular disappointment with the lack of business value from their IT investments.

In this chapter we provide a framework for navigating IT investments through to ultimate business value. We begin by giving an overview of an integrated approach to the 'IT navigation for business value' challenge.

5.2 Integrated navigation: an overview

A sound way forward on full lifecycle management appears also in the companion volume *Make or Break Issues in IT Management* (see Berghout and Nijland, 2002). Our own distinctive approach to navigation consists of several interrelated activities:

1 identifying net benefits through strategic alignment and prioritization;
2 identifying types of generic benefit, and matching these to assessment techniques;
3 developing a family of measures based on financial, service, delivery, learning and technical criteria;
4 linking these measures to particular measures needed for development, implementation and post-implementation phases;
5 ensuring each set of measures runs from the strategic to the operational level;

Lifecycle Evaluation

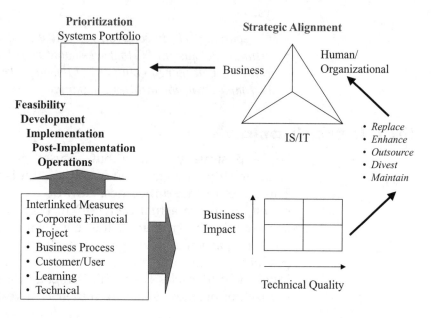

Figure 5.1
IT evaluation and management cycle

6 establishing responsibility for tracking these measures, and regularly reviewing results;

7 regularly reviewing the existing portfolio, and relating this to business direction and performance objectives.

A key element in making the evaluation cycle dynamic and effective is the involvement of motivated, key stakeholders in processes that operationalize the evaluation criteria and techniques. Our previous research points to the need to operationalize these practices across a lifecycle of six interrelated phases – alignment, prioritization, feasibility, development and implementation, post-implementation and operations (see Figure 5.1). These are described briefly below.

5.2.1 Alignment

Earlier chapters have pointed out how lack of alignment between business, information systems and human resource/organizational strategies inevitably compromised the value of all subsequent IT evaluation effort, to the point of rendering it of marginal utility and, in some cases, even counter-productive. At the same time the importance of recognizing evaluation as a process imbued with inherent political characteristics and ramifications was emphasized, reflecting a common finding amongst empirical studies (see for example Strassmann, 1997; Graeser *et al.*, 1999). Many tools have been advanced to enable the evaluation and achievement of alignment. Amongst the more well known are McFarlan and McKenney's application portfolio analysis, Willcocks's multiple objectives and multiple methods approach (Willcocks and Graeser, 2001), Porter and Millar's value chain analysis, Earl's multiple methodology, Information Economics, and Feeny's business-led IT domain navigation (see earlier chapters). In fact there is no shortage of tools. Rather, the usual deficiency in this area is the process or managerial will to use them, with a particular strong preference for, and prioritization of, financial cost–benefit analysis for most IT investments coming through most of the research on this subject.

5.2.2 Prioritization

The notion of a systems portfolio implies that IT investment can have a variety of objectives. The practical problem becomes one of prioritization – of resource allocation amongst the many objectives and projects that are put forward. Several classificatory schemes for achieving this appear in the literature. Others have suggested classificatory schemes that match business objectives with types of IT project (Willcocks and Lester, 1999). Thus, Figure 5.2 shows that projects can be divided into six types:

1 *efficiency* – doing existing things better;
2 *effectiveness* – doing the right thing;
3 *must-do* – for example, because of government regulation;
4 *architecture* – to establish a flexible, robust technology infrastructure;
5 *competitive edge* – differentiating you advantageously from your competitors;
6 *research and development* – trialling potential systems for business payoff.

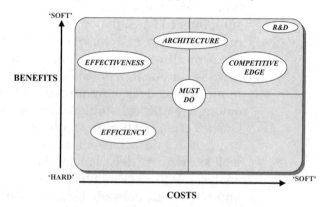

Figure 5.2
Types of IT investment

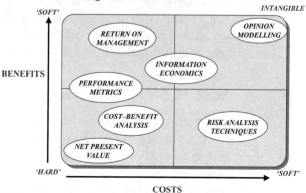

Figure 5.3
Matching IT investments to evaluation method

The type of project could then be matched to one of the more appropriate evaluation methods available, a critical factor being the degree of tangibility of the costs and benefits being assessed (see Figure 5.3).

5.2.3 Feasibility

After alignment and prioritization, the feasibility of each IT investment then needs to be examined. All the research studies show that the main weakness here has been the over-reliance on and/or misuse of traditional, finance-based cost–benefit analysis. The contingency approach outlined above helps to deal with this, but such approaches need to be allied with active involvement of a wider group of stakeholders than those at the moment being identified in the research studies. Following this, Figure 5.1 suggests that evaluation needs to be conducted in a linked manner across feasibility, systems development and into systems implementation and operational use. A key issue here is the establishment at the feasibility stage of interlinked, anchor measures (see earlier chapters, and the balanced business scorecard below). Though initially an issue during feasibility evaluation, in practice, risk assessment and subsequent management is an issue that requires attention throughout the lifecycle. Risks and their combination and virulence can change quickly throughout the lifetime of systems investments.

5.2.4 Development and implementation

The evaluation cycle posits the development of a series of interlinked measures that reflect various aspects of IT performance, and that are applied across a system's lifetime. These are tied to processes and people responsible for monitoring performance, improving the evaluation system and also helping to 'flush out' and manage the benefits from the investment. Figure 5.1 suggests, in line with prevailing academic and practitioner thinking by the late-1990s, that evaluation cannot be based solely or even mainly on technical efficiency criteria. For other criteria there may be debate on how they are to be measured, and this will depend on the specific organizational circumstances.

Kaplan and Norton (1996) were highly useful for popularizing the need for a number of perspectives on evaluation of business performance. Below we review the scorecard concept in light of its potential usefulness within an IT department and, more specifically, as an IT evaluation tool. To add to that picture, a lot of research suggests the need for six sets of measures. These would cover:

1 the corporate financial perspective (e.g., profit per employee);
2 the systems project (e.g., time, quality, cost);
3 business process (e.g., purchase invoices per employee);
4 the customer/user perspective (e.g., on-time delivery rate);
5 an innovation/learning perspective (e.g., rate of cost reduction for IT services); and
6 a technical perspective (e.g., development efficiency, capacity utilization).

Each set of measures would run from strategic to operational levels, each measure being broken down into increasing detail as it is applied to actual organizational performance. For each set of measures the business objectives for IT would be set. Each objective would then be broken down into more detailed measurable components, with a financial value assigned where practicable.

Responsibility for tracking these measures, together with regular reviews that relate performance to objectives and targets, are highly important elements in delivering benefits from the various IT investments. It should be noted that such measures are seen as helping to inform stakeholder judgements, and not as a substitute for such judgements in the evaluation process.

5.2.5 Post-implementation

One all too often routinized phase of review is that of post-implementation. Research suggests that this is one of the most neglected yet one of the more important areas as far as IT evaluation is concerned, and for keeping strategy on course to its destination of business value. Again, our own survey work showed that post-implementation evaluation was the least practiced of any evaluation approaches in the lifecycle (Graeser *et al.*, 1999). An advantage of the above schema, in practice, is that post-implementation evaluation arises naturally out of implementation assessment on an on-going basis, with an already existing set of evaluators in place. This avoids the ritualistic, separated review that usually takes place in the name of post-implementation assessment.

5.2.6 On-going operations

There remains the matter of assessing the on-going system's portfolio on a regular basis. Notoriously, when it comes to evaluating the existing IT investment, organizations are not good at drop decisions. There may be several related ramifications. The IT inheritance of 'legacy systems' can deter investment in new systems – it can, for example, be all too difficult to take on new work when IT staff are awash in a rising tide of maintenance arising from the existing investment. Existing IT-related activity can also devour the majority of the financial resources available for IT investment. All too often such failures derive from not having in place, or not operationalizing, a robust assessment approach that enables timely decisions on systems and service divestment, outsourcing, replacement, enhancement and/or maintenance. As Figure 5.4 shows, such decisions need to be based on at least two criteria – the technical quality of the system/service, and its business contribution – as well as being related back to the overall strategic direction and objectives of the organization.

A further element in assessment of the on-going system's portfolio is the relevance of external comparators. External benchmarking firms – for example RDC and Compass – have already been operating for many years, and offer a range of services that can be drawn upon, but mainly for technical aspects of IT performance. There is, however, a growing demand for extending external benchmarking services more widely to include business, and other, performance measures. There are a growing number of providers of diagnostic

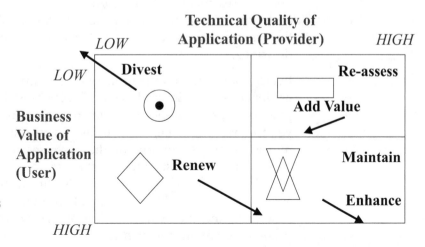

Figure 5.4
Evaluating the business and technical value of existing investments

benchmarking methodologies that help to locate and reposition IT contribution relative to actual and required business performance.

5.2.7 Evaluating IT sourcing options

Evaluation of on-going operations will point to the need to replace, enhance, divest or maintain particular systems. This leads into the final point. An increasingly important part of assessing the existing and any future IT investment is the degree to which the external IT services market can provide better business, technical and economic options for an organization. As mentioned, the possibility of outsourcing tends to drive an organization to review, improve and perhaps implement an altogether new evaluation regime. By 2002, our research showed that despite this rapid growth, few organizations seemed to be taking a strategic approach to IT sourcing decisions, though many have been deriving economic and other benefits from incremental, selective, low risk, as opposed to high risk 'total' approaches to outsourcing (Lacity and Willcocks, 2001). In Figure 5.1 we show how IT sourcing decisions need to link not just with evaluation of existing operations but also with issues of strategic alignment. In the next chapter we present two matrices to facilitate this decision-making process.

Evaluation of IT sourcing options, together with assessment of on-going vendor performance in any outsourced part of the IT service, needs to be integrally imbedded into the system's lifecycle approach detailed above. Not least because an external vendor bid, if carefully analysed against one's own detailed in-house assessment of IT performance, can be a highly informative form of benchmarking. Recent research gives more detail on the criteria that govern successful and less successful sourcing decisions.

Even where an organization does not outsource IT, our case evidence (see Lacity and Willcocks, 2001) is that it is very good practice to assess in-house performance against what a potential vendor bid might be, even if, as is increasingly the case, this means paying a vendor for the assessment. Benchmarking IT performance against external comparators can also be highly useful in providing insight not only into in-house IT performance, but also into the efficacy of internal evaluation criteria, processes; and the availability, or otherwise, of detailed, appropriate assessment information.

5.3 Getting a dashboard view: the IT cost/contribution model

So far we have provided an overview of how a sound navigation approach can be structured. The key issue we have found in all our research and practice is that organizations are increasingly trying to tie IT spend to resulting business performance, a concept that can be generically referred to as 'the value proposition' from IT. Essentially the question asked is 'what value is the organization deriving from the IT investment?'. This trend is encouraging in its message but for many organizations the 'how tos' in defining the derived value are still unclear. What is needed here is a way to immediately clarify the types of value IT investments can be expected to provide.

The Cost/Contribution model developed by Willcocks provides a starting point for examining those components of an IT investment that provide value. Figure 5.5 outlines the model.

Finding IT Value: A Cost/Contribution Framework

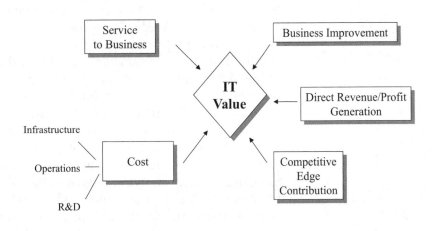

Figure 5.5
Willcocks's cost/
contribution model for
IT investments (from
Willcocks and Lester,
1999)

Note: Development Costs are allocated
directly to each contribution Focus

The basic concept illustrated by the model is that IT value derives from service provided to the business, cost controls/ efficiency, business improvements, direct revenue/profit generation and competitive edge contribution. Each of these components has an evaluation-related issue that requires in-depth examination.

- *Service to the business* – an IT department provides service to the business through speed (of response, repair, etc.), quality (of product and service delivered), and support (i.e., helping the business accomplish its tasks using IT). Consequently, this component of value requires metrics that quantify, for example, speed, quality and support.
- *Cost* – an IT department adds value to the business through 'cost' by controlling the costs of infrastructure, operations, and research and development activities. Operations costs are relatively easy to control because of the long history associated with them. Infrastructure and R&D, on the other hand, both suffer from the 'evaluation problem' of relatively intangible benefits. Since the benefits are difficult to describe directly, the IT organization will want to control very carefully associated costs. What is important here is that every IT expenditure has a strong business case associated with it, even though financial benefits may be very difficult to pinpoint in detail.
- *Business improvement* – the basic proposition to the IT department is 'can the business be improved with IT and if so how?'. Where business processes are being improved, metrics for the required improvements need to be devised and the IT contribution assessed. These metrics will be related to the specific process, for example number of invoices processed per hour, number of cars assembled in a day.
- *Direct revenue/profit generation* – this component of IT value derives from the possibility that the organizational IT department has developed some set of products and/or services to the extent that they can be sold externally as well as internally, thus bringing in a profit to the organization. The bottom line in this case is obviously money in the bank. This financial gain, and metrics showing how well the IT function manages its finances, need to be included in whatever evaluation regime is selected by the organization. Examples are shown below in the discussion on the balanced business scorecard.
- *Competitive edge contribution* – many IT investments must be made simply to keep up with industry. Some also need to be made as a competitive response. Some organizations, on the other hand, have successfully implemented technology that provides a competitive advantage to the organization. One often quoted 'classic' case is that of American Airlines SABRE reservation system. Measurement of this type of contribution to organizational value will require different approaches; again, recall that 'measurement' does not necessarily mean a bottom line number, but can rather be a set of outcomes

agreed upon by the appropriate stakeholders. Typically, however, we are looking at profit and revenue contributions by this IT use. A further measure we found to be of high importance is Relative Customer Satisfaction (RCS) – how external customers and potential customers rate your market offering relative to direct competitors.

A final caution about the Cost/Contribution model. As pointed out in earlier chapters, information-based technologies do not contribute business value in themselves but do so only in combination with other factors such as use of human resources, organizational structure and marketing strategy. This also must be reflected in the evaluation regime and measures adopted. The importance of IT evaluation as a process must be underlined, because all too often the focus is on 'magic' criteria, numbers and the 'quick fix'. From our own work it is clear that one major reason why IT evaluation approaches so often disappoint is because of the failure to erect them as sustainable processes to which people are committed, and whose results are seen as credible, useful and related to learning and improvement.

5.4 A balanced IT scorecard can really help

The Cost/Contribution model is often used where a company needs to get clarity and a quick view of what they are, and what they should be, doing with IT investments. With this tool, the investment time and effort is not large. A more thorough-going navigation tool has been devised by Kaplan and Norton (1996). The attraction of their Balanced Business Scorecard approach has been claimed to be its ability to provide, or at least offer the opportunity for developing, a holistic and integrated set of measurements linking disparate organizational activities with key corporate goals. Many organizations have now taken up this approach or their own specific variants, in applying it to IT performance. For example:

- The Unipart Information Technology (UIT) group pursued the implementation of a scorecard by trying to follow a generic scorecard format. After a year invested in the process, UIT management recognized that the scorecard effort was not providing desired results; rather the process had become mechanistic and not that useful. Consequently, UIT management focused its subsequent efforts on identifying measurements to address the primary UIT issue: that of removing cost from the business. The resulting CAPRI programme developed in late 1997 encompasses three programmes: (1) delivering more value to the customer; (2) increasing internal productivity; and (3) becoming a preferred employer. Upper management is now happy with the direction of the measurement programme, which has generated support and focus in the organization for the pursuit of identified goals.

- The BP Exploration IT group introduced a balanced business scorecard in 1993. This initial scorecard was based on the Kaplan/Norton version. Over the next several years, the scorecard was continually refined to reflect measures appropriate to the organization. The 1994 version proposed some 40 measures per site, triggering a concern over the amount of data required to evaluate 40 measures and the effort required to collect the data. IT management returned to the drawing board and developed a simplified scorecard with fewer measures. In 1997, the scorecard had metamorphosed once again into a 'performance contract' based on the 1994 quadrants as well as an added measure for Health, Safety and Environment performance. The performance contract provides the basis for a monthly Performance Management report and for Quarterly Performance Reviews.

These applications hint at the wide variety of approaches and attempts in developing scorecards, some very successful, some less so. Let us look at the rationale for a scorecard for IT, how to construct one, but also the potential risks and dangers in developing and applying such a tool.

Industry specialists and academics alike cite a number of weaknesses in broad-based performance measurement, including:

- the failure of measurement systems to provide strategic direction (Keen, 1991);
- financially based measures that short change softer, qualitative benefits;
- the historical, as opposed to predictive, nature of measurements;
- a failure of measurement systems to reinforce appropriate behaviours;
- measurements that are 'inward'-looking to the exclusion of an organization's customer and competitive environment; in other words, performance evaluation that fails to measure the value-creating factors of quality, service and speed.

Regardless of the mixed bag of success, organizations recognize the need for measurement of various sorts, but tend to rely on traditional, widely used financial measures to answer that need. Unfortunately, these financial measures usually fail to tell a complete story and, though significant to the review of *some* organizational dimensions, are not, when used alone, appropriate to today's information-age-based businesses. Many organizations have made steps in the right direction with the creation of vision statements and strategic objectives, but those statements and objectives rarely find their way into concrete measurement programmes. Additionally, management usually fails to include measurement as an essential part of organizational strategy, not least because of difficulty in conducting measurement and/or the perceived cost of measurement.

Given the difficulties with measuring performance in the organization as a whole, it is not surprising that companies struggle with measuring performance of their IT investments. And, as earlier chapters demonstrated, an oft-lodged complaint about decisions made by and about the IT function and its use of technology is a failure to align such decisions with corporate strategy. The balanced business scorecard, as proposed by Kaplan and Norton, seeks to remedy this alignment failure.

5.5 New measures are needed

The scorecard is a measurement approach that has been applied in a number of organizations, many of which have found the framework useful in resolving measurement issues. Additionally, for all the reasons provided earlier with respect to performance measurement inadequacy or outright failure, an alternative measurement method is needed. Our own research shows that the introduction of scorecard-type approaches has dominated in the methods introduced in the last five years. In reviewing over 100 organizations we have found the following cited as the most significant benefits resulting from the scorecard:

- the transformation of the measurement process into a management process;
- assisting the IT organization to focus on customer service and delivery;
- the resulting alignment of IT strategy to business strategy.

As noted repeatedly, amongst the inadequacies listed is the failure of many measurement programmes to reinforce corporate strategy *and* the failure of corporate strategy to encompass measurement as a key structure. A significant advertised benefit of the scorecard is the alignment with strategy provided by both the scorecard planning process and the subsequent use of scorecard measures. Moreover, the customer-facing content in a scorecard provides an organization with some degree of external focus rather than the use of merely internal measurements. Closer investigation will reveal that the scorecard also responds to other typical measurement programme shortcomings.

In its ultimate implementation, the scorecard concept encompasses the entire organization. The IT function can be effectively included in this panorama. Indeed, in studying over 100 applications of the scorecard, we found that a significant number of respondents using a scorecard in the IT department were doing so in the context of an overall organizational scorecard. A prime example has been BP here (see above). We also found that these organizations felt they were getting a lot more value from their IT scorecard as a result. Ultimately what is required of a measurement programme is a set of measures that address both external and internal processes and outputs for an organization. More specifically, a new class of performance measures should:

- increase the scope of the measurement focus beyond financial reporting to less tangible benefits;
- create value through a focus on quality, service and speed;
- instigate organizational learning and innovation;
- motivate appropriate long-term behaviour at all levels of the organization.

The scorecard concept will now be reviewed in detail.

5.6 What is a 'balanced business scorecard'?

A balanced business scorecard is ultimately a translation of a company's strategic objectives into a set of performance measures. As the ultimate source of the measures, the company strategy is thus the driving force behind the claims that a scorecard assists in focusing the organization on strategic vision. The use of the word 'balanced' in the description of the approach implies a set of measurements that spans the significant processes and focuses of an organization. 'Scorecard' implies measurement against a goal or target. In the words of Alan Fell, former NatWest head of IT Planning and Performance: 'the genuine balance is not just between finance and customer, it's short term and long term, it's about understanding priorities. Leads and lags'.

In the words of Kaplan and Norton (1992): 'the balanced scorecard provides executives with a comprehensive framework that translates a company's vision and strategy into a coherent set of performance measures'. An organization must start with a statement defining its strategy and mission. The organization can then use the scorecard to translate strategy and mission into objectives and measures, generally organized into four per-spectives: financial focus, customer focus, internal business processes, and learning and growth focus. Note that, although a 'typical' scorecard contains these four quadrants, many organi-zations have implemented scorecards with varying numbers of 'quadrants'.

Executives are most familiar with the financial aspect of the scorecard. The customer-facing, internal process, and learning and growth quadrants and their respective measures are used in a complementary fashion and can be thought of as operational measures that are drivers of future financial performance. Overall, the integrated financial and non-financial scorecard measures can subsequently contribute to both current and future success.

Once the quadrants are agreed upon, and characterized by *objectives* statements, such as 'reduce time to deliver', then the organization can identify specific *measures* that provide valuable feedback about the objective. For instance, the objective 'reduce time to deliver' could be measured by 'the number of projects delivered within 12 months'. To put bounds around the measurements, the organization will then establish *target meas-urement results*. In keeping with the analogy, the target measure-ment for 'number of projects delivered within 12 months' might be 'deliver 80 per cent of all projects within 12 months'.

Given that a good balanced scorecard, then, tells the story of an organization's strategy, the scorecard can be viewed as a language and benchmark against which new projects and businesses can be evaluated. The following provides detailed descriptions of the generic scorecard quadrants.

5.6.1 Financial quadrant

Despite claims that financial measures alone do not tell the whole story about any investment or process, technological or otherwise, financial measures will always be required to tell part of the story. Organizations must be able to measure costs and profits in order to manage direction of the organization and provide shareholders with a financial estimation of their investment. Simply, if an organization is not profitable in a reasonably short term, it will not stay in business.

Regardless, organizations can develop financial measures that more clearly align with their strategic, long-term goals. Such financial measures may have both short-term and long-term horizons, as well as a variety of focuses, including competitve pressures, shareholder perspective and internal profitability. In the case of competitive pressure, for instance, an organization may focus on a reduction in the financial value of 'sales backlog'. Shareholders, on the other hand, will have short-term requirements for profitability as well as a desire for organizational stability over the long-haul. Return on capital employed provides one short-term shareholder measure while profit forecast reliability is a longer-term measure. Finally, the company will want some means of reviewing financials internal to company processes, such as project cost versus profitability.

5.6.2 Customer quadrant

Many organizations have only recently begun to act upon, as opposed to merely understand, the importance of the customer. This move toward customer-focus follows a long and increasingly ineffective focus on product development and delivery. It is customer focus that generally helps the organization develop an externally focused strategy. Customers' concerns tend to fall into four categories: (1) time, (2) quality, (3) performance, and (4) service. The scorecard allows managers to translate general mission statements about customer service, in relation to these types of concerns, into specific measures that reflect what really matters to the customer. For example, an organization may choose to measure 'time to market for product' and/or a desire 'to become customers' supplier of choice'. For instance, a number of organizations studied for this book regularly administer customer surveys in order to measure their ability to satisfy the customer.

5.6.3 Internal process quadrant

While customer focus is certainly important, organizations cannot neglect the focus on the internal processes that will assist in meeting customer focus goals and measures. Popular theories of re-engineering can illustrate the need for this quadrant:

internal processes are a fundamental source of sustainable organizational advantage and people provide the coordination required to harmonize processes with enabling technology. Measures developed related to internal processes should relate to the business processes deemed critical to customer-focused goals. Examples we have seen regularly include quality and productivity measures.

5.6.4 Learning and growth quadrant

The fourth quadrant is, in effect, the measure of an organization's ability to respond to and learn from its experiences in the market. In today's world, most markets are changing rapidly, and an individual organization's strategy of today may require adjustments for continual success in the market. Consequently, this fourth quadrant should include measures of the organizational ability to improve and innovate. Measures in this quadrant should ultimately provide efficiencies to the organization that ultimately translate into shareholder value as the organization improves from learning.

In their article 'Using the Balanced Scorecard as a Strategic Management System' Kaplan and Norton (1996b) suggest that:

> 'Once the strategy is defined and the drivers are identified, the scorecard influences managers to concentrate on improving or reengineering those processes most critical to the organization's strategic success. That is how the scorecard most clearly links and aligns actions with strategy.'

In the organizations we have researched and consulted in, the learning and growth segment tended to be the most neglected and least understood. There was revealed a common confusion between the fact that all measures on a scorecard actually existed to achieve learning and improvement – a fundamental purpose of measurement – and the fact that organizational learning and growth was so central to the modern organization's success that executives needed to think through the specific, distinctive, fundamental ways in which their organization needed to learn and grow, and how these could be measured.

5.7 How to develop a scorecard

The scorecard's ability to align organizational action with strategy has been repeatedly mentioned. The first step in scorecard development is the identification and agreement on

Begin by Linking Measurement to Strategy

	Statement of Vision			
What is my Vision of the Future				
If My Vision Succeeds, How will I differ?	To My Shareholders Financial Perspective	To My Customers Financial Perspective	With My Internal Management Process Financial Perspective	With My Ability to Innovate and Grow Financial Perspective
What are the Critical Success Factors?				
What are the Critical Measurements?	THE BALANCED SCORECARD			

Figure 5.6
Linking measures to objectives

vision – the linking of measurement to strategy. Refer here to Figure 5.6 that shows how to begin the scorecard development process.

Working through the diagram it becomes possible to discern the high-level steps in the creation of the scorecard. After agreement on vision, the organization must determine the critical participants/processes that will make a difference to the success of the vision. In this respect, the example identifies:

1 shareholders,
2 customers,
3 internal processes, and
4 organizational ability to innovate and grow.

These participants/processes roughly translate to the quadrants discussed earlier. In order to pave the way for specific measurement identification, the organization must then identify the critical success factors (CSFs) for each quadrant, then translate those CSFs into critical measures. The mechanics of scorecard development and implementation will be reviewed more closely in a moment. First, it is important to note that each organization is unique; consequently, the outline provided here for scorecard development must be tailored to organizational needs. A purely generic application of the scorecard will most likely *not* breed desired results. Any given organization may differ in a number of scorecard aspects:

- from which level in the organization will the top-level scorecard generate?
- will individual incentives be tied to score card measures?
- how many different scorecards will the organization have (although all should be related)?
- how many 'quadrants' does an organization want to satisfactorily describe its strategy and related measurements?

The recommended steps for developing and implementing a scorecard emerging from the work we have done with organizations are as follows. We will use 'One Bank' as a simple illustration throughout these steps:

1 *Preparation* – select a facilitator, decide on level of management to be included in scorecard preparation. In the case of One Bank, the CEO and IT general managers bought into the scorecard concept and provided powerful driving force behind scorecard development, implementation and ongoing measurement. The organizational vision, scorecard quadrants, objectives and specific measurements were ultimately hashed out by the upper echelon of IT management, which included approximately 90 people.
2 *Education* – provide appropriate managers with scorecard information, previous strategic vision and mission statements; explanation of meetings to take place. For the bank we studied, the education process took place primarily through various workshops, discussions and offsite meetings. The bank also had the benefit of some initial measurement identification undertaken by the internal consultancy group.
3 *Independent attempt* – each manager devises his/her own understanding of strategic vision and develops a set of related measures using generic quadrants.
4 *Workshop* – all managers work together on refinement of strategic vision, discussion of quadrants. Use facilitator. Figure 5.7 provides a focusing tool for workshops. The bank we studied made use of a number of workshops during the development of the scorecard.
5 *Follow-up* – facilitator consolidates scorecard information.
6 *Workshop* – refinement of scorecard ideas.
7 *Production* – scorecard materials produced and educational programme designed for all employees. The bank we studied created two wall charts, one to document management agreements about quadrants, objectives, measurements, and the second to demonstrate how bonuses would be linked to scorecard performance.

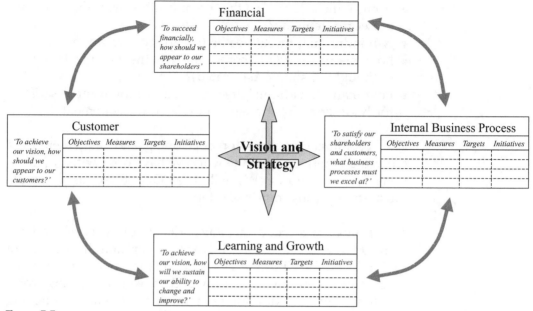

Figure 5.7
The balanced scorecard provides a framework to translate strategy into operational terms

8 *Implementation* – roll out the scorecard to the organization. The bank we studied employed its upper management echelon as the key communicators about the scorecard. The scorecard was implemented across the entire centralized IT organization; measurement data were collected and evaluated on a regular basis. Upper management met first to review results and to assign measurement responsibility to various members of management. Standard reports that documented measurement data and target comparisons were distributed throughout the IT organization as well as to upper management outside the IT organization. Managers were expected to meet with subordinates once a month to discuss overall performance and to identify any problem areas.

9 *Feedback review* – review measurement results; fine tune measures as need be and conduct management exercises that steer the organization based on scorecard results. Driven by the CEO and General Manager, the bank continually debated the efficacy of the measures contained in the scorecard. If a measure was not providing the desired management information, it was discussed and modified.

Scorecard development introduces a management process around its development and links long-term strategic objectives with short-term actions. From the aforementioned steps are gleaned the pieces of this management process:

- *Translating the vision* – management must seek to provide an integrated set of objectives and measurements that allow employees to act on the words of the vision and strategy statements. The *Vision Barrier* describes the implementers' failure to understand the organizational vision/strategy. The scorecard, when implemented effectively across and down an organization, translates the organizational strategy into concrete measurements that can be understood by all employees.
- *Communicating and linking* – management must provide an educational programme to explain the scorecard and its use to its employees. Ultimately, the organization as a whole must be driving toward a long-term strategy rather than just to short-term financial goals. The *People Barrier* describes a failure of most measurement programmes to tie personal goals, incentives and competencies to strategy. The scorecard provides the ability to create finite measurements at all levels of the organization upon which can be based individual reward and compensation.
- *Business planning* – management must seek to integrate business and financial plans. The *Operational Barrier* describes the separation of the budgeting process in most organizations from the strategic planning that a budget ultimately needs to support. In addition, process design within an organization focuses on short-term payback to the exclusion of longer-term strategic goals. As in the discussion of scorecard development, the scorecard provides a format whereby appropriate members of management must agree both on long-term strategic goals and shorter-term measurements.
- *Feedback and learning* – management must be willing to make the scorecard process a 360 degree one. As such, short-term monitoring of all scorecard quadrants provides a double learning loop to allow management to adjust scorecard measures that do not provide useful information. The *Management Barrier* describes a oft-observed organizational situation in which management/measurement systems are designed for operational control rather than for long-term strategic management. Because the scorecard measurements are ultimately a translation of agreed-upon strategy into related measures, the focus moves from purely operational control to strategic management. It is in this manner that the scorecard can be used as a comprehensive management tool rather than a mere measurement programme.

Finally, it is necessary to refocus on the 'balance' in the balanced scorecard. Balance in this context should be taken to mean effectiveness and efficiency. It does *not* mean that success in some areas of the scorecard cancels out failure(s) in other areas. Rather, an effective approach to achieving the balance would be for an organization to establish minimum threshold levels for a critical subset of measures. In other words, if all minimum thresholds are not met, then goals proscribed by the measures have not been attained. Additionally, because the scorecard is a radically redesigned approach to measurement in an organization, it is a good idea for management to establish short-term interim targets for balanced scorecard measures, in order to encourage stepwise successes throughout the organization. The bank we studied, in fact, recognized that in order to perpetuate measurement data collection, management must establish some expectations about how quickly/slowly various measures would show improvement.

5.8 The IT scope of the scorecard

Just as the scorecard can align the organization as a whole with its vision and strategy, the use of a scorecard within an IT department can:

1 align the IT department with the overall organizational strategy, thereby combating one of the oft-heard complaints about IT organizations (their failure to incorporate organizational strategy); and
2 the IT department can measure its own strategies according to the multi-faceted dimensions of the scorecard.

The integrated use of scorecards throughout the organization, including within the IT department, can focus on the measurement of *integrated* key business processes rather than merely focusing on individual functional departments.

The *financial quadrant* measurements can be used to measure the more traditional financial aspects of IT investments and projects. Perhaps the crucial difference offered by the scorecard is the ability to more effectively associate financial measures with strategically based goals. However, several respondents warned of the risk that a scorecard will be implemented without the appropriate reinforcement for the other three quadrants. In such a case, the scorecard becomes merely a vehicle for traditional financial measures.

The *customer quadrant* introduces an important facet of measurement into the IT organization. IT has been considerably lacking in its ability to focus on customer needs. If, however, the IT

IT Services Scorecard – 1 Year Targets

CUSTOMER DELIVERY	DEVELOPMENT OF IT/S

• To achieve full-year Customer Perception ratings (for Operations) of : xx (Hurdle) and yy (Stretch)
• To achieve full-year Customer Feedback rating (for Development) of: xx (Hurdle) and yy (Stretch)
• To maintain following Customer Satisfaction Survey results:
   - Overall Satisfaction (xx%) and
   - Customer First Attitudes of staff (yy%) in 1997/8 whilst implementing ORBIT
• For Overall Satisfaction, no one customer to be below xx% (Stretch)
	• To implement ORBIT recommendation & achieve Benefits as per Business Case for:
	   - Production Services Management
	   - Mainframe Joint Venture
	• To:
	   - Embed new sourcing processes for IT Service
	   - Develop and appropriate measurement mechanism with ITS Customers
	• To externally source two major development projects through framework partnerships
	• Benchmark
	   - Tier 2 & Tier 3 Support service
	   - Data Communications
	• To develop and agree with Group & Customers a Voice Telecomms Infrastructure Strategy covering sourcing, integration & value for money

BUSINESS EXCELLENCE/EMPLOYEE	**BUSINESS PERFORMANCE**

• To maintain Employee Opinion Scores in 1997/8 whilst implementing ORBIT
 	
                Hurdle   Stretch
A Communication   xx   xx
B Leadership   xx   xx
C Reward & Recognition xx   xx
• To achieve 1997/8 Business Excellence score of xxx (hurdle), xxx (stretch)
	• To - Make Real Unit Cost reduction target
	   - Achieve zero profit
	   - Maintain overall price rise to zero
	• To reduce overheads by x% in 1997/8 through implementing Zero Based Budgeting recommendation
	• To maintain
	   - service improvement in investment of £xm
	   - training investment of £xm
	• To ensure all products make contribution in the range of x% and y% by end of the plan period and to ensure no cross-subsidization between products

Figure 5.8

Measuring an IT services department

scorecard derives from the corporate level scorecard, IT's ability to focus on specific customer needs will be enhanced. Several respondent organizations chose to implement a number of surveys to obtain feedback about customers' perceptions of IT service delivery.

The *internal processes* quadrant supports IT's ability to focus on customer-facing measures. Most organizations studied saw this quadrant as critical to the desire to transform themselves into more effective, performance-oriented organizations. To that end, the bank we studied, for example, divided the internal process quadrant into the productivity index and quality index quadrants.

The *learning and growth* quadrant provides an IT organization with the ability to assimilate measurement results and experiences to attain process improvement and fine-tuned management of the organization. Note that at the bank we looked at, however, this quadrant did not fulfil that potential; rather, it was 'demoted into something about staff morale . . . rather than how

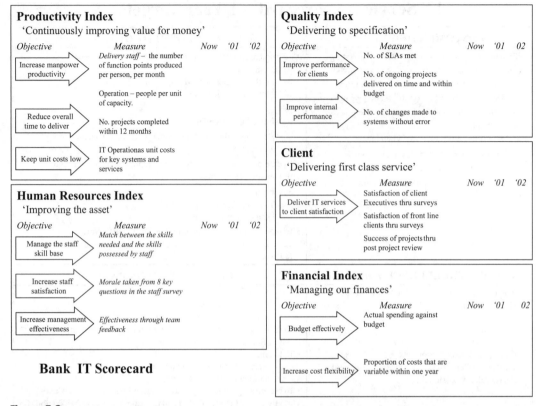

Productivity Index
'Continuously improving value for money'

Objective	Measure	Now	'01	'02
Increase manpower productivity	Delivery staff – the number of function points produced per person, per month			
	Operation – people per unit of capacity.			
Reduce overall time to deliver	No. projects completed within 12 months			
Keep unit costs low	IT Operationas unit costs for key systems and services			

Human Resources Index
'Improving the asset'

Objective	Measure	Now	'01	'02
Manage the staff skill base	Match between the skills needed and the skills possessed by staff			
Increase staff satisfaction	Morale taken from 8 key questions in the staff survey			
Increase management effectiveness	Effectiveness through team feedback			

Quality Index
'Delivering to specification'

Objective	Measure	Now	'01	02
Improve performance for clients	No. of SLAs met			
	No. of ongoing projects delivered on time and within budget			
Improve internal performance	No. of changes made to systems without error			

Client
'Delivering first class service'

Objective	Measure	Now	'01	'02
Deliver IT services to client satisfaction	Satisfaction of client Executives thru surveys			
	Satisfaction of front line clients thru surveys			
	Success of projects thru post project review			

Financial Index
'Managing our finances'

Objective	Measure	Now	'01	02
Budget effectively	Actual spending against budget			
Increase cost flexibility	Proportion of costs that are variable within one year			

Bank IT Scorecard

Figure 5.9
A bank's IT department scorecard

good is the organization at innovation and creativity, learning, changing etc.'.

In our work we uncovered many examples of scorecards actually being used. Figure 5.8 provides an example from a company that wished to remain anonymous, but was willing to share actual, used examples for purposes of illustration. The examples show how a scorecard approach has been adapted for specific IT departments, and these examples of quadrants, objectives and measures can meaningfully be called IT scorecards.

5.9 Risks in measurement systems

Before looking at the benefits, and the ways in which a balanced scorecard can minimize the weaknesses of less holistic IT assessment approaches, it is important to note several risks in scorecard creation. While it is true that 'what gets measured, gets managed', a noticeable lack of measurement implies that other things are *not* being managed. And it is possible that important aspects of organizational performance are left out of the scorecard and consequently not effectively managed under this umbrella. If careful attention is not paid to the effect of scorecard measurements on the organization, inappropriate behaviours might be enforced by the scorecard.

It is clear that initiating and sustaining a balanced business scorecard programme is not easy in complex modern organizations, as the case example of a European retailer shows (see caselet example below).

Caselet example – European retailer

In 1997, this major high street retailer struggled with aligning the centralized IT department more closely to the business. The Financial Director pushed to implement a scorecard throughout the organization. Scorecard development was only in its infancy and, as at 1998, the company lacked the experience to comment on the success or failure of the scorecard. The initial response to the scorecard effort met with mixed results: on the one hand, the organization struggled with the definition of the measurements to be included on the scorecard; on the other, upper management had demonstrated the commitment required to support a scorecard programme. Also, according to one senior manager: 'the businesses are also wary that the scorecard is "another techie thing introduced by the IS group"'.

We have found, even in 2002, many other organizations still having difficulties in quantifying performance and soft benefits, and this could inhibit full application of a scorecard approach. Thus, one major DIY retailer in the UK considered, in light of the implementation of a new balanced scorecard approach across the company, the establishment of scorecard performance measures for IT. The measures chosen focused on 'IT expenditure as a per cent of sales' and 'IT customer satisfaction' as the IT contribution to the scorecard. The IS director acknowledged that these were poor substitutes for what he saw as the key performance measures – delivery of IT benefits compared against IT investment. Unfortunately, he found this measure a great deal more difficult to describe with firm numbers in a scenario where the majority of IT benefits are soft, i.e., not readily quantifiable.

Organizations must be very careful to tailor the scorecard to their own needs. A scorecard developed according to a generic map without a supporting belief system would probably result in a complex measurement system that loses sight of strategic vision and long-term goals. A major UK manufacturer provides an example whereby the generic application of a scorecard programme did not provide desired results, but a more tailored version did. The IT Director explained:

> 'We did a lot of work at the beginning of the year on balance scorecard, we got the wrong individual involved and ultimately that didn't really lead to anywhere. I think the balance scorecard is an approach to metrics which, if it's right and it's helpful in your environment, fine. We think the alternative measurement programme we have developed will give us what we need.'

This is an important point because Kaplan and Norton in their 1996 book make great claims for the balanced scorecard approach:

> 'The cause and effect relationships embodied in a Balanced Scorecard enable executives to establish short-term targets [but] instead of simply reporting information on each scorecard measure ... managers can help validate hypothesized cause-and-effect relationships by measuring the correlation between two or more measures. Correlations among these variables provide powerful confirmation of the business unit's strategy ...' (p. 254).

However, one needs to recognize that Kaplan and Norton provide none of the promised validated, research-based cause-and-effect relationships, and in practice it is left to executives themselves to both hypothesize and test these relationships. This suggests that adopting uncritically Kaplan and Norton's Balanced Scorecard as presented may not be the wisest approach, and that detailed analysis and tailoring will be necessary if the balanced scorecard concept is to be operationalized effectively.

One other risk emerging from our work with organizations has been an excessive focus on *IT* evaluation and assessment. While it is encouraging to see IT departments take measurement initiatives, sometimes they were seen to attempt to implement a scorecard in isolation. Such an independent approach may not deliver desired results given the potential lack of connection to the strategy of the organization as a whole.

Additionally, and notoriously, measurement systems do erode quickly. While much effort in this chapter has been focused on illustrating the strategic alignment concept provided by the scorecard, it is a strong possibility that a once-aligned scorecard will fall out of date with changing corporate strategy. This possibility reinforces the need to continually revisit and critically question scorecard objectives and measures.

Finally, and most importantly, the use of the scorecard does not guarantee a 'correct' strategy; the scorecard can only translate the company's strategy into measurable objectives; failure to convert improved operational performance into improved financial performance should send executives back to the drawing board.

5.10 Emerging benefits

Perhaps the most significant contribution of the balanced scorecard to both organizational and IT measurement is the alignment with strategy and vision engendered by the effective creation of a scorecard. The scorecard, implemented across the organization, assists in conveying strategic goals to all levels of the organization and ties longer-term strategic goals to shorter-term actions via the measurements involved. In addition, the creation of the scorecard links two activities that are generally separate to the detriment of the organization: strategic planning and resource allocation. This separation generally makes for difficulty in linking change programmes to long-term priorities, since change programmes are usually a product of resource allocation and long-term priorities a result of strategic planning.

Perhaps another way to look at the scorecard with respect to IT organizational alignment with business strategy is to consider the scorecard effect on the business–IT gap that is identified as a major issue by IT practitioners and businessmen alike. The Logistics Controller of a major UK high street retailer described the scorecard process as that: 'which examines it [IT investments] from a technical perspective and from the user perspective and tries to get some agreement'. The Financial Controller of the same organization added:

> 'I think you need to get wider understanding of what the balance scorecard means for it to be of use . . . I think they [an organization] need to be very careful for it not to be seen as another techie thing that IS have introduced. Even if it's the Board that's driving it.'

Once again, the development of the scorecard requires:
1 agreement on strategic aims of the organization;
2 the distillation of the strategy into a set of measurements; and
3 continual review of measurement data and resulting ongoing improvement.

In the course of these steps additional scorecard benefits can be identified:

- scorecard development clarifies business strategy;
- the organization develops a shared understanding and commitment to the scorecard programme;
- measures reflect the clarified business strategy;
- measures are comprehensive and well-rounded; not just 'easily measured';
- the act of distilling measures for the scorecard drives to a set of agreed priorities and tradeoffs as the organization seeks to identify only those measures that truly contribute to strategy/vision attainment;
- as a management tool, the scorecard measurement data collected provides focused management information for the organization;
- accountability for measurement and performance is spread across functions.

In light of an understanding of scorecard measurements, consider an examination of the weaknesses in other broad-based measurements identified at the beginning of the chapter.

1 The failure of measurement systems to provide strategic direction: the first step in the scorecard development process is for an organization to agree upon organizational vision and strategic goals. Given this step as the basis for all further scorecard measures development, a common understanding of strategy and vision underlies scorecard measures, thereby providing the elusive strategic alignment.

2 Financially based measures short-change softer, qualitative benefits: the comprehensive scorecard contains a number of non-financial reasons for the sake of capturing those less tangible, qualitative benefits.

3 The historical, as opposed to predictive, nature of measurements: the continual measurement process that should be undertaken with scorecard development should assist management in more readily identifying problem areas and taking action to correct such problems. Naturally, the rigour with which scorecard measurements are pursued affects the timely response to measurement trends.

4 A failure of measurement systems to reinforce appropriate behaviours: the ideal scorecard measurements are cascaded throughout the entire organization and, in some cases, even tied to individual plans/goals with the hope of encouraging individuals to pursue activities that contribute to the attainment of strategic goals.

5 Measurements are 'inward'-looking to the exclusion of an organization's customer and competitive environment; in other words, performance evaluation that fails to measure the value-creating factors of quality, service and speed: again, the non-financial scorecard quadrants provide the 'outward'-looking perspective.

5.11 Putting the scorecard to work: integrated performance management

It is important to ground the scorecard concept in the actual ways in which management works, in other words to make scorecard use part of daily operations. Many software-based tools have been developed to make this possible in real-time, and here we look at one of the more robust that we have worked with, called Integrated Performance Management (IPM). Given the weaknesses with evaluation systems signalled above, and their inherent tendency to decay, it is surprising how few organizations have moved themselves on to the sort of comprehensive navigation tool we will now show at work. But, as we will spell out in Chapter 7, introducing new technology does tend to mean changes in practices that people might well be quite comfortable with, and have invested much time in learning. And more accurate evaluation, meaning greater transparency, does have its political ramifications too.

Typically, a tool such as IPM decomposes the organization into entities and associates critical objectives, processes, measurements and data with those entities to give management the necessary comprehension of the connection between organizational goals and operational activities. According to Robert White, one of the originators of IPM:

> 'Management needs to be able to focus on fewer things, but we've got to get them to do those fewer things better. And those things have to be focused on business value. Once we've got them to do that, then they need to be able to measure what it is they're trying to achieve. So we've got to have a measures framework. The moment that you say you need a measures framework, that immediately means that you are into continuous improvement ... If I'm into continuous improvement, it follows that I've got to engage the whole organization. To do that, I've got to have a common language and I've got to let everyone know how they contribute. And if I can do that, then I have an effective mechanism for moving those measures forward.'

A tool such as IPM can be used to focus on bridging the gap between corporate vision and operational activity. Whether as a general management tool for the whole organization, or for focusing on a specific problem, a tool such as IPM should aim at a decomposition of organizational activities and an explicit identification of the connections between those activities. Individuals at every level need to identify the 'entities' that comprise the organization and its goals, and work towards a model that provides a measurement framework for the organization. Such a model can address the general problems set out above but only if it embodies:

- an articulated strategy that focuses on value;
- a common language to share the strategy;
- an understanding of organizational contribution;
- measures that encompass tactical steps within the strategy;
- target tolerances for measures.

In IPM the steps required to satisfy these needs are made explicit through a process of entity modelling. Before identifying the 'how tos' of such modelling, consider Robert White's following description of resolving, at a client company, some of the organizational problems already discussed (see caselet below).

Caselet example – making the connections in manufacturing

Executives will sit in the boardroom and discuss return on capital (ROC); those executives all understand what that means. Drop down to the shop floor in the same plant, however, and say to the maintenance fitter: 'don't forget the minimal 15 per cent return on our capital' and you'll get a very blank look. That organization clearly does not have a common language, and connectivity does not exist in the organization. The organization can achieve that connectivity though in a few very simple steps.

Executive to maintenance fitter: 'You're about reliability aren't you?'
Maintenance Fitter: 'Yes.'
Executive: 'Well, if we increase reliability, don't we increase volume through the plant?'
Maintenance Fitter: 'Yes, we do.'

> *Executive*: 'So, if we increase our volume, we increase our profit and if we increase our profit, we increase our return on capital.'
>
> Not much work has been done . . . but already a connection has been made and some degree of alignment has been created; the organization has also done something about the creation of a common language because the maintenance fitter doesn't have to understand the technicalities of ROC, just where that person fits and how they contribute to that goal. If some measures are then attached to this, then progress can be tracked.

This exchange shows the simple principles of IPM: it's actually a decomposition of organizational activities aimed at understanding those activities and the links between them, as well as accountability, measures, measure tolerances, related documents and action plans. Models are created using an entity tool; each entity has associated with it:

- a description
- an objective
- related measures
- an owner
- a plan
- resources
- performance data
- document attachments
- numbers and formulae.

Figure 5.10 shows the basic entity concept with a simple model, descriptions and objectives. The process of arriving at entities and relationships, and a workable model is described in the caselet example below.

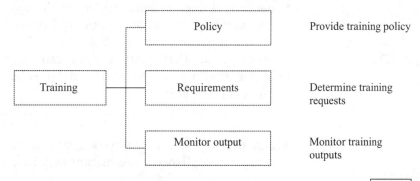

Figure 5.10
An entity example: training

> ## Caselet example: IPM – entities and relationships
>
> The demands of continuous improvement include the need for a great deal of information to be maintained and managed. Out of this wealth of information, the organization needs to isolate what is important and then figure out a way to make the selected data 'live long enough' to contribute. The data can only provide this contribution if it is in the right place at the right time *and* it is the right information. IPM is, thus, managing those data points and helping the organization translate that into information for the *next step*.
>
> An entity tool is used to create the models; entities are used to carry the said information. An entity requires a description, an objective, some measures and an owner. This entity information provides the basis for some focused activity and some ownership and accountability. To achieve that objective, plans are required. Additionally, the organization needs to understand resources: what it has, what it is planning to use, what it has actually used. Performance data needs to be provided to populate agreed-upon measures, both planned and actual. The measures and performance data help the organization understand the impact of the entity across the organization.
>
> Given the measures, the organization can set tolerances around those measures. The entity tool allows for using actual performance data that make the entity change colour to red, amber, green, depending on where it is relative to the tolerances set. Thus, the organization has a visual cue regarding the 'performance' of the entity. The entity is essentially a 'little power pack' of information that can be manipulated. Entities can be brought into relationships with other entities to create models. Rather than build great big monolithic models, models are linked . . . start small at the bottom of the organization and build up to the middle of the organization so that the whole thing remains manageable. Performance data can be rolled up to an upper-level model to obtain a consolidated view. In a nutshell, this is IPM.

When the organization agrees upon the entity models, it has already accomplished a significant task in making relationships explicit. A tool such as IPM, though, can offer a number of additional advantages.

1 'What if' scenarios – the numbers and formulae associated with the entities can be modified to represent 'what if' situations. Formulas are recalculated and graphs recreated in order to demonstrate the effect of whatever has been changed. These scenarios allow an organization to test assumptions before making a commitment.
2 The model itself provides the object of discussion as opposed to discussions aimed at attacking individual opinions. In this sense, the model is a sort of automaton (see 'Chemco' caselet example below).
3 The models provide people who are line resources with a concrete mechanism for explaining problems upwards.

Clearly, with the power of the technology available, these advantages can also be delivered quickly, and even within the context of a meeting. The caselet example of Chemco (anonymized at the company's request) demonstrates the first two of these advantages at work.

Caselet example: 'Chemco'

We were prototyping this, we had 20 people in the room from different disciplines: engineers, HR, union reps, finance people and stuff. And we prepared a 'what if' to demonstrate the 'what if' feature, and the senior finance guy who was giving the demonstration, he picked payroll numbers and he said 'now what if payroll numbers fell by 5 per cent' and he pressed the button. And away it went with the calculations. It was only after he pressed the button, he realized that he'd picked a terrible example, because he had union reps, HR people . . . you know the worst example that you could think of. It finished whirring, and up came the numbers. And wonderful things happened to profit and ROC . . . just wonderful.

The first person to speak was the HR person and he said 'that's a load of garbage' . . . we were a bit miffed by that because we were quite proud of that; it took us six weeks to put this together, so we were pretty thrilled by it.

'So why is that a load of garbage?' we asked.
HR guy replies 'well, you haven't got severance in there'.

'Alright, do you know the formula for severance?'
'Of course I know the formula for severance.'
'What's the formula for severance?'

So while he was saying it, Howard was typing it in, pressed the button again, away it went, up came the results. 'Does that help?' 'Yeah ... that's ???'

Next guy to speak was the union rep ... 'this is terrible; this is a big stick for management to beat us with ... not having anything to do with this'. Now fortunately for us, the chairman that day had issued a note that basically said ... 'look we've got a lot to do, it doesn't matter how we achieve it as long as we achieve it'. So our sponsor produced this note ... and the union guy said, 'does that mean that we can have one of these?'. 'Well yeah of course it does, because you're part of the team.' 'Well does that mean that if we achieve that result without losing 5 per cent of our people, then that's OK?' 'Well yeah ...'

Now what was happening there was that they were arguing about the model ... the model was garbage, not your opinion was garbage, not I'm right and you're wrong ...

The model and technology can also provide a mechanism for line staff to demonstrate problems upwards. This is illustrated in the 'Pharmco' caselet example below.

Caselet example: 'Pharmco'

In this case a senior 'Pharmco' manager decided he was going to increase his cash flow from previous cash flow and profitability levels. This was to be achieved by reducing spare's stockholding for the plant by 10 per cent. While this felt intuitively correct to him, he reasoned that he was going to get a very strong negative reaction from the engineers because he was reducing their cushion of comfort. He duly prepared himself for a bad reaction and planned to railroad the decision through. On announcing the decision, he got the predicted result from his team, who then said 'you've got this performance measurement thing ... what does it say?'. 'Well I don't know ... I don't know if the model is any good.' 'Well let's sort the model out.' So they worked on the model. Reducing spare's holding by 10 per cent had virtually no effect on cash flow and profitability. However, the effect on reliability was significant. It turned out that for no gain, 40 per cent of their revenue would have been put at risk.

What's going on there? An intuitively correct decision turned out not to be. So a manager was prevented from making a bad decision, but much more importantly, the team had become engaged in a debate that in any other circumstance they could not have had, so they could push upwards and say 'you're wrong and here's the reason why . . .' – this can be a powerful mechanism. And now there is the basis for change, and the basis to have the team contribute. Robert White comments: 'In the first (Chemco) example, we had HR contributing. They didn't know that they were contributing . . . they were just behaving naturally, and aggressively, and horribly . . . but we captured that. We turned that into value, is the point. And that's one of the powers of this approach'.

5.12 Building in the IT perspective

IPM is obviously not intended solely for use with IT investments. On the contrary, as a tool, it can be used from the highest levels of the organization all the way down to the line, and it can be utilized to help solve specific problems. Applying the concept to IT, though, a set of performance measures that related directly to value need to be established (by examining the organizational goals embodied in the entity model). These measures will not be just about IT, they will be about the business, because IT has no value if the business cannot extract it.

As we spelled out in the first two chapters, historically, most businesses have not acted upon this aspect of IT investments; moreover, it has been difficult to get the business to understand the contribution of IT. The business has to take an interest in IT because it infiltrates the organization and its need and use must be made explicit. The IPM value proposition provides the articulation of the related business measures, isolates out the technology measures, and provides the means to track both. Traditionally, the responsibility for these two types of measurements rests in two different places: the ability of IPM to attach accountability to entities and, at lower levels, to measures provides a way to 'ratchet up' the control over the measures and an increased understanding of the IT contribution.

The case study that follows helps to illustrate in more detail and in specific contexts the applicability of the concepts so far outlined, and the highly useful role a computerized tool such as IPM can play.

5.13 Illustrative case: international finances and property services company (IFAPS)

5.13.1 Background

As at 199X the company (whose name is anonymized by request) provided financial and property services to clients around the world. It had over 7000 employees, a market capitalization exceeding US$4 billion, and managed more than US$50 billion on behalf of 28 000 shareholders and investors worldwide. Its divisions included Financial Services, Property and Infrastructure Development and Project Management, Property and Infrastructure Funds Management and Information Technology. Significant market presence from the latter, offering a full range of IT services to corporations and government institutions, resulted from a 5-year joint venture deal signed with a major outsourcing vendor three years before. As part of the deal IFAPS outsourced all its IT employees, and all IT services and infrastructure, and took a shareholding, along with the vendor, in the new joint venture company.

5.13.2 Towards linking business and IT performance measurement

As for many other organizations outsourcing their IT (see Chapter 6), IFAPS experienced a number of difficulties as a result of loose contracting and not getting the evaluation regime comprehensively set up at the time of signing the contract. It became clear that the technology supply measures needed detailed attention, refining and updating. At the same time, as in several other deals, questions were being asked about the lack of added business value materializing from the outsourcing arrangements. Lacity and Willcocks (2001) point out the 'mid-contract sag' phenomenon frequently experienced two or more years into a deal. While the original contract may be being delivered to the letter, little additional 'added value' seems to result, especially in terms of improved business performance, despite expressions of intent by both sides at the outset.

In IT outsourcing many organizations operate on the mistaken belief that external IT vendors can be experts not only at

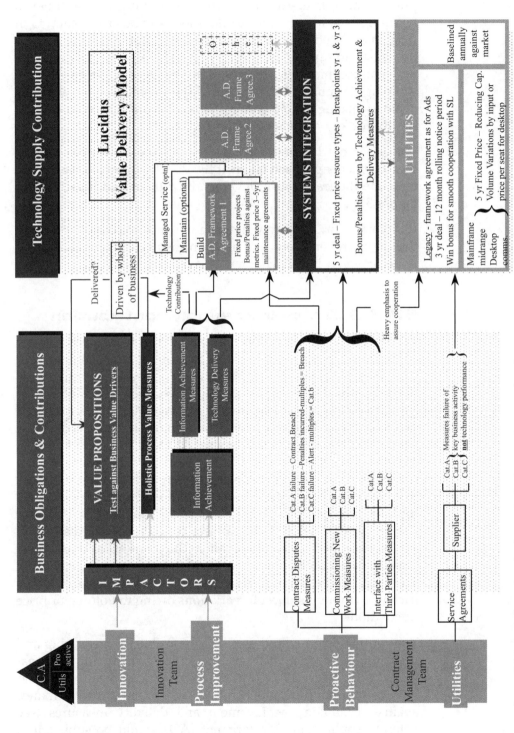

Figure 5.11 Business and technology contributions: an integrated performance measurement framework (source: Robert White, Lucidus Management Technologies – White, 2002)

technology supply, but at their own line of business as well. In practice, of course, expecting even a 'world class' IT supplier to be similarly skilled in an area not their core business, such as in this case international financial and property services, is unrealistic to say the least. If there is to be business advantage – not just technical efficiencies – to be derived from IT outsourcing, it must be driven from the business side, with the business managers and core in-house IT team accepting responsibility for key actions (see Chapter 2).

This kind of thinking was integral to the new performance measurement approach taken at IFAPS. The company used as its template the framework developed for them and illustrated in Figure 5.11.

It is worth working through this model in some detail because it deals comprehensively with all the measurement and evaluation issues covered in this chapter.

5.13.3 Technology supply contribution

For IFAPS the initial issue was to get the technology supply contribution properly measured and under management control. This required the establishment of a much stronger in-house contract team, along the lines described in Chapter 2. Its primary role was to measure and manage vendor performance on the 'utilities' (legacy systems, mainframe, midrange, desktop, comms). The way forward envisaged more than one supplier. They would be measured through service agreements erected not on technology performance but on new measures of 'failure to key business activity' – as a form of exception reporting. IT 'utilities' are one of the easier areas to measure. In this case legacy systems were to be subject to a three-year deal, with prices baselined annually against the market, and a bonus payable for smooth cooperation with the systems integrator (SI). The other utilities were subject to a six-year fixed price, reducing each year, though subject to variations owing to volume or price fluctuations.

The contract team would also be responsible for measuring and managing a five-year systems integration outsourcing deal that would run on agreed fixed prices for resources, breakpoints and with certain bonuses and penalties dependent on performance against technology achievement and delivery measures (see below). Application Development (AD) would be subject to a framework agreement based on fixed price projects, and bonus and penalties against metrics. Different suppliers may be used to deliver specific projects on more tailored contracts falling within the framework agreement terms.

A new dimension introduced into the technology supply side was the encouragement of pro-active behaviour among and across the company and its suppliers. As can be seen in Figure 5.11, this was to be achieved by measures for 'contract dispute', 'commissioning new work', and 'interfacing with third party'. Again penalties and bonuses were an essential part of the measurement and motivation mechanisms here.

5.13.4 Business obligations and contribution

With the above up and running, IFAPS would experience much more satisfaction with its IT and its suppliers (in-house or otherwise), but would still be looking hard for the elusive added business value from IT. The recommendation to IFAPS was to institute an Innovation team responsible for identifying additional business opportunities available from IT, for creating new business ideas and step change innovation. Business managers would also be responsible for process improvement ideas. In the modern corporation these would inevitably have IT implications (see Figure 5.11). Business value drivers would also be regularly identified through the strategy-making process, for example using the multiple methodology detailed in Chapter 2. Examples of business value drivers at IFAPS were prices to (external) customer, customer satisfaction and service, revenue growth and cost/margins.

But all this needed to be converted into a measurement system. The key was firstly to identify the business impactors for any new initiative and work these into a value proposition that could then be tested for alignment against the business value drivers. A business impactor can be defined as 'a point at which the correct application of information/technology will deliver tangible benefit, all other things being equal'. Business impactors and business value drivers feed into the development of a value proposition. The latter process needs to be standardized to ensure consistency and comprehensiveness within the measurement system. At IFAPS it covers:

- cost impact
- response to customer

- quality impact
- process value measures
- information achievement requirement and measures
- benefits case, release profile and risk assessment
- benefits realization programme.

It is essential that each value proposition defined in this way is strongly correlated with the general measurement system of the business, which, following what was said earlier in the chapter, should include holistic process value measures.

'Information achievement' forms a key element. Here the criteria for success to be applied to the information achievement are defined, and also the measures to check success. An important separation occurs at this point – between information achievement and technology delivery measures. The latter are concerned with the building and application of technology. Thus, measures will be, for example, budget milestones delivered to specification. Such measures are concerned with timeliness and efficiency. Information achievement measures tap directly into the impact on the business. Thus, in the IFAPS centralized knowledge base example below one information achievement target was the development of a library search engine for keywords. The information achievement measure was that a trained staff member could achieve an average search time of less than 10 seconds. The IT supplier – in-house or external – will be tracked on the information achievement measures. Where these are fulfilled, then payments, including agreed bonuses, result. Where not fulfilled, penalties start. Where a project is abandoned, then the supplier would return a pre-agreed percentage of the development costs. It should be noted that the 'Information achievement' measurement and reward system feeds into the applications development and system integration components, rather than the 'utilities' aspect of the technology supply contribution. This is because the contribution of 'utilities' is very much restricted to cost efficiency (see the Cost/Contribution model above).

Developing the value proposition in this way represents the 'engine room' of the measurement system, pushing managers to carry out the evaluation tasks and form the fundamental building blocks on which an effective measurement/management system can be erected. It is worth working through an IFAPS example at this point to illustrate the process of measurement generation.

5.13.5 Example: step change innovation through a Web-enabled centralized knowledge base

The proposal arose in the Property and Infrastructure development and Project Management Division at IFAPS. Document handling and access for external customers and internal business users was a 50 per cent manual process. Drawings were being held as multiple copies. There was a high error rate caused by use of old versions, and customer response was too slow. Moreover, overhead costs were too high because of excessive printing and paperwork for staff, cost of rework resulting from errors, and document storage and filing costs.

The proposed solution was to fully automate the process and documents to create 'knowledge'. A check was run against the business value drivers. Service would be improved by a faster design phase, reduction in customer response time and rework resulting from error. Quality consistency would be enhanced by

Targets	Measures
➤ Centralized drawing library with audit trail	• 100% current drawing loaded; nil lost drawings in year 2
➤ Central user-controlled project configurator	• 100% projects loaded; 100% project managers trained
➤ Centralized bill of materials list	• Ordered materials entry process in place and functional
➤ Standardized user-definable document pro formas	• Standard pro formas loaded; staff trained in usage
➤ Financial comparison by user-defined material group by source	• Numerical and graphic financial output available to agreed standards, and X staff trained in usage
➤ Comparison by material group by source	• As above
➤ Local Internet access to information	• Access tested from X specified remote locations plus 100% sites implemented
➤ Source access and transmission mechanism	• Nil security breaches detected on first 2 years' usage
➤ Min X users concurrent usage	• Adequate agreed volume test evidence received
➤ Administration overheads – X% reduction	• Person days in central system administration in years 1 and 2
➤ X% reduced time hardcopy printing	• % hardcopy print time removed from agreed benchmark and design process cycle
➤ X% reduced hardcopy stored drawings X	• Number of hardcopy drawings retained in targeted small/large sites in first operational year
➤ $3.5m reduction in IT overhead costs	• Specified IT overheads identified as redundant in first operational year
➤ Training costs less than $X per person	• Average training costs per person in year 1
➤ Library search engines for keywords	• X staff trained in usage; average search time less than 10 seconds

Figure 5.12
Information achievement: Web-enabled centralized knowledge base

standardization. Automation would also improve electronic and length of time of access, to clients. Complaints could be handled faster, improving the brand image, while the knowledge base offered value-added by unlocking procurement potential. The cost impact of 5 per cent design fee saving, 25 per cent reduction errors, 25 per cent reduced IT overhead, reduced hardcopy and staff savings was calculated at over US$10 million. This analysis enabled the development of detailed holistic process value measures for each item, against which information achievement targets and measures could be generated. Examples of the eventual information achievement measures are shown in Figure 5.12.

Technology delivery measures were also defined, and included project management measures such as budget variance to date – capital and staff; milestones missed or not to specification; final predicted budget variance; final predicted timescale variance.

A detailed risk assessment was also carried out. Driving out the measures then acted as the foundation for developing and tracking a benefits release profile and the benefits realization programme.

The case example demonstrates how business needs and technology development and usage can be integrated, and how a focus on detailed performance measurement can make this possible. The integrated performance measurement mechanisms were also developed with the purpose of motivating and managing external vendor performance as well as that of in-house teams. Integrated performance measurement brings a clarity and precision to responsibilities, tasks and time horizons that made the achievement of significant impacts on the business value drivers at IFAPS much more probable.

5.14 Conclusion: building a navigation scheme

Consider the following steps for setting up a navigation approach:

- engage in strategic alignment between IT investments and business objectives;
- prioritize resulting IT investments, also according to objectives;
- match feasibility assessment and lifecycle evaluation techniques to prospective benefit types;
- integrate the evaluation process across IT lifetime;

- establish metrics at (1) strategic level; (2) business process/ operations level; and (3) customer perspective level;
- engage in organizational learning and establish metrics that enhance the pursuit of this capability;
- to attain benefits from IT investments identified during feasibility assessment, the evaluation process must continue through project development and into post-implementation phases. A software tool such as IPM assists this process, and helps to embed measurement into daily management practice at all levels in the organization. It also makes IT contribution itself integrated into the measurement of business performance, thus putting the balanced business scorecard for IT concept to work.

References

Berghout, E. and Nijland, M. (2002) Full life cycle management and the IT management paradox, in Remenyi, D. and Brown, A. (eds), *Make or Break Issues in IT Management*. Oxford: Butterworth Heinemann.

Graeser, V., Willcocks, L. and Pisanias, N. (1999) *Developing the IT Scorecard*. London: Business Intelligence.

Kaplan, R. and Norton, D. (1992) The balanced scorecard: measures that drive performance, *Harvard Business Review*, January–February, 71–79, 1992.

Kaplan, R. and Norton, D. (1996) *The Balanced Scorecard: Translating Strategy into Action*. Harvard Business School Press.

Kaplan, R. and Norton, D. (1996b) Using the balanced scorecard as a strategic management system. *Harvard Business Review*, Jan-Feb, 75–85.

Keen, P. (1991) *Shaping the Future: business design through information technology*. Boston: Harvard Business Press.

Lacity, M. and Willcocks, L. (2001) *Global Information Technology Outsourcing: in search of business advantage*. Chichester: Wiley.

Strassmann, P. (1997) *The Squandered Computer*. New Canaan: Information Economics Press.

White, R. (2002) Integrated Performance Management. Internal document, Lucidus Management Technologies, Barnbrook House, Lower Mill, Cleveley, Chipping Norton OX7 4DY; Web site http://www.Lucidus.co.uk

Willcocks, L. and Graeser, V. (2001) *Delivering IT and E-Business Value*. Oxford: Butterworth Heinemann.

Willcocks, L. and Lester, S. (eds) (1999) *Beyond the IT Productivity Paradox: assessment issues*. Maidenhead: McGraw Hill.

6

Delivering sourcing strategy for IT and e-business

'The customer from hell is the naïve buyer'. CEO, major IT service provider.

'Outsourcing contracts are agreed in concept, but delivered in detail, and that's why they can break down – the devil is in the detail'. Account Manager.

'I see ourselves as in competition for resources and attention, against all the other customers of the supplier'. John Yard, IT Director, UK Inland Revenue.

6.1 Introduction

A great deal is now known about IT and e-business outsourcing, here defined as the handing over to a third party of the management and operation of an organization's IT/e-business assets and activities. Outsourcing is not the only way of using the market for external IT services. For example, buying in resources to run under in-house management control – sometimes called 'insourcing' – is also widely practised. An organization may also choose to give suppliers long-term, preferred choice status, or buy IT services more competitively, typically involving more short-term relationships. In this chapter, we build on our remarks on this subject in Chapters 1–5, and seek to summarize the growing understanding of reasons for success and disappointment, and of how best to use the IT/e-business outsourcing market. We also present two matrices to facilitate sourcing decisions. We also position use of the IT services market as essentially about risk management, and indicate what these risks are and how they can be mitigated.

In this chapter we draw upon multiple sources. The first is a case history research database of over 250 organizations assembled across the 1990–2002 period. We also draw upon three European and US IT/e-business outsourcing surveys carried out in 1994, 1997, 2000 and 2001, and additional case work into over 100 e-business developments. The most useful references for this work are Lacity and Willcocks (2001) and Kern *et al.* (2002).

6.2 IT outsourcing: towards a routine mode of managing

In the early 1990s, many company boards and government departments worldwide increasingly asked: 'Why not outsource IT?'. Much of this was a questioning of escalating IT costs and a reaction to increased competitive and recessionary pressures. Vendors were seen as being able to provide the same or superior service cheaper, offer access to technical expertise that was in short supply, change fixed costs to variable costs, and/or through headcount reduction and purchase of IT assets, improve the financial position of a client organization. IT outsourcing has also been portrayed as an opportunity to apply a core–periphery model to managing and organizing (see Chapter 1). On this analysis, all IT is sometimes mistakenly characterized as an undifferentiated, albeit occasionally 'strategic', commodity that can largely be outsourced. This can be a particularly damaging assumption as we move into outsourcing e-business components and infrastructure – by definition closely connected to the business.

A further reason for outsourcing IT is all too familiar. Faced with rising IT costs and little demonstrable business value, senior managers have often given up on the internal IT function. Finally, we are finding in most recent work into the IT needs for e-business that speed and access to scarce IT skills are becoming much more important influences on IT sourcing decisions generally, and not just for e-business activities. How has all this turned out? What practices have actually been adopted, and with what results? Are there proven sound practices in IT outsourcing, and what are the future prospects globally?

From an initial main focus on cost reduction, IT outsourcing is fast moving to becoming a complementary or alternative, routine mode of managing IT. Probably, on average, 30–35 per cent of most large organizations' IT/e-business budgets will be managed by outsourcing arrangements by 2003. The question 'why not outsource IT?' is no longer, if it ever was, an adequate base from which to make and manage outsourcing decisions. The real question now has to be: 'How do we exploit the ever maturing external IT services market to achieve significant business leverage?'.

The high-profile mega-deals are often referred to as 'strategic alliances' or 'strategic partnerships'. One could be forgiven for believing this type of total outsourcing to be the dominant trend, but globally, this is the reverse of the case. In fact, a rich picture emerges of organizations taking one of three main paths to IT sourcing (see Figure 6.1).

A 2000 survey by Mary Lacity and Leslie Willcocks (*Inside IT Outsourcing: a state-of-the-art report*) covered IT and e-business sourcing. It found that by far the dominant mode is selective sourcing, especially in the USA (82 per cent of organizations) and UK (75 per cent). A mixed portfolio, 'best-source' approach typically sees 15–25 per cent of the IT budget under third-party management, with other IT needs met through buying in resources under in-house management (insourcing), and through internal IT staffing. Many organizations (USA 10 per

	In-house Commitment	Selective Sourcing	Total Outsourcing	Total Outsourcing
ATTITUDE	Core Strategic Asset	Mixed Portfolio	Non-Core Necessary Cost	World Class Provision
PROVIDERS	IT Employees Loyal To The Business	Horses For Courses	Vendor	'Strategic Partner'
EMPHASIS	'Value Focus'	'Value For Money'	'Money'	'Added Value?'
DANGERS	High Cost Insular Unresponsive	Management Overhead	Exploitation By Suppliers	Unbalanced Risk/Reward/ Innovation

Figure 6.1
IT sourcing: main approaches (source: D. Feeny, L. Willcocks, M. Lacity, personal correspondence, 2000)

cent, UK 23 per cent) have no significant IT outsourcing contracts. Here IT is perceived as a core strategic asset, with IT employees loyal to the business and striving to achieve business value in a way in which external providers are deemed not to be able to do total outsourcing (80 per cent or more of the IT budget under third-party management of a single or multiple supplier(s)) is a distinctly minority pursuit. In the USA some 8 per cent of organizations take this route, in the UK about 2 per cent; worldwide we found there were just over 140 such deals.

Figure 6.1 shows that all arrangements have inherent risks. A mainly in-house function needs to be continually assessed against the market if it is not to grow unresponsive and cost-inefficient. One common underestimated factor is the management overhead cost of outsourcing IT and e-business. From reviewing over 300 case histories we estimate that this is falling typically between 4 and 8 per cent of total outsourcing costs, even before the effectiveness of the consequent management arrangements is assessed.

We have found that total outsourcing deals focusing primarily on cost reduction can achieve these, but often at the expense of IT operational service and business strategic inflexibilities – pretty big deficiencies where e-technologies are tightly coupled and critical to business success. Alternatively, incomplete contracts, or negligible profit margins through over-tight contracts, can, and have, promoted hidden costs or opportunistic vendor behaviour. Finally, in the 1990s 'strategic partnerships' were often high risk. Many experienced significant restructuring of the deal 18 to 24 months in. Contracts were often found to need more detail and more service performance measures. Sometimes the innovation expected from the vendor is not forthcoming. In others, the risk–reward element is too marginal to the overall deal to affect behaviours, and a more traditional fee-for-service arrangement becomes the basis of practice on the ground.

6.3 A mixed track record

Here we present findings that consider actual practices adopted against outcomes. A recent survey of USA and Europe (Lacity and Willcocks, 2001) found 56 per cent of organizations rating supplier performance as 'good' or better. Many respondents were realizing benefits, primarily some mix of cost reduction (52 per cent), refocusing of in-house IT staff (45 per cent), improved IT flexibility (42 per cent), access to scarce IT resources (42 per cent), better quality service (41 per cent) and improved use of IT resource (39 per cent). The majority of respondents characterized problems/issues as 'minor', but some customers were having severe/difficult problems in some areas. Some qualifications are necessary, however. It is important to recognize that these results are positively conditioned by three characteristics of respondent practice: the vast majority pursue the *selective IT outsourcing* option; most use *multiple suppliers*, most have *short-term contracts* (four years or less in length) and respondents generally targeted *infrastructure activities*, mainly mainframe operations, PC support, helpdesk, network management, mid-range operations, disaster recovery. The *least* commonly outsourced IT activities involved IT management and applications – in particular IT strategy, procurement, systems architecture, project management.

The 79 per cent of organizations using multiple suppliers pointed to several main advantages – the use of 'best of breed' providers, risk mediation and vendor motivation through competition. They also pointed to higher transaction costs and hidden post-contract management overheads in terms of time, effort and expense. In parallel research we have found much 'disguised' multi-supplier outsourcing in the form of sub-contracting. In some large-scale contracts we have found up to 30–35 per cent of the work actually sub-contracted to other suppliers, especially in the areas of technical consulting, desktop hardware and installation, e-business development, network specialists and software specialists.

There was evidence of lack of contract completeness, with only 30 per cent of respondents including all ten major clauses cited by us as vital to any outsourcing contract. There was a noticeable negative gap between anticipated and actual benefits. In most cases organizations were getting benefits but invariably less than they had expected. Only 16 per cent reported significant cost reduction, while another 37 per cent reported 'some' cost reduction. Other main benefits, each reported by between 33 per cent and 44 per cent of respondents, included: refocus in-house IT staff, improved IT flexibility, better quality service, improved use of IT resource and access to scarce IT/ e-business skills.

More worryingly, a number of organizations encountered 'severe/difficult' problems in six areas as a consequence of outsourcing. These were:

1 *Strategic* – supplier does not understand our business (37 per cent); corporate strategy and IT no longer aligned (35 per cent); poor strategic IT planning (24 per cent).
2 *Cost* – costs for additional services (38 per cent); cost escalation due to loopholes (31 per cent); cost monitoring/control (27 per cent).
3 *Managerial* – poor supplier staffing (43 per cent); managerial skills shortage (28 per cent); in-house staff resistance (26 per cent).
4 *Operational* – defining service levels (41 per cent); lack of supplier responsiveness (38 per cent); getting suppliers to work together (35 per cent).
5 *Contractual/legal* – too loose (41 per cent); contract monitoring (41 per cent); inadequate SLAs (35 per cent)
6 *Technical* – suppliers' IT skills shortage (33 per cent); outsourcing led to systems duplication (20 per cent); failure to upgrade IT (17 per cent).

These outcomes provide a fairly detailed 'worry list' and pre-emptive agenda for action for any senior managers contemplating IT outsourcing. Some flavour for how these findings, and the principles they imply, translate into specific IT/e-business initiatives can be got from the caselet examples below.

Caselet example: Siemens, i2 and strategic partnering

In late 2000 Siemens, the German and electronics conglomerate with some 440 000 employees worldwide, signed i2 as its strategic partner in one of the world's largest e-business infrastructure initiatives at the time. Through this initiative, Siemens intended to reduce spend on materials, reduce inventories, improve product development and quality, and buying and selling efficiency, increase e-procurement from 10 per cent to 50 per cent of purchasing, develop a global knowledge database and have all its employees Web- and intranet-enabled within 12 months.

Siemens created a central fund of some £590 million, with its divisions spread across 190 countries also providing further funds. According to CEO Heinrich Pierer, the plan was to run all processes electronically, from procurement to marketing, and from development to control. The company will use i2's software to manage its global supply chain and to standardize all its related customer and supplier processes. The company hoped to recover the central investment in the first 18 months of its e-business development, and aimed to save up to 5 per cent of its £42 billion net sales.

Siemens had a core capability on hand in Siemens Business Services, which, together with IBM, would manage the transformation using i2's Trade Matrix platform and integrated suite of e-business applications for design, buy, plan, sell, fulfil and service. Siemens would also use i2 content management and consulting services. The e-business strategy would be driven from three centres in Munich, Atlanta and Singapore forming the central platform for all Siemen's e-business activities.

The plan was to use i2's architecture to integrate with Siemens' existing technology, including its 360 ERP systems, representing one of the world's biggest SAP installations. Siemens had already implemented i2 on top of SAP in its PC Division – an implementation that proved difficult. Interestingly, though Siemens is a major SAP user, it decided against using mySAP.com/CommerceOne to e-enable its business processes. Siemens also looked to develop further systems in association with IBM and CommerceOne.

Learning points

- Siemens recognizes the significant advantages of having a standardized, global infrastructure for e-business, in order to achieve its business targets. However, the criticality of these developments, going to the core of business operations, means that it must put in risk-mitigating features in the implementation process, including parallel running of old systems, and in the design features of the infrastructure.
- The company has significant in-house infrastructure capability heavily involved in the development and implementation process.
- The right technology partner is critical. It is clear that i2 architecture and applications have been adjudged superior, even though there will inevitably be implementation difficulties integrating these with the SAP and other legacy systems.

Caselet example: United Airlines and time-to-market

By 2000, United Airlines (UA) had an annual budget of over US$550 million and some 1500 IT staff. In 1999 it wanted to give its 28 million frequent flyers the ability to redeem mileage for free flights, to check account status and to receive other third-party travel discounts. It outsourced this e-development because of issues of time-to-market and lack of internal capability. Internal Travel Network, in which UA had shares, was hired to develop advanced flight booking and to run the UA infrastructure and back-end systems. This involved creating a transaction server, based on BEA Systems' Tuxedo running on an HP-UX server, linked to UA's Mileage Plus database running at the time on an MVS version of IBM's DB2 database.

The consulting firm Sapient was also hired to develop e-commerce software, to add navigation features to the on-line reservation system. This was launched in mid-1999. United worked with Sapient on these developments, including on software that integrated customer profiles with tools that let users choose seats, rental cars and hotels. The early results were promising, with a 25 per cent increase in the number of Mileage Plus passengers accessing the site each month of operation. The site was designed to generate more sales through its travel discounts and reservations capability. By 2000 over 5 per cent of UA's sales were through the on-line channel, and UA planned to make this 20 per cent by 2002.

Learning points

- Even large organizations with large numbers of IT staff increasingly find it necessary to use external partners to develop systems, in order to get the systems implemented quickly, and because of lack of appropriate internal resources. For UA it resulted in an enhancement of its competitive position and a doubling of on-line sales in a year.
- UA took a selective, 'best-of-breed' approach, choosing one supplier for infrastructure and another for the e-commerce software and front-end systems.
- UA made sure it was heavily involved in the projects – an important feature of effective e-development projects that is discussed in Chapter 8.

Caselet example: American Insurance Group (AIG) – a mixed approach

In 1999 AIG, an insurer with over US$38 billion in annual revenues, had an Internet staff of 40 in an IT department of 1500. This proved insufficient for the on-line insurance and claims-processing applications under development. In particular, AIG lacked strategists and architects. Therefore AIG worked with the consulting form SGI to gain access to skills for Web site design, graphics and the general appearance of the site. AIG also outsourced its HTML coding and its less mission-critical systems, for example the on-line directory. AIG also hired Icon to create the front-end design for its Trade credit Web site, which went live in mid-1999. AIG did not outsource all its applications. It did not outsource those applications identified as critical to its corporate operations. It managed its back-end systems, and the e-systems that were about managing corporate assets, for example the secure on-line insurance buying over its extranet.

A senior vice president at AIG offered this advice on outsourcing:

- Always choose a reputable outsourcer. If a small integrator is used check the track record and the experience levels.
- Make certain that you own the code written by the outsourcer.
- Define in detail the deliverables and dates in the contract, but allow flexibility in the contract for changes in business needs.

AIG is another example of an organization with skills resource problems that chose a selective outsourcing route, but in doing so put into the way it proceeded many risk mitigation practices.

6.4 Managing the risks in outsourcing IT and e-business

It must be fairly clear so far that sourcing IT and e-business is never easy and that outsourcing is particularly fraught with difficulties. As indicated earlier, by 2003, on average 30–35 per cent of a corporation's IT/e-business budget will probably be outsourced. Having one-third of your IT under external control needs a clear understanding of the attendant risks, and how to mitigate these. Moreover, the research consistently demonstrates that, despite growing maturity of vendors and their clients, the practice of IT outsourcing continues to be a high risk, hidden cost process. Surveys regularly find up to one-third of organizations encounter serious and difficult problems in their IT/e-business outsourcing deals. Hidden costs, followed by credibility of vendor's claims continue to be the top single risks that actually materialize as significant negative outcomes in outsourcing. Such risks are widely commented upon by, and a considerable matter for, concern amongst practitioners considering or involved in IT outsourcing. Nevertheless it is a surprising fact that risks in IT outsourcing have received little detailed and sustained attention. This section will fill this gap by developing and illustrating a risk analysis framework that will facilitate analysis and learning about risk and how they can be managed.

Risk is here taken to be a negative outcome that has a known or estimated probability of occurrence based on experience or some theory. Although there is a limited literature on which to draw for the identification of salient risks, an exploratory analytical framework can be distilled from our own case study and survey work. Drawing on this work, the main reasons for failure/negative outcomes in IT outsourcing deals have been various combinations of the factors shown in Figure 6.2. Here we will divide the risks into Context, Building to Contract and Post-contract risks.

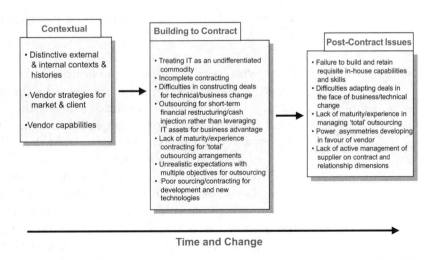

Figure 6.2
Outsourcing IT: risk analysis framework

6.5 Contextual risks: competitiveness, strategic intent and vendors

In 1994 John Browne, CEO of oil major BP, stated: *'Failure to outsource our commodity IT will permanently impair the future competitiveness of our business'*. In a highly competitive sector, the risk here was loss of focus on core competencies if the company did not outsource. In the group, BP Exploration's total outsourcing contracts with three suppliers proved largely successful in this regard. A 'best-of-breed' approach was adopted to supplier selection; contracts were kept to five years – considered a reasonable period to master the speed of business and technological change; and in-house measurement systems and retained capability proved largely up to the management tasks set by leveraging IT for business advantage and for monitoring and relating to multiple suppliers.

However, surmounting the contextual risks shown in Figure 6.2 can be elusive. Some studies suggest that strategic *disadvantage* can be one outcome from outsourcing. In a 1998 study of 54 businesses over five years, carried out by Weill and Broadbent published in *Leveraging the New IT Infrastructure*, they found those outsourcing at a faster rate had indeed achieved lower costs, but had also experienced greater strategic losses compared with organizations that did less outsourcing. Some of the losses included:

- significantly increasing information systems staff turnover;
- longer time to market for new products;
- lower perceived product and service quality than their competitors;
- slower rate of increase in revenue per employee; and
- lower return on assets.

Our own research supports the notion that companies pursuing growth and faster time to market run the risk of incurring strategic and operational inflexibilities if they outsource principally for cost reduction purposes. For example, in 1994 Xerox signed a 10-year global single-supplier deal. Where cost reductions did take place, they may have restricted Xerox's ability to cope with a major change in their marketing structure. In late 1999 Xerox lost control of its billing and sales commissions systems, with big consequences for profitability. In other words, there must be a match between business strategy and what outsourcing is set up to achieve. Consider also Capital One, the

US credit card group with 12 000 employees, 1000 of them in IT. According to the president Nigel Morris:

'If you have a business that churns out products, then outsourcing makes sense. But IT is our central nervous system [. . .] if I outsourced tomorrow I might save a dollar or two on each account, but I would lose flexibility, and value and service levels.'

During 2000/1, he continued to build his e-business initiatives from within, including infrastructure. Further risks reside in not understanding a supplier's competitive and client strategies and its key capabilities. For example, while outsourcing and e-business remain growth markets, vendors will be tempted to devote their attention and energies to winning new contracts rather than servicing existing ones. On the first issue, a supplier may well be keen to enter a new market place, as for example Perot Systems was in the early 1990s in the UK, or EDS in Australia in the mid-1990s. Alternatively, a supplier may seek increased rate of growth by offering favourable deals with the view that as other, more profitable contracts come along they can shift their key human resources to these, and can also find ways of increasing revenues and profits from the original contracts.

When suppliers make losses or have slim margins – unless of course the client is a reference site – one must also look out for opportunistic behaviour, attempts to reinterpret contracts and introduction of new modes of revenue generation. Checking that a deal is based on reasonable profit for the supplier can be a risk-mitigating exercise here. Government agencies particularly need to heed this point. In the past, because of requirements to select the cheapest supplier, they may secure fewer tenders in the first place. Subsequently they experience difficult relationships with their vendors because the contract does not allow for reasonable profit. These issues are particularly pertinent when considering the burgeoning 'netsourcing' and business process outsourcing markets (see Kern *et al.*, 2002).

Some large suppliers also have long-term strategies to dominate vertical markets, for example military logistics, pharmaceuticals, health. In these cases a supplier may well offer very favourable terms and service over the early years of a deal, but the overall objective would be to make switching costs prohibitive and to build up a monopoly of experience and track record in that market in order to dissuade competition. The risk then is that power asymmetry develops in favour of the vendor who secures the client on a long-term basis, on price and service regimes over which the client has little real power to leverage behaviour. Clearly it is in their long-term interest for client companies to retain sourcing flexibility through encouraging competition, thereby retaining the power to influence the vendor.

Companies must also be wary of suppliers' claims on capabilities and resources. Even the largest suppliers, in fact, experience skills shortages, or 'stickiness' – especially in the e-business area – in making the skills they do have available to specific clients. When in the mid-1990s EDS claimed in its bid to South Australia government it had 100 000 people available worldwide, the challenge for the client was to determine how many were realistically not already committed, and able to travel to and work in Australia. Unless they stipulate otherwise, clients may well get their old staff hired back to them, gaining no real influx of new skills. Often suppliers have to subcontract. As commented on earlier, in the big deals we studied, frequently more than 30 per cent was a multi-supplier contract in disguise, especially in the areas of technical consulting, desktop hardware and installation, e-business, network specialists and software specialists. There are a number of risks here. Suppliers do not always manage other suppliers better than the client could. They may charge more and add less value than if the client undertook the work. Moreover, responsibilities and intellectual property rights can be less than transparent. It becomes all too easy for responsibilities to fall through the cracks of these increasingly complex relationships as one supplier plays the client off against others – something to check for in application service provider (ASP) offerings, and in e-business work opened to the IT services market in other ways.

Some companies have addressed these risks by taking an equity share in the supplier to whom they have outsourced IT. The best known example is GM–EDS. Others include the Commonwealth Bank of Australia taking equity in EDS Australia and Lend Lease taking equity in IBM Global Services (Australia). There are similar examples amongst e-business providers and clients. This may prove an excellent business investment but the jury is out as to how far it helps mitigate outsourcing risk. Where the equity holding is managed by an asset management unit rather than the CIO, as has sometimes been the case, that unit will support whatever strategy the supplier has for maximizing its returns ahead of pressing for better service for its own organization.

6.6 Building to contract: pitfalls and pick-me-ups

In our research, IT outsourcing deals in failure mode invariably exhibited all the practices shown in Figure 6.2 in their build up to contracting. Problems and disappointments occurred if any one of these risky paths was selected. In 1992 East Midlands Electricity (EME) totally outsourced to a single supplier on a £150 million 12-year deal. Within three years the Board accepted that significant parts of the IT viewed as an 'undifferentiated commodity' were in fact critical to the evolution of the company's business strategy. The company began to rebuild its in-house resources but was restricted by its outsourcing contract, the terms of which Perot showed no signs of breaking. Eventually the contract was terminated five years early in 1999, as EME's acquisition by Powergen triggered a let-out clause.

Bringing together many of the ideas flagged earlier in this chapter, some of the most disappointing deals were total outsourcing long-term, single-supplier deals signed in the early 1990s either as financial rescue packages or to achieve cost savings. The failures exhibited a potent mix of characteristics. Contracting for ten years or more is done to establish the strategic nature of the relationship with the supplier. However, contracting for IT services for such a length of time is very difficult. As John Cross, IT director at BP pointed out in 1999: *'In the course of five years we experienced two generations of technology'*. Incomplete contracting is frequently the result. The e-business world sees an even more frightening set of timescales for regular technology upgrading. Future proofing against such technology trajectories becomes an important skill in arriving at deals with external services.

Another feature of long contracts is that power asymmetries develop in favour of the vendor. In many of the deals we have seen the supplier sought to recoup their investments in the second half of contracts and found many opportunities to find excess charges for services not covered in the original contract. The explicitness of the contract and service measures emerged as critical, not least because in practice people move on, and contracts can be continually reinterpreted to favour one side or the other. None of this is helped when the client does not build requisite in-house capabilities to keep control of its IT destiny.

Successful large 'total' outsourcing contracts are often mainly for stable, well understood areas of IT activity such as infrastructure/mainframe operations. But again, some companies, for example Macquarie Bank, see infrastructure development for e-business as fundamentally an in-house task (see Chapter 9). Less typically, Philips Electronics and the IT services vendor, Origin, entered a strategic alliance, where the company spun off its entire IT function in a shared risk reward and joint venture with an existing supplier. Another success involved a short-term contract to wind down a public sector agency about to be privatized. Others have gone down the multiple supplier five- to seven-year contract route, looking to spread their risks. Others we have researched, such as British Aerospace–CSC and Inland Revenue–EDS, were single-supplier deals that took on board the above prescriptions, had detailed contracts and were also high profile, with the suppliers wary of adverse publicity in specific countries or markets.

6.7 Post-contract management as risk mitigation

Failures in dealing with these issues of context and building to contract flow through into what actually happens at the post-contract stage – 'when the rubber hits the road' as it were. But even if a deal is well set up, IT/e-business outsourcing can still seriously founder at the post-contract management stage. Risks arise from not staying flexible in the face of unexpected but inevitable business and technical change, not managing the relationship dimension well, not leveraging the relationship for business and mutual advantage, and not putting into place tactics for maintaining a power balance between the parties. Short-term contracts, multiple suppliers, the possibility of competition, the possibility of future work have all been used to incent the supplier. For example, one Technology Director, asked why he went for short-term contracts, commented: *'It's amazing the service you get when the contract is coming up for renewal'*. The issue here is ensuring that the supplier's focus and priority is on your case. John Yard, IT Director in the 1993–2003 UK Inland Revenue–EDS deal, has made the point explicitly: *'I see myself as in direct competition for the supplier's attention with all its other customers'*. Such a creed becomes particularly pertinent in face of the exorbitant demand for e-business services.

In all this, the most neglected area of risk mitigation and leveraging outsourcing for business advantage has been that of retaining requisite capabilities and skills. Feeny and Willcocks (1998) spelt out nine key capabilities needed to run any IT sourcing arrangement. These capabilities are detailed in Chapter 2 and remain highly relevant for organizations moving to e-business. A major reason is that the existence of these essentially human, high performance capabilities leads to sound analysis and sourcing decisions, good contracting and management, and the development of productive relationships with suppliers – the foundations, in fact of an outsourcing relationship advantage.

In practice, though, too many companies see outsourcing as an opportunity to off-load headcount – a real risk if done indiscriminately. The core IT capabilities model implies far fewer staff but all with distinctive, high performance capabilities. Frequently these are skills not available from existing, retained staff. IT outsourcing requires as much managing, in fact, but of a different kind from that in more traditional IT functions. As one IT director told us: *'Eventually we had to hire some new people; it really did require new skill sets'*. It has also become clear that appointing one person, usually called the 'contract manager', to fulfil several of these roles detracts from the high performance requirement, though this may be a necessary, pragmatic trade-off in smaller client organizations.

6.7.1 Risk profiling: summary

Generally, selective sourcing to multiple suppliers on relatively short-term detailed and regularly revisited contracts has so far been the more effective approach to mitigating the risks from using the external IT/e-business service market. As we shall see in Chapter 8, on IT/e-business development projects, in situations where the technology is new and unstable, where there is little relevant IT experience of the technology and business requirements are unclear or changing, we have found 'insourcing' the lower risk approach. This is not to say that total outsourcing is not feasible; it means rather that risk analysis, and mitigation techniques, become even more compelling, required practices.

We have also seen a small number of organizations achieve strategic business goals by outsourcing IT on a large scale, for example facilitating and supporting major organizational change at British Gas in the 1990s; achieving direct profit revenue generation through joint venturing with a supplier partner at Philips Electronics; redirecting the business and IT into core competencies as at BP Exploration; and strengthening resources and flexibility in technology and service to underpin the business's strategic direction, as at Dupont/CSC/Accenture. All underwent and managed the potential risks detailed in Figure 6.2.

6.8 Sourcing IT capability: how to make the vital decisions

In this section, to assist IT sourcing decisions, we bring together the thinking and learning of the chapter so far into two summary matrices to aid decision-making. Before that, let us look at two cases that illustrate the principles in action. The companies in question are Cisco and Dell.

Caselet example: Cisco and IT sourcing

By late 2000 Cisco had outsourced most of its production to 37 factories. Suppliers made all components and carried out 55 per cent of sub-assembly work and 55 per cent of final assembly. All factories were linked via the Net, and an intranet was used for most internal work at Cisco. The internal pages received 28 million hits a month. Use of the Web was saving Cisco an estimated US$500–800 million a year. Of all sales, 84 per cent were through the Web site, which allowed customized configuring and checking by customers. Of all customer queries, 85 per cent were handled on-line.

All this has enabled a high degree of virtuality. According to one respondent: *'we can go from quote to cash without ever touching a physical asset or piece of paper. You've heard of JIT manufacturing, well this is not-at-all manufacturing'*. However, Cisco has been careful to control and dominate the value network. Thus, it has maintained three factories itself to understand and give flexibility to its manufacturing base. Cisco designs production methods and uses the Internet to monitor operations closely. It also controls research and development. So for new production methods, for example: *'the source code is developed here and maintained here. So the innovation is all at Cisco'*.

Caselet example: Dell's sourcing strategy

Dell has explicitly described its strategy as that of vertical integration. During 2000 it was making more than US$40 million a day (over 50 per cent of total sales) via the Internet. It success is invariably put down to its customer focus. However, an underlying vital component has been sourcing strategy and management. According to its CEO: *'I don't think we could have created a $12 billion business in 13 years if we had tried to be vertically integrated'*. With fewer physical assets and people there are fewer things to manage and fewer barriers to change. Through IT-enabled coordination and control of its value network of suppliers and partners, Dell can operate with a 20 000 rather than an 80 000 workforce. In the supply arena it has focused on making long-term deals and commitments with as few leading suppliers as possible. Datalinks measure and feed back supplier performance in real-time. Close ties with suppliers (*'their engineers are part of our design and implementation teams'*) mean that Dell buys in innovation from its suppliers. Information technologies allow speed and information-sharing and much more intense forms of collaboration. It also means that suppliers can be notified precisely of Dell's daily product requirements. This has also allowed Dell to focus on inventory velocity and keeping inventory levels very low.

Dell has also sought strong partnering relationships with key customers. Seen as complementors, customers are often involved in research and development, where Dell's focus is on relevant, easy-to-use technology, improvements in the customer buying process, keeping costs down and superior quality in manufacturing. Dell also offers service centres in large organizations to be close to the customer. Thus Boeing has 100 000 Dell PCs and 30 dedicated Dell staff on the premises.

For present purposes, what is interesting are the criteria these companies are using to make sourcing decisions. Clearly Cisco has adopted practices that leverage complementors and suppliers whilst enabling Cisco to dominate the value network it has created. At Dell the criteria would seem to be sixfold.

1 Dell focuses its attention on all activities that create value for the customer. This includes R&D involving 1500 people and a budget of US$250 million, that focuses on customer-facing activity and the identification of 'relevant' technology. It tends to outsource as much as possible all other activities that need to get done.
2 Dell carefully defines its core capability as a solutions provider and technology navigator. It uses partners/suppliers as much as possible to deal with such matters as products, components, technology development, assembly.
3 A key core task is coordination as against 'doing' tasks such as manufacturing and delivery.
4 A key core capability is control of the value network through financial and informational means to ensure requisite speed, cost and quality. What does Dell control? Basically the company appoints and monitors reliable, responsive, leading edge suppliers of technology and quality.
5 Dell takes responsibility for seeking and improving all arrangements that give it speed and focus in the marketplace and in its organizational arrangements.
6 Dell treats information management and orchestration as a core capability. This is an outcome of two strategic moves on its part. The first is to convert as much of the physical assets ('atoms') it manages into digital form ('bytes'). The second move is to outsource as much as possible of the remaining physical tasks and assets, while rendering management of the digital world a core set of tasks.

In Dell's and Cisco's external sourcing practices we find strong examples of what other organizations have been discovering as the more effective ways of managing suppliers and complementors. In particular, Dell revealed itself as having massive clarity about what was core and what was not. This enabled it to place 'non-core' activities as candidates for external sourcing, and make decisions on the best type of external sourcing. A further lesson from Dell and Cisco, especially where strategic partnering was being undertaken, was the critical importance of maintaining financial, managerial and information control in the relationship with any external supplier/partner, thus offsetting many of the risks identified above.

6.8.1 Using the decision-making matrices

How do these effective decisions get made? In Figures 6.3. and 6.4 we provide two matrices, born of experience and research, to facilitate decision-making. With IT, sourcing must start with the business imperative. In Figure 6.3. we identify two ways of defining business activities. The first is in terms of a business activity's contribution to competitive positioning. As a broad example, does a Web site represent a source of competitive advantage or is it merely 'useful', for example providing some company information. In IT, mainframes and payroll applications are frequently perceived as commodities, while British Airways' yield management system gives the company a competitive edge in ticket pricing and is regarded as a differentiator. The vertical axis allows us to assess whether a business activity critically underpins strategic direction and its delivery or merely makes incremental contributions to the bottom line. This creates four quadrants.

Let us use the Dell example to illustrate the thinking here. 'Order Winners' are those business activities that critically and advantageously differentiate a firm from its competitors. The six Dell items listed in the previous section fall here. The strong steer here is to carry out these core activities in-house, buying in resources to work under internal control where expertise is lacking and a build-up of internal learning is required. 'Qualifiers' are business activities that must be carried out as a necessary minimum entry requirement to compete in a specific sector. For airlines, aircraft maintenance systems are a minimum entry requirement to compete in that sector, but do not differentiate the airlines from each other. Often critical differentiators can become commodities and move to this quadrant.

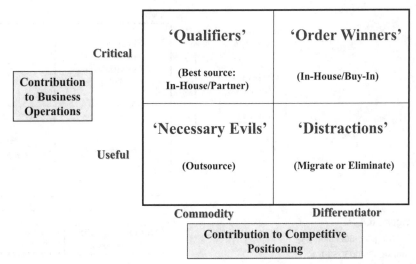

Figure 6.3
Strategic e-sourcing by
business activity

Thus, unlikely as it might seem, Dell's excellent customer service could become an industry standard and as such could become redefined as a 'Qualifier'. During 2002 assembly, manufacturing and delivery were being defined by Dell as 'Qualifiers'. These should be best sourced and can be done by third parties, where they meet the right cost and competence criteria (see below).

'Necessary Evils' (as one manager called them) are tasks that have to be done but are not core activity and gain no strategic purchase from their fulfilment. Dell has tended to cut down on administration, inventory and payroll tasks for example, but would seek to outsource as much of these sorts of activities as possible. 'Distractions' are failed or failing attempts to differentiate the organization from its competitors. The goal here must be to eliminate the activity or migrate it to another quadrant. Thus in 1989 Dell opened retail outlets, but soon discovered this development was not going to be successful and fell back on its direct business model. A more profound mistake is not to notice until too late the value shifts in a specific competitive arena, for example IBM against Microsoft and Intel in the late 1980s/early 1990s PC market. When Levis Strauss moved to the Web in the late 1990s it did so in a way that was precisely a 'Distraction'. Up to 2002 Dell had made few mistakes in this area, even in a recessionary market. In fact, its low cost Web-based distribution strategy had given it a critical competitive edge. Perhaps this resulted from its CEO's explicit recognition that *'looking for value shifts is probably the most important dimension of leadership'*.

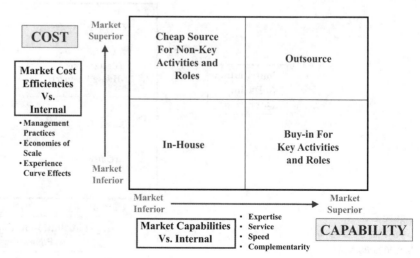

Figure 6.4
Strategic e-sourcing by market comparison

It is not enough, however, to identify a potential use of service providers or business allies. What is available, on what in Figure 6.4 we define as the 'market', also requires detailed analysis. If the market is not cheap, capable or mature enough, then the organization will need to seek a largely in-house solution. A second matrix is needed to fully capture the major elements for consideration.

In Figure 6.4 we plot the cost efficiencies and the capabilities the market can offer against carrying out tasks internally. Where the market can carry out a task cheaper and better, then outsourcing is the obvious decision but only for 'Qualifiers' and 'Necessary Evils'. An example is Federal Express providing customer delivery for Dell. Where the market offers an inferior cost and capability then in-house sourcing will be the best alternative (assuming that 'Distractions' are best not sourced at all). Where the market offers a better cost deal, then this should be taken, but only for non-key activities ('Necessary Evils'). Where the market offers superior capability but at a premium price above what the in-house cost might be, then there may still be good reasons for buying-in or close partnering with the third party, not least to leverage and learn from their expertise, and apply it to 'Qualifying' and 'Order Winning' tasks.

Thus the two Figures help to summarize the main criteria that can be utilized for making e-sourcing, and in fact, many other business sourcing decisions. Use of the matrices requires decisions on trade-offs in order to establish the least risky ways external parties can be leveraged to organizational advantage. But as this chapter has sought to illustrate, making the right sourcing decisions does not guarantee their successful implementation. As in the cases of Dell and Cisco, internal capabilities must be developed to manage the risks, relationships and performance issues inherent in the extensive use of external service providers and business allies.

6.9 IT sourcing: emerging practices and prospects

From 1996, we have seen some organizations responding to the growing experience base and the undoubted risks inherent in IT outsourcing by focusing more on certain practices or adopting new ones. Some judgements can be passed on the efficacy of eight practices we will highlight in the following, and which look set to continue. The three most effective emerging practices have been:

1 *Transitional outsourcing* – outsourcing legacy systems to enable in-house focus on building the new IT world. Thus, in 1996 NASDAQ stock exchange outsourced legacy systems to Tate Consulting Services, while the in-house IT staff continued to develop client/server systems.

2 *Smarter contracting* – some companies include a customer-written contract with the Request For Proposal, for example Elf Alochem who signed a four-year, US$4.3 million contract with Keane for accounting systems management. ICI did something similar in eventually signing a five-year contract with Origin in the UK. Others have built in competitive bidding for services beyond the contract, though competition does not always protect the customer from sitting suppliers who are reluctant to support contracts with other vendors. Various flexible pricing mechanisms are being adopted successfully to alter prices within one contract. Other practices include negotiating shares in their suppliers' savings, adopting 'open book' accounting on suppliers' costs, using third-party benchmarks and market rates to test supplier prices annually, or seeking the best prices in line with what suppliers offer to their most favoured customers.

3 *Offshore outsourcing* – taking advantage of programming and software development expertise and lower prices emerging in countries such as India, Ireland, Israel, Malaysia and Mexico. Thus, Sainsbury, the UK retailer, budgeted £30 million to deal with the year 2000 problem, with the work being done entirely in India via satellite link. Subsequently, Sainsbury was so satisfied with the results that it has expanded the work outsourced in this way. There is evidence that the cost advantage is eroding for some types of work, and control is always an issue. As we found in a case study of Holiday Inns, distance needs detailed contracts and clear definitions of responsibilities and IT requirements. One response has been 'near-shore outsourcing'. Thus, with its proximity to the USA and with potentially fewer control, cost and time-zone problems, Mexico can compete successfully against a country such as India, the market leader.

Five other practices have been growing, some are successful in some respects, but all raise questions.

1 *Value-added outsourcing* – combining client and vendor strengths in order to market IT/e-business products and services. As one example, Mutual Life Insurance of New York and CSC planned to market software and services to the

insurance industry. To be successful, the partners must truly add value by offering products/services demanded by customers in the market. Too often the added value service part of the contract is marginal to the major client–vendor focus. It is also rendered less attractive when participants discover that it requires up to nine times the initial development cost to transform a home-grown application into a commercial one.

2 *Equity holdings* – taking ownership in each other's companies. Examples include the 1996 Perot Systems–Swiss Bank deal (25 per cent share in Perot posited, while Perot took shares in software company Systor AG – owned by the bank), Lend Lease (35 per cent holding in ISSC), Commonwealth Bank (35 per cent stake in EDS Australia) and Telstra (26 per cent stake in joint venture with IBM). However, it is not clear that the incentive of joint ownership is strong enough to influence behaviour at the operational level, and there are instances of suppliers becoming complacent on service to the partner, while focusing attention and resources on pursuing new contracts elsewhere. With their investment in the supplier, the customer's Board is also likely to support such expansion, but could face dilemmas in doing so. Interestingly, Swiss Bank (now UBS) signalled the end of the 'strategic alliance' with Perot in January 2000 when it bought back Perot's 40 per cent stake in Systor. UBS remained Perot's biggest customer, accounting for more than 25 per cent of its revenues, but the focus was only to be on the management of legacy and computer operations.

3 *'Co-sourcing'* – performance-based contracts by which the vendor seeks to achieve and get rewarded on improving the client's business performance, not just delivering on its IT goals. Such deals work well, when the supplier core capabilities are contractually structured to complement customer needs. However, despite claims, not all vendors have the necessary business know-how in what is a client's rather than the vendor's core business. Moreover, many suppliers are not really geared up to deliver this type of arrangement, as opposed to fee-for-service contracts. We have also witnessed problems experienced in delivering improved business performance. There are many factors that influence business performance and suppliers do not always have overall control of these. This can be frustrating when the supplier has taken the risk of being paid mainly out of business improvements, has put in the necessary effort but, because of other parties, is not making the standard, and thus does not get rewarded appropriately.

4 *Multiple suppliers* – this approach pursues the logic of hiring the 'best-of-breed' supplier for specific IT activities. Thus in 1993, British Petroleum Exploration (BPX) arranged five-year contracts with SEMA, Syncordia, and SAIC. In 1996 JP Morgan signed a seven-year US$2.1 billion contract with four major suppliers. With this approach the risks of going with a single supplier are mitigated, but there are problems and costs in managing and organizing suppliers. From 1998, BPX gave up on getting suppliers to manage each other and has moved back to a more traditional, direct relationship with each supplier.

5 *Spin-offs* – creating a separate company out of an effective IT function. In practice companies such as Mellon Bank, Sears Roebuck and Boeing have had limited success with their spin-off companies. They need a core IT competence to attract external customers. Too often the empowered IT function has too few marketing and customer service skills, is too dependent on the former company for business, and has difficulties in getting new business without a strong track record in an increasingly competitive IT services marketplace. Two success stories are Origin and EDS. Origin was formed originally from Dutch software house BSO and NV Phillips software and development staff. In the early 1990s Phillips also transferred its communications and processing staff to form Origin, which has developed into a competitive IT services company. EDS was initially sold to General Motors in 1984 but, following a buyout, became its own company in 1996. Clearly EDS has been able to attract many external customers, being now amongst the largest IT services providers worldwide.

By 2002 there were six other developments, though at the time of writing it is too early to make a full judgement about their likely impact and levels of success, especially in a recessionary climate.

1 *Application service providers.* Firms such as Oracle, SAP, Microsoft and others are offering remotely hosted software spanning the complete enterprise, while Compaq, for example, offers to install and run a firm's new systems. By mid-2000 some 400 firms fitted the application service providers (ASP) definition – provision of 'pay-as-you-use' access to centrally managed applications distributed over the Internet and other networks. Early adopters have been primarily small to medium-sized firms. Amongst the advantages cited are: reduced total cost of ownership, improved efficiency of

internal IT staff, access to latest technology/applications and skills, accelerated application deployment and transfer of ownership risk. Our own studies show some major concerns around: speed of market development, viability of ASP business models, security of proprietary information, availability, scalability, adaptability of software, degree of customization possible, bandwidth capacity and contract lock-in.

2 *Business process outsourcing*. This has been reckoned to be the fastest growing market with revenues moving from US$6.1 billion in 1997 to an estimated US$16 billion in 2002. As one example, in early 2000 BP Amoco (subsequently BP) announced the outsourcing of its human resource function, including its IT components on a US$600 million five-year deal with Exult, based in Irvine, California. BP outsourced the administrative and IT/Internet burden, reserving for itself only 'the things that require judgement and policy'. The risks inherent in such a large IT project are considerable, of course. On the other hand, BP estimated there would be a US$2 billion reduction in operational costs as a result of this type of outsourcing.

3 *Backsourcing*. Over several years a few organizations have cancelled contracts and brought IT back largely in-house – for example East Midlands Electricity in 1999 cancelled its 1992 12-year total outsourcing deal with Perot Systems, five years early. By 1995 East Midlands had redefined the importance of IT to the business and began rebuilding its in-house skills. In 1999 it terminated the contract, taking advantage of a clause permitting this in the event of a merger (East Midlands merged with Powergen in 1998). More often we have seen a steady creep back of some previously outsourced IT activities, as a result of changing requirements and contexts or from the realization that the activity was in fact better positioned in-house all along. Partial backsourcing was also evident in Xerox's deal with EDS, although the consequences caused considerable contractual turmoil.

4 *Shared services*. As an example, seven oil companies share Andersen Consulting accounting services in Aberdeen, Scotland. Participant companies include Elf, Talisman, BP and Saga Petroleum. In practice these companies have defined accounting services as a non-competitive area, and have outsourced these in order to reduce costs. The development of shared e-procurement exchanges throughout many sectors from early 2000 onward carries a similar logic, with these typically being run by a technology provider such as CommerceOne or Oracle.

5 *New joint ventures.* As an example, FI Group and the Royal Bank of Scotland established in 1999 an independent entity – First Banking Systems – to develop commercial software and manage IT/e-business systems planning and architecture. Some 310 bank staff and 120 FI staff were transferred to First Banking Systems, and given a budget of £150 million over five years. FBS is jointly owned – 51 per cent by Bank of Scotland, and 49 per cent by FI.

6 *Complex Internet hosting/e-commerce projects.* This was a major growth area into 2001. Some estimated it would generate for IT service providers global revenues of US$18 billion during 2002, despite the slower increase in IT budgets experienced in 2001. Our evidence points to the importance of keeping business responsibility and control for e-business projects in-house, and to the dangers of ceding too much management control to the IT function or IT service providers.

As, in the new millennium, the IT outsourcing focus shifts to supplier-supported e-business projects, the use of application service providers, business service providers, managed network services, new forms of outsourced e-fulfilment, and customer relationship management, some really critical risk issues arise. As radical, new forms of large-scale IT outsourcing are mooted, and it is asserted that there are new management rules for the new economy, it should be remembered that the 'new' principles underlying large-scale outsourcing, for example, at Cisco Systems, are not that far from those underlying the original 'virtual organization' – Benetton – in the late 1980s. Ignoring all we have learned about the risks in IT outsourcing and how to manage them would be a very risky business indeed.

6.10 Conclusion

In many countries in the world private and public sectors are wading into a series of further potentially large IT outsourcing waves, stimulated by moves to e-business, application service provision, business process outsourcing and the like, as well as more familiar forms of, and reasons for, outsourcing. It is useful to stand back and look at what has been learned so far about IT outsourcing practices. It should be said that good and bad IT outsourcing experiences, like everything else in IT and its management, are *not* sector specific. For example, financial institutions in all countries do not manage IT outsourcing any worse or better than any other organizations or sectors.

Organizations fail when they hand over IT/e-business technologies without understanding their role in the organization, and what the vendor's capabilities are. One rule of thumb is: never outsource a problem, only an IT/e-business activity or set of tasks for which a detailed contract and performance measures can be written. Too many client companies see outsourcing as spending – and as little as possible – and ditching their problems, not managing. In fact, this is one of the potential temptations that the developing ASP market proffers. In practice, outsourcing requires a great deal of in-house management, but of a different kind, covering elicitation and delivery of business requirements, ensuring technical capability, managing external supply and IT governance. A cardinal insight from our own work is that organizations still expect too much from vendors and not enough from themselves or, put another way, vendors are still much better at selling IT services than their clients are at buying them.

The key is to understand and operationalize four capabilities necessary to pursue IT/e-business outsourcing effectively:

1 The ability to make sourcing decisions and arrive at a long-term sourcing strategy, building in learning, and taking into account business, technical and economic factors. On this front, our research identifies two proven practices in outsourcing. Firstly, selective outsourcing decisions and total in-house/insourcing decisions achieve success more often than total outsourcing decisions. Secondly, senior executives and IT managers who make decisions together achieved success significantly more often than when either stakeholder group acted alone.

2 The ability to understand the IT/e-business services marketplace, the capabilities and weaknesses of relevant vendors, and what their business strategies are and imply in any likely outsourcing deal with an organization. Our work shows two proven practices here. Firstly, *informed buying* is a core IT/e-business capability for all contemporary organizations. Secondly, organizations that invite both internal and external bids achieve success more often than organizations that merely compare a few external bids with current internal performance.

3 The ability to contract over time in ways that give suppliers an incentive and ensure that you get what you think you agreed to. Two proven practices here are that short-term (four years or less) contracts achieve success much more often than

long-term contracts (seven years or more); and that detailed fee-for-service contracts achieve success more often than other types of contracts.

4 The ability to post-contract manage across the lifetime of the deal in ways that secure and build the organization's IT/ e-business destiny, and effectively achieve the required service performance and added value from the supplier. The evidence is that this is one of the weakest areas in outsourcing practice and is rarely adequately thought through at the front of outsourcing deals. Typically, a minimum of nine core capabilities emerge as necessary in response to problems confronted during contract performance. These cover leadership, informed buying, vendor development, contract facilitation, contract monitoring, technical fixing, architecture planning, relationship building and business systems thinking (see Chapter 2).

Institutions need to assess their capabilities against these four vital components before outsourcing IT/e-business to any significant degree, and then build these capabilities where they are lacking.

Finally, it should be underlined that IT sourcing strategy and its execution is a key to driving out business value from IT, but only one key. Put another way, attaching a strong IT outsourcing arrangement to a poor or unclear business strategy, in association with a lack of maturity on the business side in its ability to manage IT strategically, can achieve only so much. In such circumstances even a well set up and managed IT outsourcing arrangement will still have the sceptical question asked of it: 'But where's the business value added from all this outsourcing?'. In truth, the answer may lie not in the outsourcing arrangement at all, but elsewhere.

References

Feeny, D. and Willcocks, L. (1998) Core IS capabilities for exploiting IT. *Sloan Management Review*, April.

Kern, T., Lacity, M. and Willcocks, L. (2002) *Netsourcing: how to rent applications and services over a network*. New York: Prentice Hall.

Lacity, M. and Willcocks, L. (2000) *Inside IT Outsourcing: a state-of-the-art report*. Oxford: Templeton College.

Lacity, M. and Willcocks, L. (2001) *Global Information Technology Outsourcing: in search of business advantage*. Chichester: Wiley.

Weill, P. and Broadbent, M. (1998) *Leveraging The New I Infrastructure*. Boston: Harvard Business Press.

7 Change and delivery 1: mobilizing the organization

'The higher the organizational level at which managers define a problem or need, the greater the probability of successful implementation. At the same time, however, the closer the definition and solution of problems or needs are to end-users, the greater the probability of success. Implementation managers must draw up their ... plans [for IT systems] in light of this apparent paradox'. Dorothy Leonard Barton (Leonard-Barton and Kraus, 1985).

'If you want to know how an organization works, try changing it'. Kurt Lewin (1980).

'He who has a why to live, can bear with almost any how'. Friedrich Nietzche.

7.1 Introduction

For any IT/e-business strategy, the implementation stage will reveal where prior analysis, design and planning have been inadequate. Frequently what have been termed 'implementation problems' are in fact the results of failures in these earlier activities described in Chapters 3 and 4. Implementation will bring its own unpredictabilities that need to be handled. Not least of these are human factors. In fact, in the usual implementation scenario it is only at this stage, when changes become manifest and real, that people seriously begin to question what is going to happen.

People become even more important for other reasons also. As information-based technologies enter the core of organizational functioning, IT implementations increasingly also represent major business change projects. Indeed e-business projects are by definition precisely that. People's responses, adjustments and learning become crucial areas of managerial concern. Moreover, the value of IT is only as high as its business utilization. This means that it is not enough to merely install a system. A system has to be institutionalized, so that there is a leveraging fit between technology, skills and processes.

In fact we have found that these human and organizational costs of technical change and innovation are now typically three to four times the technical costs of implementation. This suggests that the behavioural and organizational change dimensions deserve sustained senior management attention to getting them right. If this is not a sufficiently compelling financial argument consider the IT truth we detailed in earlier chapters: IT has no inherent business value. The message is clear. It is in the interests of all organizations, even, indeed especially, the most commercially driven, to assign much more importance to people factors rather than technical issues when implementing computer-based information systems.

This is not the accepted view, and indeed at the root of many implementation problems is the overriding influence of traditional systems analysis and design practices and traditional managerial attitudes to IT. In particular, human and organizational issues are reduced merely to limiting resistance to change, the need to organize training, and the need to have enough staff of the right type available in the right place at the right time. In this way an over-concentration on the technical can result in failure to deal with non-technical, emerging issues. In turn, problems in these areas can begin to interfere with technical issues. Here the crux of the problem lies in the manner in which implementation is defined and conceptualized.

This chapter examines the proposition that implementation is organizational change, and points to the uses and limitations of Organization Development (OD) approaches to handling technological change. Various implementation strategies are examined. The key role of culture is examined. Participation and its uses are discussed and various guidelines proposed for minimizing implementation problems. Finally, a key focus of the book is developed into a political-cultural contingencies approach to systems implementation. This places at centre stage the *organizational context in which digitization occurs.*

7.2 The dimensions of transformation: e-business as an example

As 'pure play' dot.coms and those moving 'from bricks to clicks' faltered throughout 2001 and into 2002, it became evident that there were few quick fixes to be had in moving to e-business. In an April 2001 *MIT Sloan Management Review* article, 'Pathways to e-business leadership', Leslie Willcocks and Robert Plant report findings from a study of 78 corporations from 1999 to 2001. They showed the management success factors that distinguished the winners from the laggards. They found evolutionary, but no overnight, successes (see also Chapter 1). In *Moving To E-Business* Leslie Willcocks and Chris Sauer (2001) detailed the evolutionary process as consisting of four stages (Figure 7.1). In researching for this present book, we found most organizations becoming really stuck trying to move through the 're-engineering on steroids' phase of Stage 3. The technical issues are large enough here, involving the building of an e-business infrastructure that embraces legacy and ERP systems, together with Web-based technologies, new technologies and software as they become relevant to the business. But the real killer is attempting to integrate the technology platform with new processes and skills while working through legacy organizational structures, culture and management processes. This links back to the point

Figure 7.1
Four stages of moving to e-business (source: Willcocks and Sauer, 2001)

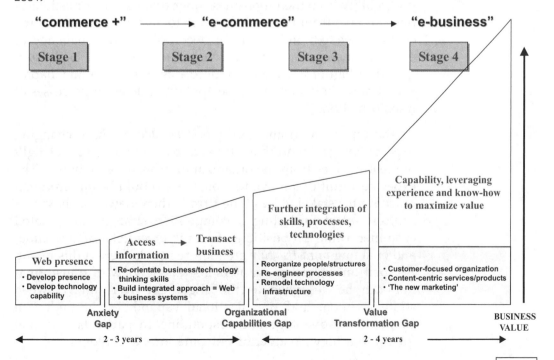

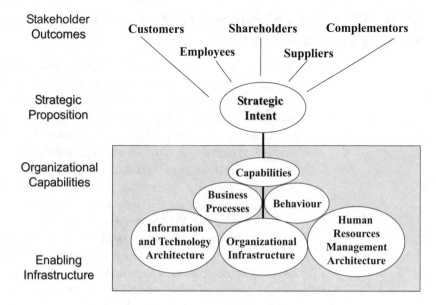

Figure 7.2
Framework for targeting IT-enabled change (adapted from Keith Ruddle, in Willcocks and Sauer, 2001)

made in Chapter 4 about the critical importance of linking IT strategy with re-engineering.

In fact, into 2002, very few organizations had matched Dell, Cisco Systems, Fidelity Investments and Charles Schwab in making it through to Stage 4 in being able to leverage significant profitability from their e-business investments. On our estimates this can take from two to four years to achieve. The size of the changes needed, and a way of decomposing the challenge of e-transformation into its interconnected components, is suggested in Figure 7.2. We introduced this framework in Chapter 3, and now show how it can be applied in detail to processes of transformation.

At the top of the framework are *stakeholders*, whose changing expectations and requirements need to be monitored in the light of the outcomes from the organization's business activities. The expected result of a move to e-business should be an improved outcome for stakeholders. The firm is then viewed as having a *strategic intent*, including a competitive strategy and related customer value propositions. Specific *organizational capabilities* and enabling *infrastructure* are required to deliver on this intent. As spelt out in earlier chapters a strategic view of transformation can be described as the alignment over time between strategic intent and organizational capabilities, grounded in competitive advantage and responding to particular external forces, to achieve a superior outcome for stakeholders.

Clearly such dynamic alignment is very difficult to achieve, and brings on-going change headaches. Firstly, capabilities have to be delivered through the execution of *business processes by people adopting distinctive, culturally determined behaviours*, the latter built on certain values and belief systems (see below). Secondly, this delivery has to be enabled by various interrelated elements of *architectural infrastructure*. These are: *information and technology infrastructure* (management information systems, IT systems, information strategy); *organizational infrastructure* (structures, management control systems, communication and coordination mechanisms); and *human resource management architecture* (skills, people development, processes, reward and motivation systems). Let us illustrate an effective journey of targeted change by describing the successful transformation of Charles Schwab into an e-business.

7.2.1 Case study: how Charles Schwab moved from bricks to clicks

US-based broker Charles Schwab had no exposure on the Internet before 1996. By mid-2000, it had about 7 million customers (Active On-line accounted for 3.7 million), and US$800 billion worth of funds under management. In 2000 it handled some 1.7 million trades a week, with over 70 per cent made on-line on its schwab.com site. It also operated in several countries outside the USA and throughout 2001/2, despite adverse trading conditions, continued to be the largest single Internet-based broker.

Schwab's move to the Web was driven from the top, though the company had a history of innovation. In October 1995, its stand-alone e.Schwab Web site was launched to provide investors with account and research information. In March 1996 it was the first major brokerage firm to offer discount and limited trading via the Internet. In 1998 electronic brokerage was integrated into the main body of the company. Pricing and availability were reorganized so that every Schwab customer could deal with Schwab through any channel, and experience consistency in Internet pricing and service. This move cost the company some US$125 million, but paid off in terms of subsequent revenues.

By the end of 1998 58 per cent of transactions were on-line, representing US$4 billion worth of trades each week. The site offered trading of stocks, mutual funds, US treasuries, listed corporate bonds and options. It also supplied a range of tools to give access to an investor's account holding and to information providers. Available also were interactive investment guides, calculators for retirement and college planning, and real-time quotes. Internet trading has allowed reductions in commission throughout the industry. In 1999 Schwab charged US$29.95 per trade; the equivalent via phone was US$80. However, the company's growth strategy is not explained by being the cheapest. For example, at that time, E-Trade was charging US$15 per trade, and subsequently there have been several price wars in USA and elsewhere. Rather, for CEO Charles Schwab, 'the transforming event is the ability to deliver personalized information to the customer at virtually no cost . . . this is possible because the Net is totally imbedded in the centre of our business'.

By 2000 Charles Schwab was offering an array of financial services and products, investment guidance and trading and brokerage services through a network of over 300 branches, offices, telephone service centres, automated phone services and the Internet. For Schwab, technology and customer service would seem to be two sides of the same coin. According to its CIO: *'technology allows us to deliver on a twin commitment: offering customers convenient access to a wealth of services, and delivering exceptional service at reasonable prices'*. Throughout 2000 it continued to expand its services on-line, for example in April establishing an alliance with E-LOAN to offer customers a complete mortgage solution, including the ability to research, compare and apply for a mortgage loan on-line. By March 2000 Schwab.com was averaging 40 million hits a day. Customers could screen thousands of mutual funds, track investment performance, get real-time stock quotes, enter trade orders, view asset allocation models, participate in on-line forums with investment experts and conduct research. Additionally, using MySchwab.com – a free link with Internet portal Excite – customers could create customized investment information such as Watch lists of stocks, and receive current news and content. By late 2001 on-line trading generally was down some 47 per cent at some times compared with 2000. Nevertheless Schwab remained the leading on-line broker.

Here one can see a process of migration over a five-year period. Schwab started with a reputation and strong brand in retail stockbroking and investing. Innovation was valued by top management and the nature of the *strategic intent* was heavily determined by learning about what customers valued and used, and by realization that the Internet needed to be integrated into the core of the business. As a result Schwab developed on the Web a range of differentiated services as well as offering competitive pricing. New *behaviours* were developed based on customer orientation, new services and experimentation. Within three years *business processes* were re-assembled to fit with the Web-based business. On the information and technology front, the Web site 'front office' was developed with high functionality and easy-to-use facilities. It also featured such aspects as personalized pages for research and account management, and customized services and information. Meanwhile the *information and technology infrastructure* eventually included effective use of database management, XML and related technologies, management information systems and effective collection, analysis and uses of information. Schwab became very certain in the 1990s of the opportunity to differentiate itself by the use of leading edge technology and by 2000 had done so.

On *organization infrastructure*, Schwab greatly restructured itself for the virtual world in terms of roles, responsibilities and by moving from budgets to dynamic management measurement tools. It had already decentralized the company into 'customer enterprises' in 1994. It further flattened its structure in the late 1990s when it re-invented itself into what it called the 'new model for full-service investing'. On *human resources management architecture* Schwab established strong values through the co-CEO's style of leadership. It also looked to provide individual incentives for risk and growth, moved to 360-degree appraisals, and separated out personal development from any fixation with quantified performance measures. It also sought to cultivate commitment through gender parity and diversity.

Such a case reveals that there can be no quick technology, or any other, fix when moving to e-business. It is indeed a long haul, even for those moving quickly, but especially for large 'bricks and mortar' companies. The framework allows the organization moving to e-business to isolate the many factors that need to be focused on. It also stresses that it is the *integration* of supporting infrastructure with processes, behaviours and strategic intent that will serve to determine ultimately the degrees of success experienced.

7.3 Managing the change process: beyond the quick fix

From these considerations it becomes necessary to reconceptualize implementation as a process involving the introduction of changes connected with computer-based systems into social and political organizational areas where the acceptance and the very definition of the success of those changes tend to be continually renegotiated. In Peter Keen's words:

'*Implementation is not just the installation of a technical system in an organization but the institutionalization of its use in the ongoing context of jobs, formal and informal structures, and personal and group processes. Installation does not guarantee institutionalization. Implementation includes the technical process of installation and the behavioural process of managing change*' (Keen, 1981).

Organizational members are often unwilling to change long-established attitudes and patterns of behaviour. Furthermore, given the introduction of a computer system, people's behaviour and attitudes may not change at all, or may change for a short time before reverting back to older patterns. The ways of working that result influence the extent to which the new

Lewin/Schein approach	Kolb/Frohman approach		Systems development life cycle approach
1. *Unfreezing*	(a)	*Scouting* Organization and change agent jointly explore mutual needs and abilities Entry point selected	1. *Definition* Proposal defined Feasibility assessment Information requirements analysis Conceptual design
	(b)	*Entry* Problems, goals stated. Development of mutual contract and expectations Establish trust, commitment and felt need for change	
	(c)	*Diagnosis* Collect data to define problems Detailed assessment of organization's and change agent's resources for change Establish feasible goals	2. *Development* Physical systems & database design Program development Procedure development
2. *Changing*	(d)	*Planning* Define operational objectives Identify alternative solutions, action steps and possible resistance to change Develop action plan	
	(e)	*Action* Putting into practice 'best' solution Keeping practice flexible in the face of unanticapted consequences	3. *Installation and operation* Conversion
	(f)	*Stabilization and evaluation* Assess 'success' of change and need for further action or termination	4. *Maintenance*
3. *Refreezing*	(g)	*Termination* Confirm new behaviour patterns Ensure handover of responsibility and ownership of system to client is complete Cease work on project	5. *Post-audit*

Figure 7.3
Addressing behavioural change in strategic IT and e-business projects

system is utilized as was originally designed, if at all. Lewin, and later Schein, addressed such problems by developing a model for intervening at the individual, group or organizational levels. Figure 7.3 shows this useful model and its development by Kolb and Frohman (1970).

From these models a crucial point emerges. As discussed, physical systems implementation may be treated as a late stage but, as Chapter 4 suggested, the implementation of the necessary behaviour change to support the emerging system must occur right from the beginning of the project. Failure to grasp the significance of this point for systems development can lead to the so-called 'people problems' frequently experienced at the implementation and subsequent operating stages.

Advantages of the models include the emphases on change as process rather than a 'one off', and the need for careful planning. The overall approach suggests the need in IT-based projects for:

1 establishing a felt need for IT;
2 establishing the support required to see the project through to satisfactory systems operation;
3 monitoring the progress of the project, and responding to resistance to the change process and the emerging system;
4 developing user commitment to the system.

Under item 2, establishing support may mean not only securing top management support but also making that visible to the organization. Establishing change-agent credibility is crucial. User understanding and active acceptance of objectives and methods are also needed. A project champion who can make available required organizational resources is important throughout the project. Such methods are aimed at creating a 'critical mass' in favour of and actively supporting the computerization process. At the end of the project, commitment (item 4) should be expressed as the users 'owning' the system, willing to use it and able to do so without the change agent's presence. In Lewin's terms, this means refreezing – locking the new behaviours into place so that they become the norm.

These models emphasize the much-neglected need to focus on behavioural change when implementing any IT system. When the IT system is linked strongly to strategy delivery – as we saw in the Charles Schwab case – a more all-encompassing integrated approach to change and delivery is needed. Ralph Kilmann's (1989) well researched work provides the basis for such an approach. In Figure 7.4 we update and develop his framework to take into account our own experiences with strategic projects.

Kilmann rightly points out that there will be barriers to change. He also rightly points out that few organizations take a sufficiently holistic approach to dealing with these barriers and mobilizing the organization for change. Kilmann argues convincingly that there are two types of barrier that managers can do little about. One is the *setting* – the external environment with its dynamic complexity, and external stakeholders. The other is the *psyche* of people – the innermost qualities of the human mind and spirit that translate into what people want, fear, resist and defend – that cannot be changed in a short period of time, if at all. However, an accurate understanding of organizational members' psyches is essential to managing organizations and solving problems. The setting and human psyche are the relatively unchangeable givens that any planned change must understand and work with.

The good news, however, is that all the other likely barriers shown in Figure 7.4 – strategy, structure, reward systems, culture, people's assumptions, technology, management skills, how groups are organized and perform – are manageable and changeable, provided that an integrated, planned approach to

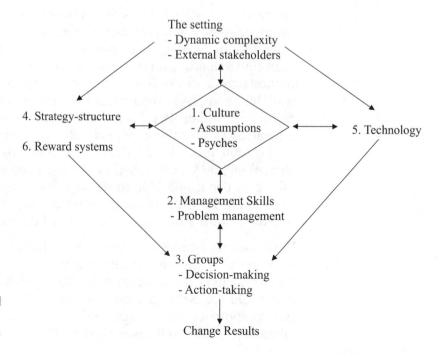

Figure 7.4
Managing barriers to success in IT-based change: an integrated approach (adapted from Kilmann, 1989)

change is adopted. So what does this consist of? Our own version gives much more detail to the technology issues than does Kilmann, but is consistent with his findings. The first three tracks that need attention are culture, management skills and team-building. These adjust the behavioural infrastructure of the organization. Without first developing an adaptive inner organization, any adjustments to the outer organization – strategy, structure, rewards, systems and technologies – would be cosmetic and short-lived. However, there must also be from the start a strong sense of how all these factors fit together. For example, it is not enough to have a strategy without also at the same time establishing how technology can leverage, or even change that strategy, and whether a supportive culture is feasible. This means adaptation becomes a vital component of the implementation process in order to achieve politically feasible 'fit' between the factors.

If this is not achieved, then action on a single factor, however powerful, will be negated by the barriers posed by the other factors. For example, if the strategy is based on false assumptions, then all technology can do is provide an efficient underpinning for what might be tantamount to 'disaster faster'. How groups are rewarded influences the decisions and actions they take. As we have seen in the Charles Schwab case, implementing and institutionalizing the changes may well take several years. However, Kilmann suggests the following sequence as the most effective approach. He also suggests starting with a single, primary business unit first. In this case, the integrated change may well take up to a year, and the figures below reflect this example.

1 *The Culture Track*. At the centre of the barriers to success framework in Figure 7.4 is *culture*, defined as shared values, beliefs, expectations, norms, the unwritten rules of the game, 'the way things are done round here'. Connected to culture are *assumptions*, that is, beliefs taken for granted to be true but that may turn out to be false under closer analysis, e.g., the technology is not important to the future of our industry, the consumer will buy what the firm produces. The key diagnostic questions here are: does this culture support the behaviour needed for organizational success? Are the critical assumptions that affect all major business decisions up-to-date, based on reality, explicit and understood?

Kilmann found many cultures to be dysfunctional and negative, embodying norms such as 'don't argue with the boss, don't share information with other groups, don't be bearer of bad news, laugh at those who suggest new ways of doing things. We can add that many senior managements and organizational members may also have a negative view on IT, seeing it as a cash sink, a cost to be minimized, irrelevant to this business, with a poor track record, and the CIO positioned as a specialist functional manager (Feeny, 2001). Kilmann also found that organizational members typically preferred to work in more positive cultures. He suggests a six-month culture track focusing on enhancing trust, communication, information sharing and willingness to change, and identifying the culture and norms the organizational members wish to commit to – for Kilmann, the conditions that must exist before any other improvement effort can succeed. All organizational members need to participate in this, and the team-building track.

2 *Management Skills Track*. Managerial styles and skills must be diagnosed to see how well these fit with strategy and dynamic complexity of the environment. In settings of dynamic complexity the problems may not be clear and managers may need to handle change constantly. The question here is: do managers throughout the organization apply the right skills for addressing complex problems? Typically this management skills track will start three months into the culture track and may well run for some eight months. The purpose here is to provide all management personnel with new ways of coping with complex problems and the hidden managerial assumptions that may prove misleading.

3 *Team Building Track*. In modern organizations, complex problems need multiple contributions from members of one or more groups. Kilmann found a close link between group decision-making, action and organizational results. The *team building* track infuses the new culture and updated management skills into each work-unit – thereby instilling cooperation organization-wide so that complex problems can be addressed with all the expertise and information available. Team building should start some six months into the planned change, as the culture track ends, with managers being brought back into their organizational units to ensure the newly internalized culture and management skills are transferred directly into the job.

4 *Strategy-Structure Track*. After some nine months, and halfway through the team building track, the originally formulated strategy and structure will need revisiting. *Strategy* refers to all the documents that indicate direction: statements

of mission, purpose, goals and objectives. *Structure* refers to the way resources are organized into action: charts, policy statements, job descriptions, formal rules, regulations, work procedures. Is there clarity and agreement about objectives? Does the way of working and developing culture support strategy or require adjustments? Does the structure actually enable or inhibit direction and productive ways of working? These questions will be addressed by small groups of leaders from every part of the organization and their conclusions acted upon by senior change managers. Thus, this track develops either a completely new or a revised strategic plan for the firm, then aligns divisions, departments, work groups, jobs and all resources, with the new strategic direction.

5 *Technology Track*. Our experience, as suggested in earlier chapters, is that information-based systems and technologies need to be 'first-order thinking' done at the time of, and included in, first formulation of strategy, and that a robust feasibility analysis of organizational readiness to accept and deliver the technological changes is also carried out then, and an implementation plan drawn up. Half-way through track 4, it will become obvious what organizational culture, managerial skills and readiness are in place, and changes in strategy and structure will also need to be adjusted to. The groups in track 4 will need to regularly consult with those responsible for technology delivery, and driving out business benefits from the IT/e-business projects.

6 *Reward System Track*. The reward system includes all documented methods to attract and retain employees and, in particular, to motivate them to high levels of performance. The *reward system track* sees a small group of leaders establishing a performance-based reward system that sustains all improvements by officially sanctioning the new culture, use of updated management skills, cooperative team efforts, working within the new strategy, and delivering the requisite technologies. The new reward system will start to be developed half way through the strategy-structure track when it begins to become clearer what the objective measures will be for success at individual employee and group levels.

It is important to evaluate the results from each track, not least so that, in a large organization, planned changes can be implemented flexibly, and more effectively, in other business units. However, for Kilmann, evaluation is not merely a reality check at the end of the process but something that needs to be performed throughout. It also needs to be part of a further 'shadow' or 'politics' track that runs parallel to all the other tracks from the very start, and right through to the completion of the change process. We focus below particularly on the implications for delivering the technological aspects of business strategy.

7.4 Managing the shadow track: a political approach to IT-enabled change

This section outlines the basics of a political approach to IT-based change implementation, which is developed from Kilmann's idea of a 'shadow track'. Bringing a computer system into effective operation in an organization is not solely about getting the politics right. However, getting the politics wrong has turned many an IT project into a long-term damage limitation exercise. How can this be avoided?

IT people commonly see the planning, designing, organizing and controlling of IT-based projects as rational behaviours. However, these activities are also essentially political. One must ask – whose plans, whose designs and whose objectives? Furthermore, organizations are inevitably political arenas with individuals, groups and coalitions attempting to influence others and events to protect and meet their own needs, interests and goals. An organization where members' goals, perceptions or interests do not conflict is a rare one indeed. 'Playing politics' may not always be the primary activity, but it is an ever-present one to some degree. Two important considerations arise from this.

Firstly, the design and development of IT/e-business systems inevitably implies the ability to bring them into successful operation. However, while IT professionals may rarely be questioned in technical matters such as analysis and design or hardware and software selection, such expertise and associated technical qualifications may form an insufficient power base these days for fulfilling the responsibility for seeing a project implemented. Unfortunately, IT professionals too often ascribe a rationality and a common sense to their projects that is not shared by those directly affected by implementation outcomes. As a result, they fail to acquire and mobilize power and develop strategies to achieve objectives, and the system flounders at the implementation stage. Of course, faced with gathering signs of organizational hostility toward what they themselves regard as a technically high-quality product, IT professionals may well have fled from responsibility for project acceptance long before implementation.

Secondly, organizational politics breed in times of technological change. The extent of political activity during systems implementation will depend on the extent to which power has been mobilized behind the project, and other options and paths of resistance are closed off before implementation. Political activity will become more obvious where there persist unclear goals and outcomes, different goals, the need to allocate limited resources, differing definitions of organizational problems and differences in information made available. Mangham's (1979) finding is that:

> 'In circumstances in which people share power, differ about what must be done, and where these differences are of some consequence, decisions and actions will be the result of a political process.'

Just looking at the implications of technology for an organization, the introduction of new technology will release political energy because of its anticipated and actual organizational and social impacts and the manner in which it is designed and implemented. A political approach may be more appropriate where the technological change impinges on core activities, will be pervasive and cut across departmental boundaries and will have numerous users. However, even in minor applications, the existing power structure will be disturbed in some way by new technology. It also represents a new organizational resource around which ownership struggles will cluster. In this way, the implementation process will reproduce, but also amplify, existing strains in the organization's political system.

In practice, political activity may well reach its highest throughout implementation as people's fears become realized. This can be a function of people avoiding facing up to the implications of computerization at earlier stages. Also, failure to participate in change will be rational behaviour as Kilmann points out, where the rewards for doing so do not seem commensurate with the efforts necessary, where there is a good chance of feeling manipulated and where the cultural norms of the organization do not encourage trust and openness in interpersonal relations. It also may be a function of the approach to implementation. Historically, IT has been implemented with the minimum of participation, the output of selective and reassuring information, and little regard for the industrial relations implications. Such an approach is marked by highly political activity during implementation and subsequently.

Thus, it is crucial to understand a particular organization's political structure and how different types and levels of IT and digitization relate to political activity. Such understanding is the first step in planning and implementing IT. A political perspective implies the possibility of resistance and the need to gain organizational acceptance for technology. This is where contingency comes in; that is, being prepared to adapt the system to the political circumstances prevailing, while also being willing and able to operate in and change those circumstances. As Markus (1983) puts it:

> 'If the implementer can divorce the need to see a system up and working from the need to achieve a particular result, several degrees of freedom exist.'

7.4.1 The concept of power

A central concept that needs to be understood when managing change is that of power. Power is inherent in organizational relations. Its exercise both creates and arises from societal and organizational context. Matters such as how labour is divided, how the organization is departmentalized, and how different categories of worker are rewarded are all the products of political activity. In turn, these results give for different people various degrees of control over information, decision-making, resources, punishments and the access of others to these. Power may also arise on an individual basis; for example, in terms of expertise, personal qualities and ability to be liked and persuade others. As a social relation within an organization, power becomes expressed as people pursue aspirations through action to try to achieve outcomes. It is an interdependence relating to how skilfully people mobilize or deploy resources (power bases) and how important and scarce those resources are perceived or experienced to be by the parties in the relationship.

Power implies influence, control over resources and sanction. However, there is power in the threat of sanctions, in the potential of power. As Pettigrew (1985) puts it:

> 'Control . . . may not be enough; there is also the issue of skilful use of resources. The most effective strategy may not always be to pull the trigger.'

Power is exercised not only by those who are in the dominant coalition but also by, as well as through, lower-level stakeholders in an organization. Participants in a power relationship are rarely on equal terms but always have some influence over each other, because power relationships imply some degree of mutual dependence for all parties. As far as computers are concerned, even low-level operators in computer systems can corrupt data, modify software in unrecognizable ways and damage the system in serious and costly ways.

But as IT has become strategically important to organizations, so they hand over an important power resource to certain individuals and groups, not least IT professionals. This highlights the importance of gaining the acceptance and support of key personnel once IT is up and running. It may also be wise to gain acceptance by those involved at and affected by the introduction stage of a computer project. How can these two objectives be achieved? An important power resource lies in the establishment of the legitimacy of change and subsequent operation. Establishing legitimacy is tied in with politics as the management of meaning. This involves developing amongst employees shared norms and internalized values and beliefs that elicit their cooperation and commitment in system introduction and operation (see the Culture Track above). Given the vulnerability of computer systems to low-level participant activity, it is not surprising to find hi-tech companies such as Microsoft, IBM and Hewlett-Packard developing cultures based on high rewards, attractive personnel policies, encouragement of initiative and pleasant work conditions. In some hi-tech companies, computer technology for home-working and tele-working has developed further this marriage between enhanced business performance through cost reductions, labour flexibility and 'putting people first' personnel policies. The development not just of power bases but also of an organizational culture that will support and sustain technological change lies at the heart of a political-cultural contingencies approach to introducing IT/E-business systems into organizations.

7.4.2 Change agents

An argument can be made that IT professionals should not be involved where political problems are likely to result; they lack the political skills needed to handle these. A counter argument is that such skills have become an important part of an IT professional's job if a computer application is to be successful (see also Chapter 2). Additionally, IT professionals' interventions in an organization are necessarily political for reasons already advanced. But further, political problems will inevitably develop, given the trepidation and ambivalence generated historically by the IT professionals' specialist culture, the trade language and the mystery of an expertise needed but inaccessible to many organizational members.

In fact, it is a mistake to assume that IT professionals have not had enough power in the past. The problem has more often been too much power applied in ways that distorted and harmed the very implementation they were promoting. The culture of expertise and the identification of IT with 'improvement' and 'progress' are in fact hard to argue against in organizations. We have found over the years a number of instances where otherwise unpalatable changes in work practices, reward systems and structures were accepted because the otherwise bitter pill of change was often coated in the sugar of 'IT progress and investment'.

IT professionals and systems implementers may well exploit this mystique of technology; managers will accept their legitimate claims and hand over responsibility for computerization

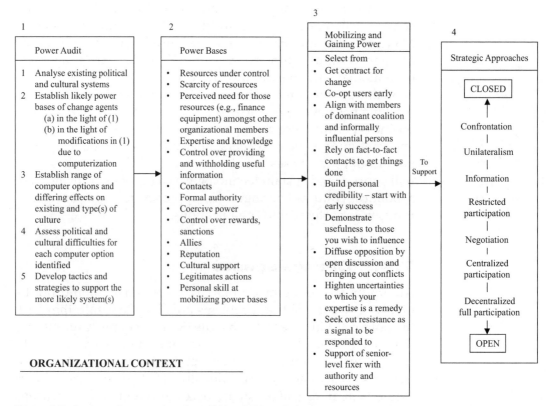

Figure 7.5 Strategy for managing the politics of IT-based change

to IT specialists; the latter can then make policy decisions in management's absence almost without being aware of doing so. The difficult problem over the last decade has been for IT professionals to come to accept how dangerous such a narrow 'political' approach can be for the successful implementation of IT-based business projects. As we pointed out in Chapter 4, at implementation, what becomes a crucial determinant of system success becomes system compatibility with, and its use and acceptance by, the emergent political and cultural structure. IT professionals need to develop wider political skills and sensitivity to promote this outcome. As we will see in the next chapter it is also important that business managers also accept their own responsibilities for effective delivery. All need to ensure that a shadow track is managed so that politics do not become a barrier but a support for IT-based change. How can this be achieved? Figure 7.5 shows the process.

7.4.3 The power audit

A first step is analysing the existing political and cultural system of the organization. This means establishing membership of the dominant coalition and the sources of their influence. It also requires close analysis of lower-level participants, their power bases and the manner in which they, as well as the dominant coalition, are likely to support or resist any level of IT adoption, and how crucial such responses might be to system development and implementation.

A second step is establishing the likely power bases of the change agents in the context of the existing political and cultural systems; also, how these power bases can be modified in the course of IT implementation (see Figure 7.5).

The third step is to establish a range of possible IT options and their differing effects on the existing distribution of power. More radical shifts in power distribution will require different strategies and alliances, and a much more careful political approach.

The fourth step requires an assessment of the political and cultural problems likely to be engendered in the course of developing and implementing each of the IT options identified. A preliminary assessment of the political feasibility of each proposed system can then be made.

The fifth step is to develop strategies and tactics to support the more likely systems and make an assessment of how successful differing combinations of systems, tactics and strategies are likely to be.

The power audit assists the change agents in understanding the existing power structure and culture, who is influential, who will resist different types of system, who will be affected in what ways by different proposals and how different change strategies will be affected when different individuals and groups mobilize their power. It will end with an understanding of the political complexity of computerization but also a clearer idea of the political feasibility of different types of system, design method-ology and change approaches.

7.4.4 Mobilizing/gaining power

How can influence be managed? Political goals need to be formulated and an ends–means analysis carried out (i.e., what do we wish to achieve and how do we go about achieving it?). Targets to be influenced are then identified and incentives desired by the targets determined. Implementation involves mobilizing these incentives and monitoring the results.

The management of politics and culture must continue through-out the technology project. In organizational settings, a political approach is rarely just a matter of accumulating enough power at the beginning of a project to do what you like thereafter. Various approaches to influencing the process of IT implementa-tion are possible. Keen (1981) suggests that the IT function be headed by a senior-level fixer with resources and authority to negotiate with those affected by any new system. A steering committee including senior-level managers will become actively involved in highly political aspects of the computer project. Under this umbrella, systems staff can establish credibility and influence events tactically:

- make sure you have a contract for change;
- seek out resistance and treat it as a signal to be responded to;
- rely on face-to-face contacts;
- become an insider and work hard to build personal credibility;
- co-opt users early.

Other tactics might include presenting a non-threatening image, aligning with powerful others, developing liaisons, developing stature and credibility by attending to a client's immediate needs before gaining approval for a less well understood project, and diffusing opposition by open discussion and bringing out conflicts. In research on internal consultancy by systems analysts, programmers and operations researchers, Pettigrew (1985) found at least five power resources that can be mobilized. A crucial one is expertise. The change agent can increase client dependence by heightening uncertainties to which the application of their expertise would be a remedy. Internal consultant activities across departmental boundaries also give privileged access to, and so control over, organizational information. Political sensitivity and establishing relations with those with power is also important, as is the gaining of 'assessed stature' by identifying and serving the interests of relevant others. Group support by departmental colleagues and related consultant groups is a further power source that needs to be developed.

7.4.5 Implementation problems

There are three problem areas in implementation to which our political approach needs to be specifically addressed. One is resistance to change, another is the danger of the change process running out of control and the third, and related, problem is how to maintain influence over the political dynamics of change. We need to reiterate that IT implementation must be seen in the context of wider objectives than the limited goal of gaining acceptance for a specific system. This implies that system modifications may be necessary in the face of politico-cultural problems. But, anyway, implementation should serve as an important period for learning about system design imperfections at the technical level as well.

Techniques for reducing resistance to change include:

- the need to make visible any organizational dissatisfaction with present systems;
- addressing people's attention to the consequences of not computerizing;
- building in rewards and reasons for people to support the transition and the future system;
- developing an appropriate degree, level and type of participation for different affected parties;
- giving people the opportunity and time to disengage from the present state;
- setting up temporary structures to maintain control over the project in the transition period.

Keen's (1981) recommendations above are relevant here. Also, adequate planning and resources are needed to see the transition through. There is also the need to develop and communicate clear images of the future to organizational members, and establish multiple and consistent leverage points, aimed not just at individuals but also at social relations, task and structural changes (see also Chapter 4). It is also important, as Kilmann suggests above, to build in feedback mechanisms to monitor developments as early as possible.

Keeping power on the side of the IT-based business project and handling the power dynamics of change is crucial. Here one needs to ensure that leaders and key groups maintain active support for change, that a culture and climate of success is created, but also that enough stability remains, and the pace of change is judged, so that the changes remain acceptable to involved parties. The selection and implementation of a strategic approach is also a crucial aspect.

7.4.6 Strategic approach

'*Contingency*' implies retaining a flexible approach to IT/e-business implementation and building in opportunities to modify design where it is seen to be deficient. A contingency approach also means adopting a *change strategy* appropriate to the organizational circumstances in which those responsible for implementation find themselves. As Kilmann suggests, such a strategy involves intervening in the technical, political and cultural systems of the organization at one and the same time.

Change strategies range from being *closed* to *open* (see Figure 7.5). Closed strategies are marked by a minimum of communications and consultation, negligible participation in design and implementation by the vast majority of interested parties, and the development of systems by IT specialists to achieve managerial objectives that tend to be control- and finance-focused. Closed strategies are linked closely with the introduction of centralized computer systems. Closed strategies are often linked with confrontational industrial relations at implementation, though this is not a necessary relationship and depends on the power realities pertaining. Often these mean that little confrontation is necessary and the system is introduced unilaterally by systems professionals and management. This may be a sensible approach where the system is technically sound and designed to minimize dependence on user skills and cooperation, or where organizational culture supports authoritarian management styles.

Kilmann points out that in these circumstances, the approach he advocates is inappropriate; it just would not work. Most organizational members would not voluntarily support the proposed changes.

By 2002 such closed strategies would be less appropriate for many IT-based business projects (see next chapter). However, for illustrative purposes, an example of a closed 'confrontation' strategy that was successful was the development and highly publicized implementation of the computerized photocomposition and print systems by News International at their Wapping site in 1985–86. A feature of confrontation strategies is the need to secure cooperation of at least part of the workforce. At Wapping it was the journalists. The following account gives some of the flavour of closed systems implementation:

> 'For most it was the first time they had been in the heavily fortified compound . . . the first journalists to reach the new newsroom were astounded. The entire floor had been laid out as an electronic newsroom with everything in place. A desk was ready for all of them with an ATEX terminal on each. Phones were in place, the switchboard had just been installed, and all around them were genial men and women, many of them American or Australian, who welcomed them to their new workplace and asked to call on them for any help they would need. The day which for all of them would normally be a day off was designated as a time to familiarize themselves with the new technology . . . everywhere were new faces, many of them women, who knew how the system worked and keen to make it work in practice.' (Lloyd and Hague, 1986).

More open strategies stress participative design, communications, consultation and willingness to modify technical systems, job design and work organization in the face of user feedback. Open strategies tend to be associated with negotiated change by agreement and consultative machinery in the formal industrial relations sphere. Some strategies are more 'open' than others. Prototyping and 'Time Boxing' tend to be closely linked to open change strategies (see next chapter). Clearly, one best change strategy for all circumstances cannot be advocated. Open strategies are more relevant where there is underlying support for the aims of the project, where there is a large number of affected parties, where there are differing views on how computerization can be achieved, where power to resist introduction is widely distributed and where user involvement will provide vital information for system development. Closed strategies will tend to be preferred where the benefits of participation are low, where there is widespread agreement and support for computerization, where the promoters of the system are all powerful or where the level of disagreement and hostility about the system is so high that participation is perceived to serve little purpose.

7.5 Conclusions

Where dependent on traditional systems design methodologies, IT project management has been technically oriented, with human issues perceived as mainly arising at the implementation stage. Furthermore, implementation itself has often been viewed as a discrete 'one-off', late event in a systems project. The failure to consider many human issues as significant until late in the project means that when they emerge there is often a reluctance amongst implementers to adapt, let alone abandon, the computer-based system in which so much time, money and labour has already been invested. People-management as an essential and primary implementation task can then become a self-fulfilling prophecy with a vengeance, with human issues and problems, and lack of user acceptance, persisting throughout the system's subsequent use.

A key task, then, is to manage behaviour and politics as intrinsic parts of IT-enabled change from the beginning. Particularly crucial is the management of the politics of computerization. From a project and change-management viewpoint, this means ensuring that the system becomes sufficiently politically acceptable to be used effectively, and that a culture exists to sustain its continued use. However, technology will only form part of the overall change process. In this chapter we have located delivery of business and IT strategies in a holistic approach to managing programmed change. However, we need to stress that the principles outlined here would seem to apply to all change projects in contemporary organizations. Politics do breed in times of change. The politics or 'shadow' track is planned for and followed, or managers find their way there by chance, unexpectedly, and invariably under less favourable circumstances.

References

Feeny, D. (2001). The CEO and CIO in the information age, in Willcocks, L. and Sauer, C. (eds), *Moving to E-Business* London: Random House.

Kilmann, R. (1989) *Managing Beyond The Quick Fix*. San Francisco: Jossey Bass.

Kolb, D. and Frohman, A. (1970) An organizational development approach to consulting, *Sloan Management Review*, Autumn.

Keen, P. (1981) Information systems and organizational change, *Communications of the ACM*, Vol. 24, No. 1, 20–34.

Leonard-Barton, D. and Kraus, W. (1985) Implementing new technology, *Harvard Business Review*, November.

Lewin, K. (1980) Discussed in Schein, E., *Organizational Psychology*. New York: Prentice Hall.

Lloyd, J. and Hague, H. (1986) *Financial Times*, 27 January, 16.

Mangham, I. (1979) *The Politics of Organizational Change*. London: Greenwood.

Markus, M. (1983) Power, politics and implementation. *Communications of the ACM*, Vol. 26, No. 6, 430–445.

Pettigrew, A. (1985) *The Awakening Giant: continuity and change in ICI*. Oxford: Blackwell.

Willcocks, L. and Plant, R. (2001) Pathways to e-business leadership, *MIT Sloan Management Review*, April.

Willcocks, L. and Sauer, C. (eds) (2001) *Moving To E-Business*. London: Random House.

Change and delivery 2: managing IT-based business innovations

'There are three routes to failure – gambling, sex and technology: "Of these gambling is quickest, sex the most pleasurable, but technology the most certain"'. French President Pompidou.

'By all means specify a time, by all means state a budget, but never do both at the same time'. Old project manager's advice on achieving perceived success.

'There are only six things that can go wrong with a project. The problem is that it's a different six each time'. Senior Manager, financial services company.

8.1 Introduction

In the previous chapter we located technology innovation in a broader organizational context. In this chapter we pursue this theme further by looking at further practices that seem to work when implementing IT-based business innovations. In particular we use the example of Enterprise Resource Planning (ERP) systems implementations to identify ineffective and effective principles. As we shall see, these days, effectiveness is highly dependent on adopting a time-box philosophy, prototyping, breaking projects down into smaller ones that each deliver business value quickly, and new forms of project governance. Throughout we illustrate the principles with case studies drawn from our research.

Applied to more recent IT-based innovation, Pompidou's observation quote above remains an all too apposite indictment.

Consider a typical finding represented by a 1995 Standish Group study of 175 000 projects in the USA. It concluded that 30 per cent of projects, representing US$81 billion expenditure, delivered no net benefits. Our own end-of-millennium study found 26 per cent of projects producing very disappointing results, while 5 per cent were complete failures (Willcocks and Graeser, 2001). Regularly such studies show that 70 per cent plus of IT-based (and 90 per cent of ERP) projects are 'challenged', meaning over budget and late. Introducing new information technology, even just to support the existing business model, emerges as a high risk, hidden cost process. The risks are even greater when, as for example with many Internet and ERP applications, real *business* innovations are also being looked for. The top reasons for disappointment cited in studies also remain stubbornly familiar: incomplete definition of business requirements, insufficiently detailed technical specifications, changing business requirements and lack of business user input in the development process (see, for examples only, Willcocks and Griffiths, 1996; Avital and Vandenbosch, 2000).

Faced with a catalogue of high profile failures ranging from Taurus in the London Stock Exchange (cost to LSE and the City: £400 million), California's driver licence and registration system (cost: US$50 million) and its state automated child support system (cost: US$100 million) and the failure of Confirm, a US joint venture attempt to develop a reservation system for hotel rooms and cars (cost: US$200–300 million) – serious question marks can be placed against whether IT-based business innovations are really worth the risk. However, our own work shows a consistent picture of how business innovations based around IT occur, how the technology-related, organizational and project management risks can be mitigated and managed, and how IT-based innovation can be translated into real business advantage.

A central feature is releasing the learning potential inherent in the juxtaposition of customers with organizational members, and co-location and co-working of users, technical specialists and external expertise. This enables not just the transfer but also the creation of new explicit and implicit knowledge, which Nonaka and Takeuchi (1995) and Leonard-Barton (1995), for example, show to be all important for any knowledge-creating, innovating company. In practice, our 15 years of research and practice in a range of IT-based business innovations identifies enduring organizational and cultural factors that explain success, irrespective of the differing technologies being implemented. Even with new technologies, there are still consistent principles to be applied, and many lessons to be learned from history.

8.2 IT-based business innovation revisited

The first lesson, in fact from earlier chapters, is that technical innovation in itself rarely translates into business innovation. Significant payoff arises only when IT is applied to a new business idea and model. Otherwise no matter how advanced the information technology, the most that can be expected is that some existing business idea will operate more efficiently (Feeny, 1997). Consider Direct Line in UK insurance in the early 1990s. Against traditional insurance sector models Direct Line (DL) achieved some five years of competitive advantage by identifying what the customer disliked most – delays and administrative complexity in getting a policy and making claims, and high price. Focusing initially on the 9 million motor vehicle insurance niche, and low risk clients, DL used the telephone and IT-supported receptionists to arrive at policies and claims within minutes. Significant reductions in operating costs were passed on to customers in much lower prices. Interestingly, the IT was not particularly new, but it was configured to effectively support the new business model.

As Chapter 1 made clear, the Internet is all too often a technical solution in search of a business problem. The few successes so far in business-to-consumer e-business suggest that the above logic applies. For example, the computer manufacturer Dell has used the Internet as a channel to eliminate all intermediaries except a courier service. Prospective buyers visit the Web site, choose a custom PC configuration and place an order. Dell's automated assembly line and just-in-time ordering achieves cost savings and allows dispatch sometimes within 2–3 working days. Virtual store front and direct selling to end users reduce the costs of salespersons, intermediaries and physical assets. Prices can be lower, with customers receiving reliability assurance from the brand. Dell's Web site regularly makes large revenues indeed (Willcocks and Sauer, 2001).

The second lesson concerns the two main processes by which a business-led approach leads to focused, innovatory IT investment. We described these briefly in Chapter 2 but let us revisit them in the context of implementation issues. In the first, the trigger point is articulation of a business issue or opportunity –

for example, a breakthrough in unit costs, reduced time to market, differentiation through new value-added services – that, if successfully addressed, would radically advance the organization's achievement of its vision and strategy. The business issue is owned and addressed by the organization's executive team, including its head of IT. The team accepts that 'breakthrough' thinking is unlikely to be achieved amid the hurly-burly of day-to-day business or routine board meetings. They adopt an 'away day' culture, taking significant time out from operational activity.

The team adopts some high-level methodologies – positioning frameworks, value chain concepts, etc. – which serve as a common language and structure for debating the issues at hand. Through its own membership or through external guest members the team has access to knowledge of how other organizations have addressed this type of issue, including organizations in other sectors and including examples of potential IT contributions. The target output is not an IT investment case, but an integrated design for a new business initiative, spelling out requirements for IT as well as other functional requirements. Target changes in business metrics become the driving force (Willcocks *et al.*, 1997).

A second effective process starts from being close to the customer. In practice few IT-based business innovations have materialized from formal planning processes, routine organizational IT investment committees, or from IT departments working alone (see earlier chapters). It has been pointed out that even the classic cases of 'competitive edge' IT, such as SABRE in airline reservation systems, Baxter in medical supplies ordering and Merrill Lynch in account management systems, developed mainly incrementally, through a process of learning over time and from a strong external focus. More recently, observable effective innovation in many sectors continues to originate from close interaction between customers and those working at the sharp end of the business (Willcocks and Plant, 2001). This provides an external view, allows the identification of genuine customer requirement and how existing or potential IT can be optimized to fulfil an updated customer value proposition. But innovation will founder at this point unless it gains a high-level project champion, with funding achieved outside the formal IT investment decision process. Continued customer involvement is also required to refine the innovation, and a high internal marketing and political effort is needed to convert the opportunity into organizational reality (Earl, 1989).

However, the overriding factor then becomes the implementation process adopted. The main features of difficult projects continue to be large size, long timescales, complex, new or untried technology, and lack of clear, detailed project staffing and management structure (Willcocks *et al.*, 1997). Moreover, traditional 'waterfall' methods of systems development seem particularly inappropriate for implementing IT-based business innovations. In what follows we look at Enterprise Resource Planning (ERP) implementation as a typical large-scale IT-based business innovation, and comment on our findings as to what in a major 27-organization study we found to be working, and not working. We then bring together from diverse pieces of research, and from our practitioner experiences, the principles that have proved effective in managing IT-based business projects effectively.

8.3 The example of ERP implementation: record so far

By 1999 what Ross *et al.* (2002) call the ERP 'quiet revolution' was generating over US$20 billion revenues annually for suppliers and a further US$20 billion to consulting firms. If 2000 and 2001 saw a fall-off in business globally, then some believed that once the distractions of Y2K deadlines were over, new ERP business, plus the need to support and capitalize on the sunk investment in IT infrastructure ERP already represented, would guarantee further take-off. Once again, at first without many noticing, IT not only raised itself high above the cost parapet, but also set off traditional alarm bells about questionable business value. For many firms, ERP represents the return of the old IT catch-22 with a vengeance – competitively and technically it's a must-do, but economically there is conflicting evidence, suggesting it is difficult to cost justify, and difficult to drive benefits from (Shanks *et al.*, 2002).

The problem has been further complicated by the coming of Web-based technologies. Thus, Sauer and Willcocks (2001) found many organizations struggling to integrate their legacy and relatively new ERP systems with e-business initiatives and technologies. The goal of a relatively seamless e-business infrastructure seemed particularly difficult to achieve in 'bricks and mortar' companies trying to move to the Web, a finding explained by Kanter (2001) and Willcocks and Sauer (2001) in terms of cultural, organizational and political issues, together with less than good organization and project management for e-business (see also Chapter 7).

Critical success factors, and reasons for failure in ERP implementations, have now been quite rigorously and widely researched, and are also discussed in detail elsewhere (see Shanks *et al.*, 2002). But authors such as Markus and Tannis (1999), and Ross (1998), point to some distinctive characteristics of ERP that require different treatments from many other IT implementations: packages requiring a mix of old and new skills, often a 'whole organization' suite of applications, software embodying generic best practices that imply large-scale business process re-engineering, integrated software requiring further assembly of the *technology* platform, the constant need to keep up with evolving functionality, software and technology related to ERP, the degree of customization that is possible or prudent. However, what is more noticeable is how the difficulties experienced in ERP implementations and with their business value are not untypical of most IT projects, especially where they are large and complex, expensive, take over a year or more to install, use new technology and impact significantly on the organizational culture and existing business processes.

Our own work on ERP success and failure factors complements previous findings but differs in one essential respect. In a study of 27 ERP projects in the 1999–2001 period we found serious neglect in ERP implementations in identifying the most effective roles for the CIO and IT function. Moreover, in case studies we have found failures in this area to be correlated strongly with subsequent difficulties in achieving delivery and business value. This chapter will spell out the several ways in which we have found the CIO and IT function, and relatedly it must be said, often senior business executives, 'asleep at the wheel' on ERP, and the more effective capabilities and practices some organizations have been drawing upon. Our work also enables us to describe a consistent picture of how business innovations based around ERP, and IT generally, occur, how the technology-related, organizational and project management risks can be mitigated and managed, and how IT-based innovation can be translated into real business advantage. In practice, our ERP and broader research into a range of IT-based business innovations and transformation projects identifies enduring organizational and cultural factors that explain success. Irrespective of the differing technologies being implemented, we have indeed found, with Markus and Tannis (1999) and Ross (1998), that there are still consistent principles to be applied to IT-based business innovations, and many lessons to be learned from history.

8.4 ERP: efficiency or transformation?

The roots of the ERP 'revolution' technologically were two-fold: firstly pre-written software available off the shelf with sufficient flexibility to match most needs; and secondly, an underpinning of data structures shared across many applications (so that data on a given invoice were not passed step to step but accessed from a common data structure). The first step promised a great improvement in software implementation productivity – no time wasted reinventing the wheel and writing endless new software. Seen in that particular IT context, the promise has been delivered, but the context has been one of IT resource productivity alone. The second step promised both IT and operational productivity improvement (including quality improvement and less room for error) through more simple implementation of seamless processes.

The challenge of the ERP revolution has been how best to use the new capabilities. This is where the failure to deliver begins to be real in many organizations we and others have studied. The opportunity was to automate and simplify complex paper-based transactional systems. In reality the *status quo* was more than the paper-based system – it was a whole generation of business processes and how business was done. The real value-adding opportunity was therefore to radically reshape how the business was done (business process re-engineering) and exploit the new automated, seamless ERP capabilities in the process. 'How a business is done' is, however, not simply the transactional processes that they supposedly serve. The human processes reflect an accumulation of human skills, human process and preferences (human ways of going about things) and so on. So the real route to value in ERP includes major human and organizational change processes as a necessary part of the process. Simply put, it is about a transformation involving identifying business strategy and objectives, and designing integrated processes, technologies, information systems and skills to deliver on these. These are, of course, themes continuous from the previous chapter.

8.4.1 A case in point: Guinness

Consider a successful implementation we studied. Guinness is the brewing division of Diageo, formed in 1997 through the merger of Guinness plc and Grand Metropolitan plc. Guinness operates in 150 markets and its turnover exceeded £2.5 billion in 2000. Needing to enhance its logistics and systems to increase sales growth, make better use of its assets, sell new products globally, and reduce stock levels and back-office costs, senior management resolved to transform and establish new common business processes and IT systems throughout its five trading divisions.

Both cultural and organizational changes were needed as the company had very separate businesses each operating globally, with their own IT departments, systems and processes. IT architecture was regional in nature in both governance and organization. While the infrastructure in terms of e-mail, UNIX and desk top was reasonably consistent across regions, the applications base was very mixed, with, for example, Ireland having a lot of legacy systems and Europe a lot of locally purchased packages. A strong point was the selection of SAP R/3 as the new core ERP platform, since this had already been implemented in the UK between 1997 and 1999.

From February 1998 Guinness ran an Integrated Business Programme and a year of implementation work saw SAP R/3 going live at Guinness UK, extended to Ireland in July with Customer Order Fulfilment going live in both places by November 1999. Throughout 2000 both were further rolled out in the USA and elsewhere. Guinness used R/3 implementer Druid to help put in finance, sales and operations planning, procurement, customer order fulfilment and product supply suites. But Guinness also had to implement workflow, data warehousing, advanced supply chain solutions and integrate some legacy systems as well. It also resolved to continue to use Manugistics for production planning. Guinness also changed its organization architecture to a shared service model, with, for example, finance being one dedicated department servicing all business divisions. Centralization of most back-office processes has been implemented and has been found to work satisfactorily, and is reflected in having only one corporate IT function, with only some systems infrastructure and software development decentralized.

Guinness has tended to achieve its goals with the ERP implementation by making some radical organizational, skill and business process changes, at the same time as restructuring the IT base and the way IT was organized and managed. The strong factors enabling success mentioned by management were: creating a project team from staff drawn from all parts of the business globally; detailed communication to and buy-in from all relevant stakeholders from the beginning and

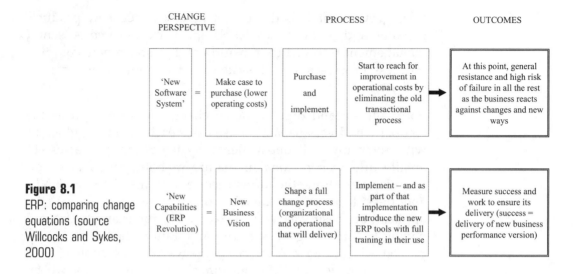

Figure 8.1
ERP: comparing change equations (source Willcocks and Sykes, 2000)

throughout; strong leadership from the top; a focus on changes to the business as a whole rather than just on the ERP implementation, e.g., breaking down local cultures, building secure and stable networks and a single IT department; and implementing in a fast, focused manner. A further aspect was being flexible about some aspects of implementation. Thus IBP left out the Far East and Africa operations that remain fundamentally stand-alone. The IBP also recognized that sometimes localization should take precedence. For example, in Ireland most pubs were still owner-managed rather than owned by big chains as in England. This meant their order-processing systems had to be different, with Ireland not using SAP R/3 exclusively, but having a Siebel front-end.

In these respects, Guinness can be located as following the orientation and practices typical of the second change equation illustrated in Figure 8.1. The dangers seem to come when an organization allows itself to follow only the first change equation, or deludes itself into believing that it is delivering on the second, without adopting the necessary transformation practices this requires.

8.5 ERP, the CIO and IT function: asleep at the wheel?

In this context, on what occasions, and in what ways can it justifiably be said that the CIO and IT functions have been, on ERP, 'asleep at the wheel'? Our research has identified three 'asleep' modes and one main 'wide-awake' set of capabilities and practices in ERP implementations. The three 'asleep' modes are: technological determinism, supplier/consultant driven, and absent relationships and capabilities. These are now described.

8.5.1 Scenario 1 – 'technological determinism'

ERP software has particularly lent itself to the notion of being a packaged total solution to a whole range of technical and business problems. This itself has become a problem when the CIO is technologically focused, the IT function's skill base is technical and the organization is functionally driven, with the IT function seen by itself and the rest of the business to be the prime 'owner' of IT issues. A relatively mediocre previous IT track record on business systems delivery and value becomes the basis on which ERP is handled and implemented. Invariably ERP is regarded as a 'new software system' and the change equation that results, typically and disappointingly, is that shown in Figure 8.1. In our study we found examples of such outcomes, especially in the early implementations in the 1995–97 period in two banks, an aerospace company and several manufacturing companies and public sector organizations. As one example a senior business executive in a UK-based multinational manufacturing company commented on a two-year ERP project begun in 1996:

> 'When I think back, the whole thing was seen as a technology infrastructure development. We were also promised a solution to Y2K problems. I recall the business case premised on infrastructure renewal, there was little there on business benefits ... it was assumed they would come ... [but] a lot on streamlining of technical functionality, indeed on a global basis.'

In such examples typically the ERP project is abandoned into the often eager hands of the IT function, whose view is to deliver technical capability on time and within budget. The Change Equation posited is the first shown in Figure 8.1. In itself this often proved more difficult than at first appeared, because of lack of relevant in-house IT skills, attempts to customize the ERP, and the complexity of linking with legacy data, systems and technologies.

215

8.5.2 Scenario 2 – 'supplier/consultant driven'

A second scenario has been where senior business executives have taken the significant decisions without meaningful CIO and IT input, either because they see ERP as 'too important and enterprise-wide' for the IT function to be left with the responsibility or because the IT function has a poor track record and ERP is seen, somewhat like large-scale IT outsourcing, as both a way of replacing the IT headache with a packaged solution, and also a way of giving substantial IT work to external suppliers and consultants whose core capabilities are seen to lie in this area. This tendency has often been fuelled by suppliers and consultants increasingly selling ERP not into the IT function, but into the boardroom itself. One noticeable feature of this scenario is how far the CIO is regarded neither as a peer within the top team, nor as an ally with loyalty to the business rather than to the IT function and to the technology.

Too often an outcome here is considerable cost overruns: one respondent mentioned the cost being ten times that posited in the first feasibility study with suppliers. A second is lack of buy-in by the organization. The ERP is implemented, but the re-engineering and training necessary become long and painful, subsequently, while the continued use of external contractor staff cause a sharp rise in the maintenance and development budgets for ERP. While Change Equation 2 is posited (see Figure 8.1), the means to deliver it are not really present. Respondents in two-fifths of our case studies recognized this scenario in various degrees. As one example, in one US-based manufacturing company operating globally, the ERP expenditure between 1997 and 2000 was estimated to be US$500 million. The Board made the decision to launch a so-called 'global business integration project' largely in negotiations with suppliers and consultants. Subsequently the IT function was supplying some 300 staff to the project, believed little in its value, but was receiving a high level of complaints from business units for their lack of ability to deliver on other pressing IT-related business requirements.

8.5.3 Scenario 3 – 'absent relationships and capabilities'

All too many IT functions and CIOs have not been in a sufficiently prepared state to step up to the admittedly difficult business challenges represented by new technologies, increased competitiveness and changing, ever-pressing requirements from the business. Quite often, of course, the business itself has not set a suitable context in which CIOs and IT functions can flourish. Where IT is seen as a cost to be minimized, and as a cost efficiency tool and not as a potential strategic resource, and where the CEO and/or senior business executives are permanently disengaged from a business transformation agenda through IT, there is in fact little chance for the IT function to contribute significantly to business imperatives. Inflexible human resource policies on pay and career and contracts will also exacerbate the skills shortage problems many, even large, corporations face in today's volatile IT labour markets.

Translated into ERP development and implementation, it can be seen how a third scenario has developed. Either Change Equation may be posited. In either case, the IT function is made largely responsible for ERP, but is in no real state to be successful. It lacks the technical skills, but also lacks the capabilities needed to manage the external suppliers they hire to fill the planning and operational skills gaps. It also has not managed to build up the relationships with the business side at CIO and operational levels, nor helped to reorientate business thinking and motivation sufficiently to cause the business to step up to their key responsibilities in the re-engineering, change and transformation aspects of ERP implementations.

In practice this scenario was the most common one we found, even to certain degrees in the ERP implementations that were proving successful. As one CIO in an insurance company commented:

> 'In the last three years I have not had time to rethink the skills base . . . it's been one thing after another . . . in some ways ERP was a blessing, there were so many problems I could shovel into it, but I can't say we were ready for it, the complexity, the management of the suppliers, the problems with the business . . .'

8.6 On being wide-awake: core IT capabilities

In practice, however, the need to identify and build key in-house IT capabilities before entering into ERP projects emerges as one of the critical – and neglected – success factors we have identified throughout our practical and research experiences. It will be recalled from Chapter 2 that Feeny and Willcocks (1998) have identified nine core IT capabilities. Here we comment on their role in ERP implementations.

- *IT Leadership*. In successful ERP the CIO must at least have built strong relationships with her/his business executive peers, must behave as a knowledgeable strategic partner with the business, and be able to align investments in IT with strategic business priorities. The IT function will have built, and will continue to strive to retain, credibility for its ability to deliver on promises.
- *Business Systems Thinking*. In the ERP context the failure to have integrated business, process, technology and skills thinking and planning at what Markus and Tannis (1999) have called the Chartering phase has been an all too frequent reason for sub-optimal ERP business performance.
- *Relationship Building*. ERP potential cannot be leveraged without strong coordination of effort and goals across business and IT personnel.
- *Architecture Planning*. Again this cannot be abandoned to ERP suppliers despite the seeming attractions as a total packaged solution. The client organization needs to maintain control over its IT destiny, its ability to plan for future technology requirements of the business, while retaining the ability to have informed discussions with ERP suppliers.
- *Technology Fixer*. This capability to handle non-routine technical problems as they are disowned in the technical supply chain must be retained in-house. Ross (1999) reports that this happened at Dow Corning, and we saw it also in several of our examples of success. With ERP, suppliers and consultants cannot be expected to have the commitment or the specific business and technical knowledge to deal with the unusual company-specific problems that arise. Retaining such talent in-house may involve paying them more to stay than they would receive as contractors, but several respondents reported that this was precisely the trade-off between cost, stability and effectiveness they were willing to make.
- *Informed Buyer*. This and the remaining three core capabilities are vital in ERP implementations, where so much use of external contractors, supplier staff and consultants is made.
- *Contract Facilitation* to ensure success of existing contracts through user–supplier management and multiple supplier coordination.
- *Contract Monitoring* to hold suppliers accountable to existing service contracts and to the developing performance standards of the market through benchmarking and other means.
- *Supplier Development* to identify and seek added value from supplier relationships by looking beyond contractual arrangements to explore long-term mutual benefits.

These nine core IT capabilities must be retained in-house. Where, as frequently is the case in ERP projects, these key skills may be lacking, one solution is to build them over time by 'insourcing' – buying human resources off the market to work closely with the in-house team and ensuring that a transfer of learning takes place. These capabilities represent the minimal IT function needed to plan for and implement ERP for business advantage.

8.7 Implementation as innovation: 'dolphins not whales'

Once these capabilities are in place, the overriding factor then becomes the implementation process adopted. The main features of difficult projects, ERP or otherwise, continue to be large size; long timescales; complex, new or untried technology; and lack of clear, detailed project staffing and management structures (Willcocks *et al.*, 1997). Moreover, traditional 'waterfall' methods of systems development seem particularly inappropriate for implementing ERP-type projects if they are to be genuine business innovations.

For these reasons, in a highly competitive sector, Ford Europe in the early 1990s moved to a different 'time box' approach with very positive results. From 1997, with 500 IT-based projects at any one time, British Airways has been adopting more rapid application development techniques and taking 30 per cent off typical delivery times. In 1999 the Woolwich bank finished piloting the UK's most advanced and integrated suite of call centre and Internet-based banking services, developed and built in just six months. In 1998 Daiwa Europe, the Japanese financial securities company, achieved an IT–based innovation in eight months meeting the deadline of 1 January 1999, and allowing the company to trade in the euro. What is common to each example? The significant differentiator is not new tools for faster systems development, such as computer-aided software engineering (CASE), object-oriented programming (OOPs) and rapid application development (RAD) tools, but innovations in staffing, culture, project disciplines and learning. Let us distil out the rationale, and major features, of an 'implementation as innovation' approach.

8.7.1 User versus specialist focus

Projects embodying IT-based business innovation are, firstly, business projects and, secondly, are inherently unstable.

Detailed business requirements, as opposed to the overall objective, are unclear and subject to rapid change. Flexibility for further learning and innovation is required. Additionally, the technology itself (less so the ERP software) may be under-developed, lacking stability and detailed technical specification. Technology maturity refers to where a radically new technology is being utilized or where a radically new business application of an existing technology/software is being made or where relevant in-house technical expertise is lacking. Increasingly in fast-moving business environments, as IT becomes increasingly organizationally pervasive, development can no longer be left primarily to IT specialists or external IT suppliers. If second-wave ERP is to happen then ERP-based business innovation requires a user-focused approach involving multi-functional teamwork, personal relationships and business goals. Only when technology maturity is high, and a detailed contract and deliverable can be pre-specified, does it become low risk to hand over those aspects of development and operations to in-house IT specialists or outsource to external IT suppliers.

8.7.2 Governance and staffing

Our ERP study, and earlier IT-related studies, consistently show that effective IT-based business innovations require a high-level sponsor and a project champion, both taken usually from the business, not the IT side. The former will provide only up to 5 per cent of his/her time, but be involved in initiating the idea, underwriting the resources required, and protecting the project into business adoption and use. The project champion will provide between 20 and 60 per cent of his/her time. The role involves communicating the vision, maintaining motivation in the project team and the business, fighting political battles and remaining influential with all stakeholders, including senior management.

A small 'dolphin' multifunctional team is needed to implement the time box philosophy described below. Effective project managers have three distinguishing characteristics: credibility with the salient project stakeholders, a track record of success with *this* size and type of project, and skills in controlling the detailed actions needed to keep a project on its critical path. Additionally potential users of the IT, drawn from the best people available, will be assigned to work full-time on the project, along with in-house IT specialists. External IT resources may be needed to fill skills gaps. Certain users and managers may need to be brought in to provide additional knowledge and opinion on an occasional basis. The multi-functional team will also contain people with 'bridge-building' interpersonal skills. Co-location of team members also helps the key processes of team building, knowledge sharing and mutual learning.

8.7.3 Time box philosophy

The primary discipline here is that the IT-based business innovation must be delivered within a six- to nine-month period. Moreover the IT must be developed within the overall IT architecture for the organization, and not as a separate 'portaka-bin'-type system. If on a hard look this cannot be achieved the project does not start. However, it can be decomposed into smaller projects, each of which will deliver tangible business benefits. Time discipline reduces the risks of the project not meeting business requirements, ensures that big projects, or 'whales', are reduced to a series of more manageable 'dolphins', means that business benefits flow regularly rather than being delayed, and ensures the team has to remain focused and fully staffed over a more realistic, limited period. Within the project further time-boxing will place time limits on each part of the development, to reduce drift from the overall business delivery target.

Development proceeds on the basis of the 80/20 rule, with the business accepting in advance that the first systems release may well only provide 80 per cent of the functionality origi-nally demanded. As the marketing director for Ford Europe puts it: '"80 per cent systems are OK" is now part of the culture here'. As the head of distribution development at the Woolwich comments: 'We decided to build it as quickly as possible and accept that we would make mistakes along the way'. However, in the new culture mistakes and failure are treated as positive contribu-tions to learning. Iterative development by prototyping ensures close interaction between developers and users with a workable system built quickly and constantly refined. The knowledge exchange and incessant testing and learning leads to a culture of rapid improvement, with sometimes radically new discoveries on business utilization of the systems. Proto-typing and user involvement also sees the developing system becoming business-owned, thus easing acceptance problems traditionally experienced when IT specialists hand over IT to users.

221

8.7.4 The supplier/consultant role in innovating

External perspectives and knowledge can contribute much to the process of technical and business innovation. Furthermore, with the need for rapid delivery of systems to the business and all too typical in-house shortages of both routine and key skills, suppliers can perform an important 'fill-in' role. More routine, easily defined tasks within the overall project can be outsourced. Our own research suggests that with IT-based innovation, suppliers are most effectively utilized as resources brought in to work under in-house direction and control. The responsibility and detailed direction for innovation must stay with the business, but 'insourcing' external skill can, if properly managed, release valuable transfer-of-learning effects. These suggestions are mapped in Figure 8.2, which is adapted from Feeny *et al.* (1996), which also summarizes the argument made above on the roles of users versus suppliers/specialists.

The alternative – of outsourcing to a third party the management and resourcing of IT-based innovation – places the external supplier in an invidious position. Consider one European insurance company, intending in the mid-1990s to achieve competitive advantage through transforming its policy and administration systems. A major supplier was given aggressive timescales to deliver detailed business requirements for the systems. However, the supplier had no great in-depth knowledge of insurance and greatly underestimated the complexity of insurance work and information. The method used for driving out requirements was new and relatively untried. Project

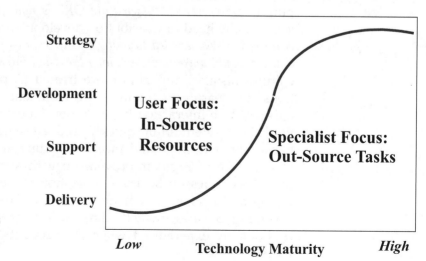

Figure 8.2
Sourcing and the roles of IT suppliers/specialists

management was also made the supplier's responsibility. In practice a business innovation was being abandoned to the supplier. After one year the insurance company invoked penalty clauses for non-delivery to cancel the project, with the supplier incurring significant costs.

A useful comparison can be made with the successful ERP implementation at ICI Polyurethanes between 1993 and 1998. The company started with a complex series of operations across Europe and a complex customer base covering, for example, auto manufacturers, shoe manufacturers and white goods makers. A clear change programme was led by a very systems-literate CEO and backed by a very IT-literate finance director. The internal IT function was very heavily involved in what was conceived as a business re-engineering project from the start. The main steps were:

1 a revisioning detailed planning exercise to position the business as a single pan-European operation;
2 negotiations with many national tax authorities to allow the business to operate as a single legal entity across Western Europe;
3 developing a change plan to revise the 'footprint' of manufacturing plants, systems, processes. The human dimension tackled as an integral component of the plan;
4 business processes redesigned to align with the new streamlined business 'footprint';
5 SAP R/3 implementation to support and underwrite the new processes. Heavy emphasis was placed on training and implementation exercises. Very strong focus throughout was placed on delivery on business performance metrics.

In practice the business has grown strongly in a very competitive marketplace. ERP achieved considerable business advantages including allowing vital tax negotiations to take place and enabling the eradication of 125 000 internal transactions involving the company doing business with itself. The IT function's role was integral to this success, and it followed many of the effective practices on in-house capabilities, 'user' focus, governance and staffing, time-box philosophy and use of external supply emerging from our study.

8.8 Conclusion

Much of this, of course, assumes that the business itself has matured in its ability to manage ERP and similar IT-based business innovations, thus setting the context in which the CIO and IT function can thrive (see the evolution model in Chapter 2). In these circumstances, there emerge from our practical and research experiences eight critical enabling factors if IT-enabled business innovations are to stand a chance of succeeding:

1 senior-level sponsorship, championship, support and participation;
2 business themes, new business model and re-engineering drives technology choice;
3 'dolphin' multi-functional teams, time-box philosophy, regular business benefits;
4 CIO as strategic business partner;
5 nine core IT capabilities retained/ being developed in-house;
6 in-house and 'insourcing' of technical expertise preferred;
7 supplier partnering – strong relationships and part of team;
8 ERP and IT components of projects perceived as business investment in R&D and business innovation, rather than primarily as a cost efficiency issue.

Does the arrival of Web-based technologies change these imperatives in any way? Actually, in the additional research we have carried out so far, we have found the opposite (Sauer and Willcocks, 2001). The difficulties of integrating ERP and other new technologies with legacy and Web-based technologies makes it even more critical to make sure these enabling factors are applied.

References

Avital, M. and Vandenbosch, B. (2000) SAP implementation at Metalica: an organizational drama in two acts, *Journal of Information Technology*, Vol. 15, No. 3, 183–94.

Earl, M. (1989) *Management Strategies For IT*. London: Prentice Hall.

Feeny, D. (1997) Introduction, in Willcocks, L., Feeny, D. and Islei, G. (eds), *Managing IT As A Strategic Resource*. Maidenhead: McGraw Hill.

Feeny, D. and Willcocks, L. (1998) Core IS capabilities for exploiting IT, *Sloan Management Review*, Vol. 39, No. 3, 9–21.

Feeny, D., Earl, M. and Edwards, B. (1996) Organizational arrangements for IS: the roles of users and specialists, in Earl, M. (ed.), *Information Management – the organizational dimension*. Oxford: Oxford University Press.

Kanter, R. (2001). *E.Volve: succeeding in the digital culture of tomorrow*. Boston: Harvard Business Press.

Leonard-Barton, D. (1995) *Wellsprings of Knowledge: building and sustaining the sources of innovation.* Boston: Harvard Business School Press.

Markus, L. and Tanis, C. (1999) The Enterprise Systems Experience – From Adoption To Success. Working paper presented at the 'Enterprise Systems' seminar, AGSM, Sydney, August.

Nonaka, I. and Takeuchi, H. (1995) *The Knowledge-Creating Company.* New York: Oxford University Press.

Ross, J. (1998) *The ERP Revolution: surviving versus thriving.* Cambridge, MA: Center for Information Systems, Research Paper, MIT.

Ross, J. (1999) Dow Corning Corporation: business processes and information technology, *Journal of Information Technology,* Vol. 15, No. 3, 1–16.

Ross, J., Vitale, M. and Willcocks, L. (2002) The Continuing ERP Revolution. In Shanks, G., Seddon, P. and Willcocks, L. (eds), *Second Wave ERP: implementing for effectiveness.* Cambridge: Cambridge University Press.

Sauer, C. and Willcocks, L. (2001) *Building The E-Business Infrastructure.* London: Business Intelligence.

Shanks, G., Seddon, P. and Willcocks, L. (eds) (2002) *Second Wave ERP: implementing for effectiveness.* Cambridge: Cambridge University Press.

Willcocks, L. and Graeser, V. (2001) *Delivering IT and E-Business Value.* Oxford: Butterworth-Heinemann.

Willcocks, L. and Griffiths, C. (1996) Predicting risk of failure in large-scale information technology projects, *Technological Forecasting and Social Change,* Vol. 47, 205–28.

Willcocks, L. and Plant, R. (2001) Pathways to e-business leadership: getting from bricks to clicks, *Sloan Management Review,* April.

Willcocks, L. and Sauer, C. (eds) (2001) *Moving to E-Business.* London: Random House.

Willcocks, L., Feeny, D. and Islei, G. (eds) (1997) *Managing IT As A Strategic Resource.* Maidenhead: McGraw Hill.

9 Delivering business strategy: the criticality of infrastructure

'I can't get anyone in this business, this industry to articulate what the e-commerce model will look like in two, three and four years' time . . . But I do know that is the direction we are going, that I have to spend a dollar because we have to compete, we have to change the way the industry works . . .'. Gill Lithgow, CitiPower.

'Infrastructure as a unit is becoming more important all the time to the point where the business is saying, in terms of the whole bank environment, technology is *the business'. Liam Edwards, Macquarie Bank.*

'Managing infrastructure is about changing the tablecloth without disturbing the cutlery'. Infrastructure team, Macquarie Bank.

9.1 Introduction

Effective business users of IT invariably at some point in their history have confronted and dealt with the issue of infra-structure. What we saw in the Internet Bubble of 1998–2001 were all too many e-strategies declared that were revealed as threadbare in their thinking. But even those that were not so threadbare were often held back by the gap in their ability to found e-business on a robust infrastructure. One recalls the frequent failures every Christmas, when e-tailers' systems were manifestly not up to the job of dealing with high demand from customers (Sauer and Willcocks, 2001).

An amusing demonstration of the gap was by Victoria's Secrets, a company selling women's lingerie on the Internet. Its marketing department decided to run a TV advertising campaign during the US Superbowl in 1999. The advertisement pointed out that those logging on to the site could see Claudia Schiffer modelling underwear. The site attracted some 250 000 hits in the first hour with some 9 per cent making purchases averaging US$80, but then the site collapsed for three days, incurring a loss of some US$7.4 million in sales. It was revealed that the site was not developed to deal with anything like that volume, could not transfer prices quickly and had poor connections with inventory. Such infrastructure results from 'The Wizard of Oz' syndrome – designed to look impressive to the customer; in fact it is very frail and unimpressive behind the curtain. Unfortunately, all too many, even multinational, businesses could be described in this way.

As we shall see here in three of the cases, the effective users of IT realize that infrastructure is a boardroom issue. They see infrastructure as laying down the parameters within which business can operate, and in that way allow the business to shape the future and behave dynamically, able to contemplate real options rather than pipe dreams. One will see in those three cases, also, that there is a very strong connection and interchange between the IT groups, the infrastructure teams and the businesses they serve.

In the final case, we also provide a glimpse into what an effective IT and Internet service provider looks like, how it operates and what makes its infrastructure services attractive. Though critical, infrastructure does not have to be sourced internally. As we saw in Chapter 6, provided a rich analysis is carried out and there are appropriately skilled service providers, in fact the IT service market is a perfectly safe place to go for all manner of infrastructure needs. The Vistorm case gives a glimpse of the past, but of, in our view, an even more fundamental future. The Net has provided an important new mode for delivering services, applications and infrastructure. In 2002 this marketplace was still in an embryonic stage. As providers follow companies like Vistorm in making their offerings more robust, find viable business models, and develop services and charging systems that are attractive to customers, we will see over the next five years a slow but fundamental shift in the ways in which infrastructure is delivered.

9.2 Case study one – CitiPower: strategy, infrastructure and the role of a programme office

Part of CitiPower's history was previewed in Chapter 3, but it is worth presenting it as a whole here.

From its headquarters in Melbourne, CitiPower provides electricity and other energy-related products and services to over a quarter of a million business, residential and industrial customers in the city's business district and suburbs. It is also licensed to sell gas in New South Wales and its home state of Victoria, and has offices in Sydney, Brisbane and Adelaide. CitiPower thus runs an energy distribution, but also an energy retailing set of businesses. CitiPower resulted from the break-up and privatization of the State Electricity Commission of Victoria in 1994. Subsequently it has faced some daunting challenges. There have been rapid changes in ownership, increasingly fierce competition, and constantly changing political climates and regulatory regimes in the different states in which it operates. There is a constant need for product innovation. At the same time CitiPower has been learning how to operate in a commercial environment, and trying to understand its markets – all of which implies on-going cultural change for its long-term staff.

The challenges are summarized by Gill Lithgow, appointed new CIO in January 1999: *'As an organization we have to become incredibly flexible, at the same time as getting a new identity and culture, and supporting that with tools and capability'*. The solution, starting from March 1999, has been to build a technical and process capability that enables e-business, even before many of the applications are known:

> *'everything we do, every dollar we spend in applications development or purchase, on technology spend, is cognizant of the fact that we will move progressively to e-business'*.

The important building blocks to achieve this are described here. They include the design of the e-business blueprint, the relationship of IT with the business, people and sourcing policies, and the organizational delivery of new IT, primarily through application of the Programme Office concept.

9.2.1 Inheriting and developing infrastructure

Lithgow inherited a number of problems. A major one was that CitiPower had spent as little as possible on infrastructure. For example, rather than having a strategy on server architecture, the investment had been in PCs on the desk:

> 'What I saw was an ad hoc style of management in an organization that was, in Australian terms, reasonably large. It depended on IT to deliver, to be connected to the outside world. But they had a project office of one person whose background was as a technical writer. CitiPower had new Y2K systems being built, and the old ones kept as well, at the insistence of business people. Development of its new payroll system had a threefold cost overrun . . . If it had been a greenfield site it would have been easy. Maybe what we should have done is actually gone to a different floor, and built a new infrastructure from scratch!'

At the same time as inheriting a poor infrastructure, and the need to deal with the increasingly urgent Y2K issue, Lithgow also had to address the potential for e-business and of emerging Internet-based technologies. By March 1999 CitiPower had made conscious decisions: they were only going to offer information and bill presentation and payment on the Internet site; they would await with interest developments on B2C in Australia and their sector; and they would look actively into the future opportunities for e-procurement.

Bringing these things together, it became clear to Lithgow and the executive management team that the company faced considerable uncertainty, that much needed to be done on the IT front, and that what needed to be done was fundamental and involved infrastructure development:

> 'The basic building blocks have got to accommodate large flexibility. That means you don't buy or build certain components. Because the world can change so dramatically the components have to be slotted in and out quickly, so we produced the term "object-oriented applications" . . . The absolute trick is to put in the right components, and be single minded in following it . . . From a purely architectural sense, the description of the components and how they were to be linked was produced some three months after I started.'

229

This blueprint that was developed is a whole organization infrastructure blueprint, and not a separate blueprint for e-business. The blueprint rolls up all the issues and develops a way forward for CitiPower to develop into an e-business, though the precise business strategies were yet to be worked out:

> 'I can't get anyone in this business, this industry to articulate what the e-commerce model will look like in two, three and four years' time. I see a number of players trying it, I can't see the numbers of customers, in Australia, interested enough to actually buy a product such as electricity or gas through e-commerce. So why invest in all the effort and customer-facing part? But I do know that is the direction we are going, that I have to spend a dollar because we have to compete, we have to change the way the industry works, and I had to spend a whole heap of money on Y2K anyway, so why build something that could not be utilized for an e-commerce environment?'

In some ways, at this time, CitiPower did not have an e-business strategy as such, but was intent on developing an e-business infrastructure that enabled different choices to be made when senior managers wanted to make them. Fundamentally, from mid-1999, CitiPower invested in readiness for e-business whilst dealing with its legacy of poor systems and making the infrastructure robust enough to handle current business. The latter was achieved fairly quickly. However, by late 2000, on Lithgow's judgement, CitiPower were also seven-tenths the way to having in place an infrastructure robust enough to exist in an e-commerce world. And this was being done on a controlled budget, of Aus$30 million in 1999, the same again in 2000, and Aus$25 million in 2001, knowing where most of the applications are going and the architecture it has to fit.

The point of the infrastructure blueprint is to establish the parameters for any development not just in technology, but also for processes and skills that support moves to becoming an e-business. For Gill Lithgow, the blueprint is indivisible, because even if something simple in the business is to occur, nothing is left untouched. For example, a customer making a change to his/her own address would impact on customer relationship (billing and payment), sales and marketing (offering future services), metering, contracts and settlements, to name just a few. The blueprint ensures that the necessary interconnectivity, and efficiencies, will be achieved as each new development occurs in alignment with the infrastructure's trajectory and laid down parameters:

> *'If a customer moves out or moves in, and we get 50 000 of those each year, remembering also that next year especially, they can choose where they buy their electricity, there is a whole set of things we have to do. The cost used to be Aus$365 each time, and our cost base just escalates. So we have had a massive redesign of all our processes, done it conceptually without building them, designed our IT in and around it, and we have brought the cost down on paper to about Aus$5 a time. The biggest single challenge going forward is that we have got existing operations, we have got to transform it almost overnight from one way of doing things operationally, to suddenly another way of doing things.'*

What ensures the discipline to keep to the plan has been the implementation of the Programme Office and the cultural change it has been catalysing, as described further below. But the engagement of IT with the business, and *vice versa*, also helps to explain this wider acceptance of an e-business infrastructure perspective, even without specific B2C and B2B initiatives.

9.2.2 IT and the business

The interesting thing at CitiPower has been the extent of business backing for investments in technical infrastructure projects that run across the organization and for which, notoriously, it is often difficult to find business champions. One reason is that Gill Lithgow was hired by a like-minded CEO, who had also worked with him previously at one of CitiPower's competitors. As we have demonstrated elsewhere (Willcocks *et al.*, 1997), effective CEO/CIO relationships are a fundamental building block to managing IT as a strategic resource. Relatedly, at CitiPower, IT sits at the same table as the senior executives and business heads, who share the same remuneration targets. Investment decisions are also arrived at by shared business case criteria. Moreover, according to Lithgow:

> *'I have been lucky for the last few years in working in organizations where the change in business has been massive, like building a new retail bank in New Zealand, and changing another electricity company here, so all the infrastructure stuff has been tied to the business cases for change, as opposed to the age-old problem where you have got a fairly stable business, and IT has to spend large sums of money on purely the screws and nuts and bolts . . .'*

At the same time, in order to educate senior business management, occasionally Lithgow has not wrapped pure technology projects, for example the middleware and the Aus$5.5 million server/database projects, into the various business cases for building business applications. Why is this education necessary? Because, for Lithgow, executives have to know intimately about IT, its contribution and the components that make it up:

> 'IT is not a single specialization, it is multi-disciplined. I had to find a way, and continue to find ways, of exposing things like architecture to the Board and into the Executive management team, as part of the on-going education.'

At the same time there are a number of people throughout the organization who come up with opportunities in the IT and e-business areas, and these opportunities get widely exposed, including at senior executive meetings, but the opportunities are always judged against a business case. But Lithgow, with a somewhat more back-door approach, was also able to argue successfully for the adoption of an Intranet. The existing Intranet had been poor, and Lithgow pointed out that if you can't do IT or e-business internally, and cannot set up all the processes, ownership and disciplines necessary, then you are not going to do it externally, for example with customer-facing systems, or B2B operations. Over time the Intranet has become more entrenched and used, whilst it also forms an integral part of the infrastructure being developed.

9.2.3 Implementation: skills and sourcing

A critical issue is the type of IT-based people needed to make all these developments possible. Gill Lithgow is very clear that in management:

> 'it is people who are outward-looking and technically aware, people who can think and talk in business terms, know what a customer is, and understand direct marketing and what profitability is about. Maybe it is my bias but I look for people with a broad grounding.'

The people he looks for are not easy to find, and there seems to be no one place to find them. Lithgow explains that for him skills in IT fall on a continuum (see Figure 9.1).

The typical progression for people is to be mainly technical and in operations to start with. They then move along the continuum

Figure 9.1
Skills continuum
(source: Gill Lithgow)

at different speeds to various end-points, with some making it to the end as visionaries and strategists. The trick is to know where a job candidate is on the continuum, how their personal development is likely to progress and how they slot into CitiPower's current and future needs. The people Lithgow prefers to employ cross at least one of the boundaries, that is they are at point A or B in Figure 9.1. However, he recognizes that it is not so much about individuals as having a balance of skills to form a team with the right mix.

However, skilled IT staff are a scarce resource, especially in the current Australian environment – a major reason, together with affordability, why CitiPower looks to a variety of sourcing options for its IT operational and development capability. In fact, CitiPower outsources its operational and customer information systems activity to Compaq, telecommunications to Telstra, the running of the programme office to a consulting firm InFact, while project management is done in-house. It also employs contractors on an insourcing basis as resources to work on in-house projects. All projects and all developments, however sourced, have to run through the Programme Office, and work inside CitiPower's common standards, methodologies and framework. Interestingly, a lot of the work on developing the infrastructure blueprint was done by an outside consultant, but only on the understanding that he could not then work for any competitor, that CitiPower owned the intellectual property rights to the blueprint and owned everything that was to be built according to the blueprint. A key differentiator here, of course, is knowing how to actually deliver the blueprint, which is where the Programme Office concept has a major role to play.

9.2.4 Implementation: introducing a corporate-wide programme office

Underpinning these infrastructure developments has been a delivery mechanism – the Corporate Programme Office.

In February 1999 a review of programme governance and management had revealed some disquieting facts. Some 300 existing projects were not aligned to CitiPower vision and strategy, nor managed across business functions. Project costs and progress were not tracked. No project methodology or process was in place; undue reliance was placed on individual skills and experience. The high number of projects in an organization of some 600 people revealed considerable duplication of effort and much confusion over sponsorship and the defining and prioritizing of projects.

Lithgow had experienced similar scenarios five or six times before in his 30 years working in IT in industries that included banking, gas, electricity and insurance. The danger of not translating business objectives into successful outcomes was all too obvious. At CitiPower he quickly introduced a corporate-wide Programme Office structure to maximize use of resources, control costs and reduce risks of late delivery.

By early 2001 the programme had eliminated much unnecessary activity, and was ensuring all new products fully supported the company's vision and business plans. By this date resources were only being assigned to approved projects; progress and financial status was being widely communicated; projects were being delivered effectively to the organization and the business benefits measured; continuous improvement processes were in place; project managers were highly skilled and well equipped, roles were much clearer, and key performance indicators and career development supported future performance. Moreover some 300 projects had been cut to 80. Once all projects, including those for infrastructure, had been logged, each was prioritized against business vision, strategies and potential payoff. This removed, for example, planned upgrades for commercial systems in fact due for replacement, and the installation of a Aus$1 million PABX system that would have duplicated the existing Telstra Virtual PABX service. According to Gill Lithgow:

> 'If you look at projects in cold financial or customer service terms, quite a lot just do not stack up. The classic one is spending Aus$100 000 to do something that in four months I'm going to throw away'.

At CitiPower he also found no clear idea of what people were working on, how they were spending their time, nor any clear idea of how much was being spent on IT – typically on projects 30 per cent or more than was thought. Getting control of these issues was fundamental. At CitiPower the Programme Office is able to track and operate efficiently the many different projects running concurrently. It does this through applying standard approaches to project management and reporting. A fundamental aspect here is recognizing project management as a core organizational capability, and creating the situation where people can switch from one project to another with ease.

Within this project management discipline, everything the Programme Office does must support the overall strategy and business plans of the corporate vision. Moreover business benefits must always be measured and achieved; and everything the Office does must be done right first time. This approach allows CitiPower to prioritize its valuable financial and human resources, in the sure knowledge that they are being assigned to key, strategic tasks. This becomes important because of the possible wide claims on those resources, and their possible misplacement without the discipline supplied by the Programme Office (PO).

Staffed by project managers and business analysts, the PO records decisions affecting the programme of work, and communicates these to stakeholders and interested parties, including the Executive Programme Council (EPC), made up of the CEO, Lithgow and the Executive Management Team. The EPC directs the programme, weighs up project risks and returns, sets priorities and monitors the delivery of results. Each project proposal is discussed in the line of business and with an executive team member who will present any viable proposal to the EPC.

Once a project is accepted, it is subject to common procedures applied throughout project life from change control to status reporting and outcomes. The framework includes job descriptions for all roles within the project management process. All procedures are defined in a standard format on the CitiPower intranet. A critical role is that of business results manager, delegated by the project sponsor to deliver project outcomes when they are due. The business results manager works with the project manager to define anticipated business benefits; on completion of the project these measures are transferred to the business result manager's personal key performance indicators. Given this level of accountability, this manager is involved in all key decisions and approvals during the project lifecycle.

The Programme Office clearly works at CitiPower, and a significant part of this has been the public and private support of the CEO and top management team. Moreover, every attempt has been made to make the process a business, not an IT matter. Thus, in the early stages, the Office focused heavily on business customers and projects, and by early 2001 this still accounted for over 75 per cent of the Office's programme activity. At the same time, according to Gill Lithgow, full implementation of the concept does take time:

> 'There's always a period when you are building the capability, and what people are seeing is bureaucracy. It's not until the concept starts to actually help them deliver – which can be a long time – that people become more accepting. We're getting positive acceptance now [late 2000] ... With all the training and the rollout of the intranet, we're now walking ... I typically would expect two-plus years [before we are running].'

9.3 Case study two – Charles Schwab: building the engine room for on-line investing

By 2001 Schwab had become one of the largest on-line brokerage, investing and associated financial services company in the world. It held over US$600 billion in customer assets, had over 300 branches and operated regional customer telephone service centres, automated telephone support and on-line channels. By 2001 close to 70 per cent of its business was on-line. It had also expanded globally into, for example, Europe and Australia. In Chapter 7 we detailed the Charles Schwab transformation process. But what e-business infrastructure lay behind this success, and how was it developed?

9.3.1 Starting out

In December 1995 Schwab established the target of implementing an Internet trading system in 90 days. The objective became to transform core business operations, build new e-business applications, run a scalable, available and safe environment, and leverage knowledge and information. IBM became the chosen partner because of its experience in building large-scale transactional sites, and the depth of its hardware and software solutions. Early on IBM provided RS/600 SP AIX-based systems running CICS for AIX transaction software. This was tightly integrated from the start with Schwab's existing mainframe OS/390 CICS-based applications. IBM was also asked to add Tivoli systems management software, a DB2 Universal database to store on-line client data and transactional information, and MQSeries to provide increased availability and scalability for Schwab's Web trading platform. In the first nine months the original three RS/600 systems grew to 24. By 2001 hundreds actually were powering the site.

In late 1997 servlet technology was developing quickly, and Schwab began looking at the business case for using server-side Java technology and where it might be best deployed. The objective was to increase developer productivity and hardware efficiency significantly. The Director of Web Systems Availability (WSA) presented the concept to many groups, including the Technology Review Board, a group of IT managers responsible for reviewing any major architectural change. This board had been set up to ensure, in a period of rapid business growth, that technology decisions were always examined in the light of business value, supportability and operational issues. The final decision to go ahead with IBM's WebSphere Application Server (WAS) technology was made by the senior vice-president of electronic brokerage.

Before choosing IBM Schwab also researched Sun/Javasoft, BEA/Weblogic and JRUN as alternative application servers. However, IBM seemed the better option because of IBM's early support for the JSP standard and longer-term benefits from the on-going relationship, including technical support. According to the WSA vice-president, Purna Roy:

> 'Java server pages was one of the key things that Schwab wanted and IBM was one of the earliest vendors to provide full support for that. Strong support matters a lot to us.'

Choosing IBM also allowed Schwab to stay in the existing AIX environment. Also, Schwab's critical need was for Java server pages, and IBM's technology was well ahead of, for example, Sun Microsystems, even though Sun had developed the standard.

The decision was made to deploy this technology initially to support the Account Open application, considered non-mission-critical. Schwab's principle was not to impact applications related to quote and trade placements, because downtime there would mean lost revenue for Schwab. An outage in the Open Account application could be handled by would-be customers by downloading an application form over the Web, or even visiting a local branch office.

237

As this initiative proceeded, Schwab also developed another Java desktop application for its active trader customer segment. This created the possibility of inherent synergy of the two Java-based solutions:

'The server-side Java solution of IBM WAS presented itself as a perfect server-side complement for this experimental product. A major benefit of having Java on both sides was their ability to communicate using serialized Java objects instead of the large HTML documents filled with presentation directives. This made the product significantly leaner in the usage of Internet bandwidth.' Purna Roy.

The new Schwab product, known as Velocity, in fact showed a threefold improvement in response time for a comparable transaction using a Web browser, illustrating the knock-on customer effects from infrastructure/technology improvements.

In development and infrastructure terms, WAS technology could lead to two main improvements. The first, on the server side, was to improve the efficiency of processing at the Web server level, thus reducing long-term hardware requirements. The second was to increase the productivity of its application development personnel. By implementing WebSphere's JSP support the application development process becomes more efficient as presentation and logic become more clearly separated in terms of tools and skills. The company divides its Web development team into Web page designers and software developers. Before WAS, much of the presentation logic was embedded in the CGI programs. This meant a complex coordination of tasks between the two groups, also requiring each to have a working knowledge of the other's functional area. Server-side Java meant reducing the time to make changes from days to well under a day and sometimes 30 minutes.

9.3.2 Implementation

Schwab's approach was essentially internally driven and staffed. Beginning in early 1998, the company assembled the internal team of Java and CORBA programmers needed to assist in utilizing the WAS JSP technology. IBM, Sun and other suppliers were also lined up for hardware resources and consulting support. By mid-1998 Schwab was using the Java Web Server from Sun and Servlet Express from IBM as prototypes, while also seeking further resources from senior management. In later 1998, after clearance on supportability and concerns over Java's impact on Schwab's wider IT development, more development resource was made available and the prototypes were subjected to rigorous testing.

In late 1998 attention shifted to the broader issues of how a new technology architecture would impact on IT organization areas such as quality assurance, developer training and data centre operations management. IBM Global Services helped to resolve such issues, for example training Schwab developers on the Internet brokerage side of the IT department, and reassuring the data centre staff in Phoenix. In early 1999 the Account Open application was deployed across all Schwab's transaction servers. Internal staff did the core programming while IBM (GS), with a virtual team of about 20, operated as problem solver on run-time environment, JSP technology and Java Virtual Machine. It also supplied advice all the way through, and its Java expertise allowed Schwab to learn from IBM's first-hand exposure to Java implementations elsewhere.

Initially Schwab experienced little of the increased run-time efficiency and cost savings it expected from WAS-based applications. But this stemmed from the small-scale of the initial implementation. Subsequently Schwab experienced more efficient hardware utilization, and operations and systems administration gains, producing large cost savings. However, it started to immediately gain increased productivity from its application developers, and lower development costs. The infrastructure developments also meant that new applications could be brought to market much faster than through the CGI-based development process, thus increasing Schwab's competitiveness against a growing, fierce competition.

By 2001 Schwab's infrastructure was a three-tiered system. The back-end systems ran IBM ICS on mainframes. This served as the platform for Schwab's business transaction applications and held all the company's business logic. Schwab's IBM RS/6000 Web servers were located in Phoenix, Arizona and formed another tier. Between these tiers was a third tier, collectively known as SEntry (Schwab entry) servers, whose function was to link the UNIX and CICS domains within the Company's infrastructure. Schwab had also rolled out IBM's WAS technology to all of its servers, including elements such as automatic alerts and back-up procedures. Subsequently Schwab began to deploy WAS across more applications and piloted using XML to, for example, give more flexibility in accessing data in a Mutual Fund application.

9.4 Case study three – Macquarie Bank: supporting strategy with infrastructure across seven groups

Macquarie Bank is an independent Australian full service investment bank operating globally. The bank and its subsidiaries operate in a range of investment banking, commercial banking and retail financial service markets, with some 4000 staff in offices around the world. Macquarie has more than 40 distinct, but closely related business divisions. As at 2001 these fell into seven groups:

1 *Asset and Infrastructure (A&G)* – project finance cross-border leasing, structured finance markets; specialist infrastructure and technology investment funds;
2 *Equities (EG)* – institutional and corporate stock broking services to local and offshore investors for trading on the Australian Stock Exchange; research team support;
3 *Treasury and Commodities (T&CG)* – commodity and futures trading; debt market trading; foreign exchange, financial advisory, risk management services;
4 *Corporate Finance (CFG)* – strategic advice on mergers and acquisitions, privatizations, divestments, capital raising, corporate restructuring;
5 *Banking and Property (BPG)* – property investment and advisory, business and private banking services;
6 *Funds Management (FMG)* – more than Aus$22 billion of funds managed for corporations, businesses and individuals;
7 *Financial Services (FSG)* – financial services distributed via advisers and directly. Offers managed funds, stock broking, futures broking, private investment banking, margin lending and mortgages. Newly formed on 1 June 2000.

The bank continued to be financially successful throughout 2001, and made higher profits than in the previous accounting year. To March 2000 pre-tax profits were Aus$289.3 million, a 33 per cent increase on the previous year. Some three-quarters of this was contributed by the first four groups mentioned above. Financial Services Group was scheduled to make a loss in 2000/1 as it underwent restructuring and a major investment programme in systems development.

In this context IT provided key underpinning to activities in all the groups, but was recognized as a key driver of the Bank's strategies especially in retail, e-commerce and risk management.

According to a June 2000 presentation by then CIO Gail Burke, IT represented 18.5 per cent of total bank costs in 2000; 50 per cent of this was business-driven, while 50 per cent was on infrastructure. There were 700 staff (including contractors) in the Information Systems Division at this time, a third working on infrastructure. The importance of IT can be assessed from the number of strategic initiatives during 2000/1. Thus, core systems were being replaced in four groups, dedicated architecture capability was being developed across the bank, and e-commerce capability was being ramped up rapidly through upgrades, infrastructure initiatives, an on-line joint venture with Fairfax (f2), and the creation of an innovation arm called E-Division. At the same time FSG needed new IT support for multi-channel, multi-product distribution. Here in FSG a cross-business infrastructure was required. IT would also provide the capability for customer and adviser self-service and 'single view' of accounts. An architecture needed to be built to integrate cross-product servicing and reporting.

In summary, for IT infrastructure, the busy year ahead would see the implementation of a high availability platform, including a major upgrade of the e-commerce infrastructure, the roll-out of Office 2000, a review of the WAN, improvement in remote access, and a new voice communications strategy.

That the bank could be firing off on so many IT fronts came from a long-standing recognition of the importance of IT, infrastructure and e-business to the conduct of its existing and new businesses. Contemplating how and why this happened gives a number of insights into how e-business infrastructure can be managed effectively in complex business environments.

9.4.1 Moving to e-commerce

It is important to understand the culture of a bank like Macquarie. Some would characterize it as almost a federation of entrepreneurs that trade under the Macquarie name:

> 'The philosophy is not dissimilar from a number of other investment banks in the sense that other than a couple of things that are more tightly controlled, particularly the brand and prudential risks, we've generally empowered the business heads to run their own race. And that includes, to some extent, determining what direction they take from an application point of view.' – Rahn Wood, Head of E-Division.

This enduring feature has undoubted strengths, especially where looking for revenue and growth opportunities, but does not lend itself naturally to control from the centre, unlike in trading banks that tend to be centralist in terms of determining platforms and architectures. At the same time, business staff numbers doubled in the late 1990s, as did geographic spread, again pulling further activity and weight into the business units. How does an organization with such a culture and structure get into e-business effectively?

During 1994 Macquarie ran a series of architecture projects, looking at areas such as desktop, server, mainframe, trying to sort out a 'town plan for the future'. One of the main areas ripe for architecturing was client connectivity. Here it was found that there were some seven different technologies and diverse methods being used to communicate with the Bank's clients. Many were unreliable, support-intensive or failed to provide adequate functionality. The need for an integrated connectivity solution was apparent, but suppliers were not coming up with anything that looked usable. At the same time, by early 1995, it became obvious to the IT division that the Web was going to be important very quickly. Casting ahead IT could see an evolution of capabilities – as summarized in Figure 9.2 – but knew it would have to start small. The result was the Macquarie Web site, launched in April 1995 initially as a graduate recruitment site, then, in October 1995, as a bank-wide site (http://www.macquarie.com.au), showing what our respondents called the Bank's 'brochureware'.

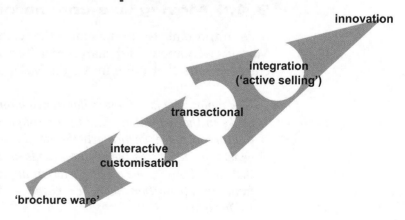

Figure 9.2
Evolution of capabilities at Macquarie Bank (source: Macquarie Infrastructure team)

At this stage, however, there was very little buy-in from the businesses, and the move to the second and third stages was delayed. Still being driven primarily by the IS division, but with some individual business involvement, in April 1996 Macquarie became the first Australian Web site to provide Australian Stock Exchange prices. 1996 saw three other developments: the provision of integrated financial transaction capability for real estate agents (DEFT Interactive), the provision of on-line research for Equities and Retail clients, and on-line provision of prospectuses. A site redesign followed in early 1997, allowing, amongst other developments, a Futures clearing application, an e-commerce application specifically for stockbrokers, and an e-service for Investment Services. In early 1998, realizing the importance of Web security, the Bank became the first Australian company with US export-controlled secure encryption technology.

One drag on development throughout was the difficulty in making strong business cases for Web developments. However, the inflection point, when the businesses began to take real ownership, was 1998, as a result of an education process but also because it became clear with the launch of Active Banking – the first Web-based banking application – and of on-line trading (DirecTrade) that:

> 'this [Macquarie On-Line] is suddenly a mission critical application now. If something went wrong large numbers of people would see it, and it would also cause a major problem. So it went from "here is a bunch of great ideas you can look at and rack your mind around" . . . to . . . "this is a mission critical system which can actually bring the brand down".' – Tony Graham, Macquarie On-Line.

According to John Scott, Division Director of Technology Investment Banking at Macquarie, the mood changed very noticeably with lots of buy-in from the business units:

> 'It went from: "you quoted Aus$250 000 to do this, but can you do it for Aus$180?" and there would be a lot of discussion around that, to suddenly: "But we can't just have these people not having access to their system, spend whatever it takes to solve the problem".'

From that period on, a lot more of the businesses were very aware of e-commerce and much more demanding, turning the tables irreversibly from being IT-driven to business-driven. It also became much more possible, but also much more necessary to take a whole-bank perspective on the issue of moves to e-business. A whole raft of applications followed, numbering 19 as at April 1999, focused mainly, at this stage, in Banking Services, Equities and Investment Services. The position the Bank had reached by this date is shown in Figure 9.2, and the route forward was clear. As several respondents put it, the future was not .com but .core. It was about putting all the basic transactions on the Web and making e-commerce a routine part of how the bank operated. As Bruce Terry, Executive Director of Investment Management, put it:

> 'There shouldn't need to be an e-commerce specialist in your Division. It should just be people doing their job, of which part of it is on-line, part of it over the phone, part of it face-to-face. It is not a special channel, it is just a way of doing business . . . and I think by now [late 2000], certainly in the retail businesses, e-commerce has become much more of a normal thing.'

Following this vision, back in 1999, the route forward was manifestly to move heavily into interactive/business integration, then on into business innovation (see Figure 9.2).

9.4.2 The infrastructure challenge

These developments had massive implications for the existing and the developing e-infrastructure. Historically, Macquarie's IS Division has been quite centralized, with the infrastructure area covered by two central groups – technical consulting and technical services. Subsequently, in the late 1990s, these were amalgamated into an Infrastructure team making up about a third of Macquarie's total IT staff. More recently, while the infrastructure team has stayed at the centre, business-aligned account teams were formed. As at 2001, their job continued to be to work with the business to define business requirements, understand and translate these into IT terms, then own the relationship with the business in delivering and supporting that IT into the business. The infrastructure challenge as the businesses move at different speeds with different applications towards e-business, has been: how do you achieve seamlessness and high service to customers, but also back-office integration, security and efficiency, for all systems and processes? As Tony Graham of Macquarie explains:

> 'We are trying to work through this now [late 2000]; how do we organize our infrastructure to support the Macquarie businesses?

Does every single person have to have the same level of security for every single application? Again, a decision was made at the corporate level that "look and feel" would be global and would be tightly controlled, and then some of the businesses railed against that. And it goes down to the technology level of how do we set ourselves up to support that – you know, the management of "look and feel" the way to roll out change quickly, those sorts of issues. And the technical people too have gone through a lot of changes as well – we have gone through different skill sets in certain areas of the bank – from artists to army in some areas where IT needs to be done in a very controlled way because of reliability and stability issues.'

Clearly there are many diverse needs across the Bank. The infrastructure team does control standards and insist on common policies and technologies in certain areas where a single view can be taken, for example networks, desktops, general processing. The Infrastructure team has also moved to providing more integrated support across the groups. Moreover, as Liam Edwards, head of the Infrastructure team points out:

'Infrastructure as a unit is becoming more important all the time to the point where the business is saying, in terms of the whole bank environment, technology is *the business. Every channel to market is now dependent on the way technology works. So there is an increasing emphasis on how do you get a lot of the technology commoditized, so that you can look for the really value-adding technologies you can overlay on top of that.'*

However, the business units still remain relatively unfettered. Even when it boils down to something as simple as a Web site, they always have the option to go outside, and no-one in IT could say 'no' unless there were real integration issues involved. For Rahn Wood, it is a two-edged sword:

'It encourages people to make their own destiny, and the thing that makes Macquarie successful is that there is a bunch of really brainy people at the application end focused on the markets . . . but it does mean that we have got a lot more ground to cover in terms of bringing people up the curve to actually recognize all the factors involved in running with some of these decisions.'

In such an environment, the process of arriving at the many benefits and synergies derived from even more common infrastructure and applications has been necessarily a gradual one. One place it has become most obviously and convincingly applied is in the recently formed Financial Services Group – a very long-term time horizon, and a lot of investment, is needed to make retail work:

> 'We have recognized that retail needs big dollars up front. Retail is like the One Hundred Years War relative to some of this niche sort of stuff that just opens up in the wholesale or institutional markets, and the quicker you can pile in there the better'. Rahn Wood.

In FSG the core technologies are developed, or bought, in order to serve the whole of that group. It is no coincidence that the former Macquarie CIO, Gail Burke, has moved to oversee FSG operations.

Clearly, in moving to an e-business infrastructure, given this diversity, but the increasing need for interconnectivity from a customer and an internal perspective, Macquarie continually needs to revisit and work out the most flexible and optimal way to support the businesses as they go down the e-business venture route.

9.4.3 Doing e-infrastructure

Macquarie infrastructure is run by an in-house team. The calculation was that if the Bank wanted to drive costs down it could, and does, do that better internally rather than through outsourcing. In fact the infrastructure costs are recovered fully every year from the businesses, though with some flexibility built in on research and development costs. More fundamentally, through its infrastructure work, Macquarie looks for real added business value from information and e-business technologies:

> 'To facilitate this, it was felt that you really needed an infrastructure supporter who understands how to respond quickly to the business'. Liam Edwards.

The move to e-infrastructure was always a centralized approach, managed by one group from 1994 on. To a large extent, this set the standard for how e-initiatives would be developed, and prevented the natural anarchy that has proliferated at the early stages in many other organizations. More recently (2000), the organization had perhaps outgrown this model, and there have been drivers to push off in different directions at different speeds. From an infrastructure perspective the problem then has become not trying to bring order out of chaos, but trying to provide a fairly flexible capable infrastructure in the face of differing drivers in the businesses. To put it another way, Macquarie has built a robust infrastructure in an Australian environment, but the forward challenge is: how do you continue to deliver infrastructure to meet fast-arriving business opportunities in an increasingly off-shore, Internet-based environment, with the increased visibility the Internet brings?

The Infrastructure team has developed a blueprint in terms of existing infrastructure, the present plans and where the end gains might be:

> 'Infrastructure development here is about, as each of the businesses jump, looking at how you make infrastructure flexible enough so that you can upgrade parts of it very quickly, because those parts impact on other parts of the infrastructure . . . it has been all about learning on the job within the context of a blueprint, as you gradually go out and implement it and take it forwards, putting in the bits that are required to take you to the next stage, and then learn again. Each time you break it into small enough chunks that are sustainable within the company, from both a cost and a service perspective. You then get the buy-in, move it towards the end-gain, and make sure you have an infrastructure that allows you to scale it, as the business growth occurs'. Liam Edwards

The approach has been necessary in order to keep a balance between keeping today's infrastructure – so that the Bank can continue to do business at the right quality and with the right image – enabling new products so that the Bank can grow, while evolving the infrastructure that is looking potentially 18 months ahead, when the businesses might be only looking six months ahead. As the Infrastructure team understood it: *'managing infrastructure is about changing the tablecloth without disturbing the cutlery'*.

In 1999 the existing infrastructure was robust, but its design had been driven by cost and previously specified requirements. It had several single points of failure and limited capacity on performance and expansion. Conversations with the businesses identified capability gaps, and implications for future infrastructure in areas such as availability, performance, scalability and flexibility, more flexible cost structure, and ability to employ new technologies quickly. One of the issues was that the infrastructure had all been built in-house and was essentially single purpose, for Macquarie Bank. But the new challenge, in face of increasingly mature IT products available on the market, has been how to integrate those into a tailor-made model and still meet the time-to-market requirements of the businesses. The solution was to rebuild the infrastructure, by putting in some enabling technologies, that would enable a level of flexibility and future proofing not at all previously available. According to one Infrastructure team member:

> 'It has been hard, like trying to set up a blueprint for a town, knowing you have got to make provision for hospitals and police stations and parks, but not quite sure when and how many people are going to be using them. It just depends on what the business comes up with, but we have a lot more flexibility through this upgrade, than we ever had before'.

The development of the infrastructure consisted of three phases. Phase One, finished in December 2000, was designed to give the infrastructure the primary resilience it needed. For example, the existing infrastructure depended on a large single machine representing a single point of failure. Vertical flexibility, a looser coupling, was achieved by splitting the major functions it was doing into independent components, thus giving flexibility at both ends – allowing future changes in Web platforms and application servers. Horizontal splitting was also achieved, giving scalability and giving resilience by having plenty of technical capacity, and running the infrastructure across the Bank's two sites rather than locating all infrastructure on one site. Phase One also started the move towards a common shared infrastructure, independent of actual delivery mechanisms such as Web servers, application servers and databases. This makes it much easier for a business to choose when to opt into, say, a Web presence, or to slot in future business products. Clearly this was not an easy development. Another analogy used by the Infrastructure team for what they were attempting was 'replacing the actor in your favourite programme tomorrow, without you noticing it'.

Phase Two, begun in early 2001, then addressed the database at the back-end. This presented an interesting challenge. A large database was needed, but this could not be split vertically and horizontally, so how could it be made resilient enough to operate as the critical foundation of the infrastructure? This depended largely on the maturity of the IT products being made available in 2001. The alternatives for making it work better would result in a very complicated set-up that may well be more trouble-prone, with the database failing in very non-predictable ways. It was not a Phase Two to get ambitious with. Phase Three involved an attempt to provide an underlying e-business infrastructure that was reusable, that allowed economies of scale, and businesses could come in and use as little or as much of it as they needed. Some of this was achieved in Phase One, and basically Phase Three is a consolidation of the first two phases.

These developments also had process and skill dimensions. Indeed, Macquarie had a number of e-business drivers for infrastructure over and above just technical capability. The infrastructure team saw it important to manage also from a process and organization perspective. Thus it was important to have in place a process to assess the infrastructure implications of a business having a requirement to put a product on the Internet, and to detail the nature of the infrastructure upgrade where needed.

Other relevant processes included service delivery, configuration management, product management, release management, a change management system appropriate for a dynamic technical environment, help desk management, capacity planning, problem management.

On skills, Macquarie was finding it easier to grow people internally rather than finding themselves short. Because the Macquarie infrastructure was not falling neatly into the mainstream. It required technical skills, but also a clear understanding of what the team was trying to deliver in the specific Macquarie environment, which was not just about technical solutions provision, but about being Macquarie-orientated. Moreover, according to Liam Edwards:

> 'Infrastructure work is moving over into some of the development-type environment. It is becoming a lot greyer, and therefore you need more generalists between the development and infrastructure worlds. And it is not that you are a Unix person or a network person anymore, but that you need some Unix, some network and some database skills . . .'.

9.4.4 Further developments

Two separate developments in Macquarie's moves to e-business are worth noting. The eDivision was set up in 2000 to do the risky things, or things with a longer time horizon, on new markets and new business models that could only be possible through going down the e-business route. The objective was disruptive innovation, that is, to provide and stimulate the level of innovation that would not be attempted elsewhere in Macquarie where it might endanger a good business, or involve going beyond the short-term bonus cycle. The eDivision acts as an incubator of its own ideas but is also open to ideas from the other Macquarie businesses. It has its own e-infrastructure and network and operates as a semi-autonomous business.

One example of the eDivision at work occurred in September 2000. Financial Enrichment is 100 per cent owned by Macquarie through eDivision in its role as a venture capital e-commerce incubator. In September it made its account aggregation service available to the 400 000 membership of the free on-line service provider FreeOnline. Enrichment is designed to revolutionize the way customers manage their financial affairs as retail bank customers will be able to view, and ultimately manage, their on-line accounts securely using a single password. Enrichment intended to extend the management tools available to on-line share broking, managed funds, mortgages and superannuation.

Another e-development was the joint venture, announced in June 2000, between f2 – Fairfax's Interactive Network – and Macquarie to offer investment services on-line. Each 50/50 partner would provide up to Aus$20 million funding for up to three years. Fairfax is a major Australian media organization and, through f2, offered editorial content from its large number of publications and archives. In late 2000 it was attracting over 2.5 million views per day. The new business would offer on-line trading, cash management, managed funds, superannuation, wrap accounts and other investment tools. An array of investment products would be available from different providers, together with access to research and information provided by both partners. The objective was to capitalize on each company's strengths, and circumvent their own relative slowness in developing similar businesses within Fairfax and Macquarie.

The joint venture had considerable, expensive, infrastructure implications, but the JV route was a lot less expensive than if Macquarie had tried to develop a potentially high risk business itself, in a very competitive sector. As it was, the systems needed to run the new business would still be worth in excess of Aus$50 million. In sharing the costs of the Web infrastructure, there were spin-offs also for developing Macquarie's off-line business infrastructure. According to Craig Swanger of Macquarie, in charge of the JV technical developments, the plan was to integrate the IT back into the infrastructure of both Fairfax and Macquarie, while operating a relatively stand-alone business. From f2 would come the network of Web sites, and from Macquarie the investment services infrastructure – both very expensive to build yourself. Several projects were being done by the JV, including the Web service and managed investments projects, but much was outsourced to the two host companies.

While this way of developing/providing infrastructure together would seem to be the most difficult, it is probably the cheapest, quickest and probably the most likely to succeed of the options available. Swanger saw dependence on Macquarie to develop infrastructure as a strength, because it was something Macquarie had to do anyway, and having a reliant external party with a Macquarie brand name put pressure on the Bank to get it done. F2 already had a relatively simple infrastructure, and the integration issues were not great, and more about capacity planning than anything else.

By 2001 Macquarie had over 20 Internet applications and over 260 products on-line to customers. There was still much to be done in terms of getting businesses to think and work cross-divisionally, on updating Intranet capability, on getting the infrastructure capability further developed to be able to handle mounting e-business demand, and anticipate events, for example, further JVs or major acquisitions of other external businesses.

9.5 Case study four: what the IT services market can provide: Vistorm

Vistorm Limited was started in 1991 as Engineering Software (later shortened to ESOFT), by Charles Sharland, an ex-Business Manager for Sun and Hewlett Packard who saw a clear market opportunity to make money by implementing pre-mainstream technical software.

According to David Sidwell, Development Manager at Vistorm:

> 'We first implemented a Firewall in 1994. We first connected two businesses together using the Internet in 1995/6. Now, over 65 per cent of Vistorm's business is now in Managed Internet Security,

where we enable businesses to develop and implement a secure Virtual Private Network (VPN). In many cases Vistorm manage that VPN remotely, 24×7, to a Service Level unattainable by the users themselves, on a monthly fee basis'.

Vistorm is now a European leader in the provision of Managed Internet Services, and was voted European Application Service Provider (ASP) of the year in 1999/2000. It offers on-line delivery of line-of-business applications to companies worldwide. It operates a large Independent Software Vendor (ISV) alliance program. With these, Vistorm takes ISV software, ASP-enables it, then delivers it to end customers on a managed, rental basis, supplying all the necessary infrastructure. Applications are hosted in managed data centres and delivered by secure Internet connections direct to the user's desktop/laptop. Vistorm's offer is fast access to 'best practice' IT management of business application software and technology support at affordable prices, and to provide world-class IT infrastructure. Vistorm also offers managed Internet security for firewalls and virtual private networks, and solutions for desktop and server security.

Its primary target market is line-of-business applications aimed at the SME and divisional corporate sectors. According to David Sidwell, Business Development Manager, there are three main parameters for selecting an ASP market:

1 *scale of application* – level of application complexity, integration and customization;
2 *user profile* – size of user population/type of user;
3 *application type* – business function/industry applicability.

These options are mapped in Figure 9.3. On this analysis, and given the company's historically developed core capabilities, Vistorm pinpointed the mid-range 'line-of-business/collaborative applications' as the most commercially and technically attractive market, because such applications were the most widely adopted by corporate (more than 500 employees) and SME middle-market (between 100 and 500 employees) companies.

Clearly, the key to Vistorm's success is its technical capability, ability to integrate applications, provision of infrastructure, capability in the Internet security arena, partnering with leading applications providers, and ability to be client and end-user focused. Its customer value proposition is faster and more competitive business operations (access to new applications faster, applications where and when the business requires,

Application Landscape

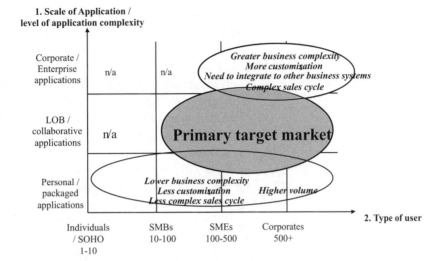

Figure 9.3
Vistorm: identifying market segments (SOHO, small office, home office; SMB, small business; SME, small/medium enterprise)

affordable 'best' applications, allowing refocus on the business). The second component of the value proposition is better managed IT costs (minimal up-front costs for technology, pay for users, predictable IT costs and less IT staff costs). The third hook is greater reliability, scalability and flexibility; customers obtain predictable service levels backed by service level agreements (SLAs), industry 'best practices', all scaled as the customers' businesses grow at their own speeds.

One illustrative customer is Redwood Financial Services, which outsources company accounts. It uses Vistorm's Open Accounts and standard Windows packages to network in real time with clients to access and update their accounts. They can also offer the Open Accounts package to clients previously reluctant to pay for superior software. Redwood pays £300 per month per user, as does the client for its users.

9.5.1 Capabilities

The following exchange between David Sidwell and the interviewer gives an idea of the capabilities an ASP such as Vistorm can provide to a desktop:

> DS So I am now just on a desktop and I could be dialling in from home, this works just the same on a 28K line as it does on what we have here. So if I just power up Excel, how fast does Excel load on your machine, your PC?

253

INT   *Not that fast.*

DS   *Let's use part of the Microsoft Test Suites as a demonstration ... here I'm calculating a random number and I will just create a grid of random numbers and refresh it. As quick as your machine?*

INT   *Uh, huh.*

DS   *Now we will do something that looks a little bit more tricky with some graphics. So we will create a graphical package there that does this and we will just go, OK let's just refresh that. So that is Excel running at lightning speed. Where are the servers?*

INT   *Well they are not here.*

DS   *They are in Manchester, connected via the Internet. Now most people cannot believe that a remote service can be faster than locally based servers. However, that's because all I have here is a thin client device, effectively just a Network card. My whole desktop is remotely delivered over the Internet and it is working quicker than most people's own laptops, without any question. Now the first thing to say about ASP is that almost every application is currently in use was written to run on a PC. It is written to hog the mouse, the keyboard, the DOLs, the CPU itself, and you put a hundred re-entrant users on a single executable and it will not work by accident. It will crash at some time, and has no error routines to inform the Systems Administrator what went wrong and where in the code. One of Vistorm's key skill sets is making applications that weren't meant to run in a remote environment not only run, but perform faster than when run locally.'*

Vistorm is set up to make technology fit a customer's business, not by selling products or services, but by creating a platform for other people that can be embedded into their business propositions and infrastructures. Managed Internet Security (MISEC) effectively delivers a secure managed Internet connection that people then build as part of their infrastructure moving forward. In itself, it is something of an ASP application because Vistorm remotely maintains it – actual monitoring software for the firewalls run centrally. The firewalls run remotely but the users have commissioned Vistorm to manage the whole thing for them – a piece of application service provision. The next part of the business the company looked at was running applications. Explained David Sidwell:

'Right now people are doing things to get connected, which is what MISEC is all about and, in future, they will be connecting to do *things, which is what SBC [Server-Based Computing] is all about. One of the dreams of IT has always been to build applications that work independent of its delivery mechanism – on any desktop, over any network, securely. We've been working with Microsoft, Compaq, CheckPoint and Citrix's product sets for years to achieve this goal and we are now one of their most technically competent partners in Europe, and possibly in the world. As early as 1996, we got thousands of users at Rolls-Royce running Windows applications across a wide range of desktops, all managed centrally. So we were doing ASP back before it was even known as ASP.*

The key to delivering applications to any desktop, over any network securely, is in having deep technical skills in the core technologies needed, and years of experience in troubleshooting the inevitable teething problems that occur. Day-by-day, week-by-week, Vistorm worked at these problems, and made many, many, many incremental changes. But the end result is that we are in a completely different market space now, with a massive step difference between what we can deliver and others, who haven't made the same paradigm shifts.'

9.5.2 Into 2001/2002

Up until June 2000 there were only three shareholders in the business, namely original founder, Charles Sharland, Tony Bolland (Sales Director) and David Sidwell (Business Development Director).

During the late 1990s the company's growth was so rapid (up to 86 per cent compound over five years), it could not continue to be financed from its own earnings. The company in fact managed to get to sales of £17 million without outside finance, but needed an injection of growth capital to maintain momentum. To that end it raised £25 million in a first round of Venture Capital through a syndicate led by 3i, that also included Compaq, Credit Suisse First Boston and Granville Baird.

By the end of the financial year for 2001, Vistorm expected to show an increase in revenues of 75 per cent to over £30 million, and that rate of growth was projected to be maintained into the next financial year. More importantly, given the temperature of the financial markets in 2001, all Vistorm's businesses were projected to come into profit during 2002. As one senior manager commented: *'Our business isn't easy, and we're always paranoid about whether we're doing the right thing or not, but we must be doing some things right'.* On our analysis, Vistorm's long-term development over the 1990s and its recognized core capabilities in specific areas seen as critical in Internet-enabled service and application provision, particularly in security, has placed the company in an advantageous position relative to many competitors. Its track record in delivery also majors on an important customer requirement in a confusing and immature market.

9.6 Conclusion: lessons from the cases

The cases provide a range of learning points. Let us take each case in turn.

9.6.1 CitiPower: delivering infrastructure through the programme office

- While CitiPower constantly reviews the business case for e-business initiatives, but seems slow into specific applications, the company has been very clear that without e-business infrastructure it would experience massive inefficiencies and problems in the new decade. CitiPower has taken a very anticipatory, infrastructure perspective on its IT development, which in fact is a much more strategic competitive positioning than merely launching into specific initiatives and applications that may or may not pay off, and for which the business case may be seriously doubtful.
- CitiPower has not developed a separate e-business infrastructure but rolled all its IT issues into the development of a single infrastructure trajectory. It sought help on the overall design, but retains strong control and ownership over its implementation.
- We have recognized many times that managing IT as a strategic resource occurs only when CEO/CIO relationships are very good, when both perceive IT as potentially transformative for the business, and when the CIO is business-focused and sits at the same table as his/her senior manager peer group. It is also important for the CIO to take responsibility for educating his/her peers on IT issues, for example on the importance of infrastructure and expenditure in this area. All these conditions are in place at CitiPower.
- E-business Infrastructure blueprints are fine, but are paper-ware unless they can be implemented. Lithgow applied skills and sourcing policies that facilitated implementation.
- The key turnaround occurred through developing the Programme Office concept and applying its disciplines to every project.

- CitiPower is an example of what can be achieved in offering a business many degrees of freedom in reach and range even when it has not clarified for itself its business strategy for the next three years. CitiPower also illustrates the huge costs and disadvantages that can result from failure to support basic operations of the business with information technology. Recall the high costs of signing on a new customer or deleting a customer that may be going to a competing energy provider.

9.6.2 Charles Schwab: building the engine room of transformation

- Schwab underwent a major transformation in moving to the Web over the 1995–2001 period. Nevertheless it put in place measures such as the Technology Review Board to ensure that infrastructure changes would always represent prudent technology decisions in the light of business impacts and a range of knock-on effects and consequences in the rest of the infrastructure. Such technology decisions remained the preserve of Schwab itself.
- The company migrated much of its business to the Web relatively quickly, but was clear that technology infrastructure and IT generally were key areas on which to retain internal capability. The 'technology architect' and 'technology fixer' roles are very much to the fore at Schwab.
- At the same time, even in an internally developed IT function such as Schwab's, senior business and IT management recognized that use of the market was essential in several ways. The company chose a selective, 'partnering' mode of sourcing from the market, looking to suppliers for capabilities Schwab did not have itself, or actually wanted to build over time.
- Schwab was clear about the development process needing to be fast, focused, based on prototyping, involving a range of interest groups and expertises and essentially about learning better how to deploy the technologies being developed.
- Schwab was always eager to learn from suppliers, and this learning fed back into improving internal capability.
- The approach described here reflects the centrality with which Schwab has viewed Web-based technologies and infrastructure when operating a major part of the business via the Internet. Outages not only hit share price, but also, in the fast-moving share broking business, create considerable customer unease. In early 1999, Schwab experienced an outage of four

hours that hit the headlines. The company was very quick to announce a further investment in its systems of US$70 million to reduce the risk of this ever happening again. This sense of IT's centrality to the business may well also explain why Schwab do not outsource systems and even relatively mature activities to any great degree.

9.6.3 Macquarie Bank: infrastructure as vital support for strategy

- The Macquarie experience shows the advantages of having a centralized infrastructure team from the beginning, that can take a single view of existing infrastructure, how it needs to be developed and how this can occur in an increasingly Web-enabled environment.
- About a third of Macquarie's IT staff are concerned with infrastructure; it runs and develops its own, historically tailor-made infrastructure, though there is some outsourcing of certain aspects of IT. Potentially it would be possible to standardize much more, and also outsource much more. However, the fact that Macquarie's businesses are relatively decentralized, with differing and fast-changing needs may well militate against this. Indeed centralized, in-house-run infrastructure is undoubtedly one of the core things holding Macquarie together and ensuring that the businesses are fully enabled technologically.
- A critical success factor has been the expansion of skills sets within the infrastructure team to embrace understanding of the Bank culture and environment. This has led on to a much more sophisticated understanding of the business-focused role infrastructure development must increasingly have if e-business infrastructure is to be developed effectively. It has also led to a subtle set of management and operational practices for negotiating infrastructure development through a host of business pressures and exigencies. This is neatly summarized in the infrastructure objective: changing the tablecloth without disturbing the cutlery.
- It is clear from the Macquarie experience that, to achieve effective e-infrastructure development, infrastructure teams now have to stay very close to the businesses as those businesses themselves evolve.
- Macquarie has developed a flexible view of its ongoing infrastructure blueprint. It would be all too easy to take a 'Five Year Plan' approach to infrastructure. In fact Macquarie regularly revisits its blueprint, sees the next Phase as very

detailed and clear, but is much more flexible about how later Phases will be achieved, though conscious of the parameters within which technologies and processes will fall, and the end-gains needed. It also sees infrastructure as a constant evolution, especially given the flow of ever-maturing technologies and tools coming on to the IT marketplace.

9.6.4 Vistorm: infrastructure through an Internet-based service provider

From a customer perspective, Vistorm represents an attractive supplier on several fronts.

- It has a ten-year-plus pedigree of consistent market performance.
- It has a core capability in security and VPNs – one of the perennial concerns we identified amongst potential customers. It has a strong and growing customer base.
- It allies with recognized brands. Its niche strategy makes clear who its best customers are going to be, and how it is customizing its products and services.
- It clearly provides for its existing customers what so many ASPs promise: scalability, predictable, lower costs, speed to application adoption, secure and responsive infrastructure, ability to integrate applications.

In these ways Vistorm demonstrates also what customers should be looking for in potential suppliers of infrastructure and applications capability.

There are learning points for an Internet-based service provider too:

- be precise in identifying the profitable market segment you sell into, unless you aim at dominating several (as is Oracle's and EDS's strategy);
- develop a core capability that customers respect, and that gives you distinctive competitive advantage – don't just be an intermediary. In Vistorm's case the security/VPN focus gives them a solid base and track record to expand from;
- application integration is a core capability all ASP aspirants needs to develop;
- control the forward technology trajectory for the client, not least by investing in the core skills and technologies needed to make applications and systems run over the Internet.

These characteristics mean that Vistorm is well positioned to ride out the downturn and take advantage of improvements in the business climate.

References

Sauer, C. and Willcocks, L. (2001) *Building The E-Business Infrastructure*. London: Business Intelligence.

Willcocks, L., Feeny, D. and Islei, G. (eds) (1997) *Managing IT As A Strategic Resource*. Maidenhead: McGraw Hill.

Index